The Book of
Withycombe

The History of a West Somerset Village
Chris Boyles

HALSGROVE

First published in Great Britain in 2003

British Library Cataloguing-in-Publication Data
A CIP record for this title is available from the British Library

ISBN 1 84114 254 9

HALSGROVE

Halsgrove House
Lower Moor Way
Tiverton, Devon EX16 6SS
Tel: 01884 243242
Fax: 01884 243325
email: sales@halsgrove.com
website: www.halsgrove.com

Frontispiece photograph: *A beautiful photograph of Combe Farmhouse, taken in the 1890s when it was still thatched. Widow Mary Hagley was in charge at the time, but here we see her three children who would later take over the reins. Annie is by the door, Charlie has the gun, and Thomas, the youngest, stands by the gate.*

Printed and bound in Great Britain by CPI Bath Press, Bath

Contents

An elegantly posed group of Levershas outside the 'Mansion House' at Court Place in an early photograph. We are probably in the era of John and Elizabeth Leversha, who may well be the older couple on the left.

Higher Rodhuish Farm and Jack Dyer (left) helping to load the hay cart. The other man on the ground was an Australian pilot, sent to the farm to convalesce during the Second World War.

Opposite: *A view of Withycombe from Buckhill, taken by Alfred Vowles.*

Acknowledgements

I would like to thank all of those people of Withycombe, and those with a connection to the parish, who have participated in the creation of this volume by lending me their photographs and historic documents, and who have passed on their invaluable knowledge to me. My thanks to Stephanie Aitchison, Keith Arscott, Gerald Badcock, Hilary Binding, Bob Bishop, Dottie Black, Ron Blundell, Gerald Bull, Eileen Burns, Anthony Case, Margaret Chorley, Jo Crossman, Dick Davey, Margaret Davies, Kath and Mike Ferris, Roy Fry, Richard and Geraldine Hagley, Jean Humber, Violet Jones, Alan Manley, Steve Milton, Dick Pearse, Donald Parsons, Wendy Richardson, Molly Ross, Joan Scudamore, Alan and Jenny Thomas, Greta Thrush, Raymond White, Ray and Barbara Young and Tony Young for contributing photographs; and to Bill Allen, Marc Hiles and Mike Uppington for information and assistance. There is also a debt of gratitude to be paid to the original photographers, both amateur and professional, for their skill in creating the images in the first place.

I am grateful to the Luttrell family for their meticulous keeping and care of the manorial documents pertaining to the village, and to the Somerset Archive and Record Service for continuing to preserve them; also for the latter's help in interpreting them and for permission to reproduce some of this material here; also to Mary Hobhouse for her help in finding and passing on information there to me. My thanks to David Bromwich and others at the Somerset Studies Library for their help and advice, and especially to the Somerset Record Society, whose volumes contain invaluable information relating to Withycombe.

Final thanks go to those whose abiding interest in the history of the village prompted me to attempt this project, among them my helpers Jean Humber and Dick Pearse. The latter's phenomenal knowledge and memory of village life has had a huge influence on this work, not least in enabling us to identify faces that would otherwise have remained anonymous. Great care has been taken to ensure that names, etc. are correct but inevitably a few mistakes will have been made, for which I apologise.

Chris Boyles
June 2003

WITHYCOMBE FROM BUCKHILL.

5

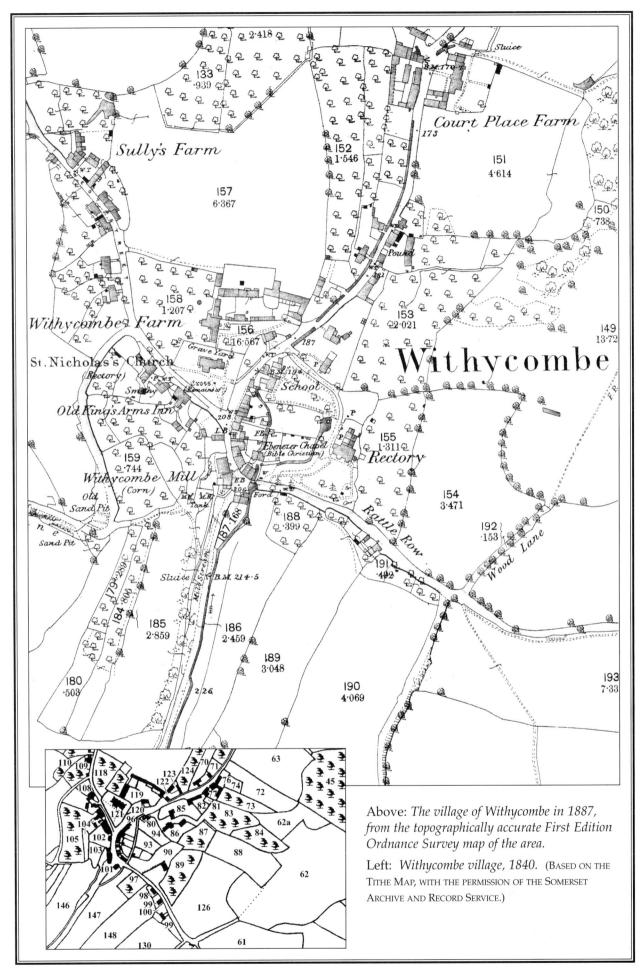

Above: *The village of Withycombe in 1887, from the topographically accurate First Edition Ordnance Survey map of the area.*

Left: *Withycombe village, 1840.* (Based on the Tithe Map, with the permission of the Somerset Archive and Record Service.)

Introduction

From its position astride the eastern edge of Exmoor, the parish of Withycombe is accordingly a mixture of hill-farm country and lowland combe, the village having formed itself on the gentler ground in the lee of the hills. The Revd James Savage described the village in 1830 as consisting of 'two straggling streets of mean houses, deep worn roads, and high old-fashioned causeways.'

What the author of the *History of the Hundred of Carhampton* was describing is evidence of great age and permanence. His 'mean houses' were the plain cottages of thatch, stone and cob that had been the local building style for centuries – not the elegant products of the Georgian and Regency eras to which the Revd and other gentry aspired certainly, but eminently practical and enduring. Where these cottages survive today they are coveted for their simple beauty and for the sense of history that seeps from their fabric, which is something no modern dwelling, however well appointed, can provide. And in Withycombe a great many have survived, most of them modernised to varying degrees. Yet if James Savage passed along the two straggling streets today he would still recognise most of them.

Not just the houses, but also the way of life of their inhabitants has rolled along largely undisturbed through the centuries, evolving only slowly. Now though, great technological leaps bring change at a frightening pace, overturning the certainties of the past. We have a village with neither shop nor – even worse, some might say – public house; and there is little employment for its inhabitants. We can only guess at what changes the next 100 years will bring. All things considered, the beginning of a new century seems like a good time to take stock of Withycombe's past.

Looking down on Mill Street from Buckhill, in a photograph taken by L.T. Blackmore around 1950. Away in the distance is the Bristol Channel, with Wales beyond.

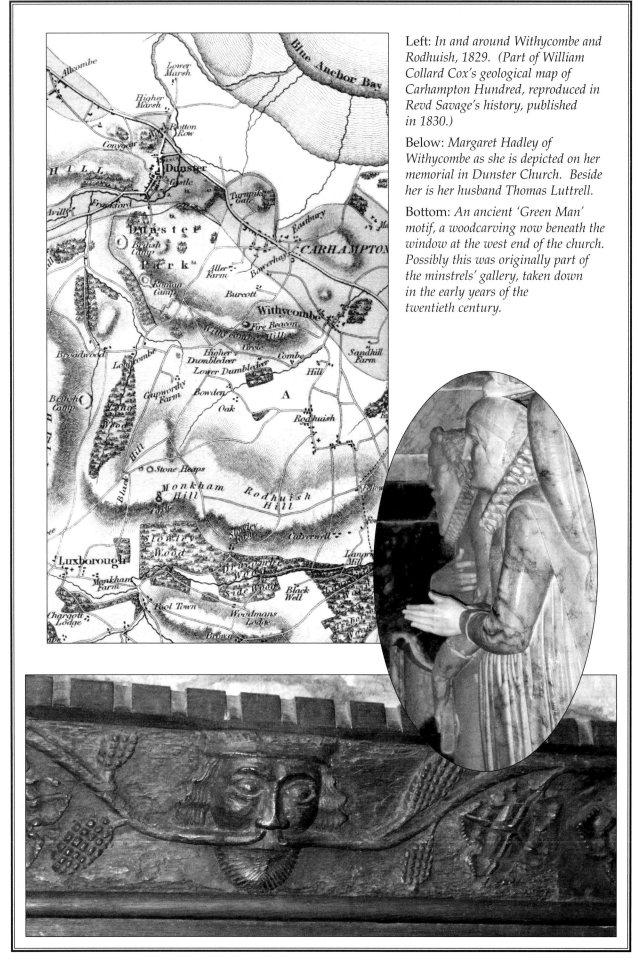

Left: *In and around Withycombe and Rodhuish, 1829. (Part of William Collard Cox's geological map of Carhampton Hundred, reproduced in Revd Savage's history, published in 1830.)*

Below: *Margaret Hadley of Withycombe as she is depicted on her memorial in Dunster Church. Beside her is her husband Thomas Luttrell.*

Bottom: *An ancient 'Green Man' motif, a woodcarving now beneath the window at the west end of the church. Possibly this was originally part of the minstrels' gallery, taken down in the early years of the twentieth century.*

One

Ancient Withycombe

The parish of Withycombe has existed for more than 1,000 years, little changing in scope and area with regard to its neighbours, at least until 1884, when it was expanded to include the hamlet of Rodhuish. During this time it has also been part of a larger administrative unit, the Hundred of Carhampton; and it has been the property (for the most part) of the lords of the local stronghold, Dunster Castle.

The parish was originally an area of ecclesiastical jurisdiction and was a structure thought not to have existed in Western Europe before the eighth century. The parish had its civil equivalent – the manor – that defined an area according to ownership of the land and the estates thereon. Manors did not necessarily correspond to parishes and the pre-Norman manor of Withycombe was smaller than the parish with which we are familiar. Land at Combe and Gildencote, adjoining areas in the west of the parish, were excluded, being manors themselves.

The manor of Withycombe existed during the Anglo-Saxon period, since at least the time of Alfred the Great (AD849–99). His success against the Danes was due in part to his skilful reorganisation of society within the manorial system: it has been suggested that many communal elements, such as the open-field system and common grazing, were introduced to some areas by him in order to free up men for military duty. There is some evidence that an open-field system of agriculture was used in Withycombe, although it is unusual for this working practice to be found so far to the west. However, there was a strategic need for Alfred's improvements here, as the area had been a target for Danish raids. On the coast of the Bristol Channel to the north can be found a safe anchorage, as the name Blue Anchor suggests; and the rivers and streams (including the Withycombe Brook) debouching into the sea here have formed a coastal plane which would have made the landing of troops a simple matter in contrast to the barrier of high cliffs to be overcome all along the coast elsewhere. In AD836 and/or 843 the Saxons had been heavily defeated by sea-borne raiders at Carhampton. Needless to say, the men of Withycombe would have been involved in the fighting.

While we do not know when the single community that we call Withycombe was established, we do know that there were people living within its modern boundaries since prehistoric times. The evidence for this has been found on the high ground within the parish, in particular on Withycombe Hill and Rodhuish Common (now in the modern parish). It has survived here because these areas were common land, free from development for thousands of years. It would be wrong to conclude from this that the lowland area was not inhabited in the prehistoric period: there is simply no evidence to decide the matter either way.

While there are indications of occupation in earlier times (the cist burial, complete with human remains, excavated in Langridge Wood, for example), the evidence becomes quite spectacular when we reach the Iron Age, traditionally said to begin around 700BC. Hilltop enclosures dating from this period have been discovered comparatively recently on Rodhuish and Monkslade Commons and at Longwood – all close to Red Girts, where the Withycombe Brook has its source; but the one on Withycombe Hill, near Higher Dumbledeer, has an entire prehistoric field system associated with it. About 20 small fields are identifiable, some showing evidence of ploughing. Early antiquarians recognised the Withycombe Hill enclosure as 'druidical remains': one Victorian gentleman, upon enquiring of a nearby workman as to the whereabouts of the hut circle, was told that the surviving stones had been taken away during the 1850s to be used for drainage.

The establishment of farming communities on the high ground in and around Withycombe coincides with the construction of Bat's Castle hill-fort to the west of Withycombe Hill. This lies beyond the parish boundary, in Carhampton; and in its creation it is surely not being too fanciful to suggest that the skeleton of the later political structure of the area was formed. Just as in later times with the Norman Castle at Dunster, here was the focus of power within the greater community, the lord's stronghold perhaps, surrounded by fields worked by his people, under his protection.

Who were these people? They were Celts, by the beginning of the Roman period of the tribe known as the Dumnonii. This tribe dominated the West of England, although Withycombe was close to the eastern border of their territory. They had no coinage of their own, preferring to barter for goods and services; and the smaller number of hill-forts that they built might suggest that they were less warlike than other Celtic tribes. They had an affinity with the sea, like the men of Devon and Cornwall in later periods, and would have taken an active part in the sea trade that took place not only between the regions of Britain but also with continental Europe. Consequently they would have had more knowledge and experience of what the Roman Empire was all about than many other British tribes, and this may help to explain the position of the Dumnonii when, in AD43, the Romans invaded Britain.

The Romans' initial plan was to secure the south of England as far as the Exe Valley and the Bristol Channel in the west – the borders of Dumnonii territory, more or less, which seems to suggest that the tribe was not seen as a threat. Indeed, it seems likely that they were one of the Celtic tribes that welcomed, or were at least prepared to tolerate, the invaders. For the people of Withycombe this would have been good news, as normal life continued here while battles raged elsewhere. However, this was still a vital area strategically, as the Romans recognised; and in the early phases of the invasion the future Emperor Vespasian was despatched to the West with a full legion to secure it.

After Britain became a Roman province there was still little sign of their occupation of West Somerset. It looks very much as if the lands were left for all practical purposes in native hands. However, the Romans would still have had a considerable influence on local life. They were keen to exploit the mineral wealth of the Brendon Hills, which were rich in iron ore; and there was ironstone to be had at Red Girts – plenty for the local populace to do then on that front, whether for trade or tribute. There were also new opportunities for the military-minded. 'Join the army and see the world' is a motto that could have been invented by the Romans, for it was their policy to post locally recruited units far away from home, so that in the event of local rebellion they would not be tempted to join in on the 'wrong' side. The Romans sought to exploit the Dumnonians' seafaring abilities and some are known to have served as marines in their overseas-based fleets.

Relations between the Romans and the local Celtic populace would no doubt have been strained at times, especially when there was serious revolt elsewhere in the country; and periodically there may have been open hostilities. However, while the Romans maintained an adequate military presence in the region to police it, one has the impression that Dumnonia was the least of their worries.

Things changed though when the Romans left and the Germanic tribes started to push their way into the South West. This was no peaceful takeover. There is evidence that at this time many Iron-Age hill-forts in the region were reoccupied and refortified, and it is probable that this occurred at nearby Bat's Castle. The main thrust of the West Saxons was to the south of Exmoor, and during the seventh century several battles were fought in the vicinity of the Dumnonian capital, Exeter, with the result that the Romano-British were driven back; and by AD682 all of Somerset was in Saxon hands.

There was no massacre of the local population though: it was the local aristocracy and their retainers who would have suffered, most of whom would have fled or been killed, to be replaced by new Saxon lords. Many of the ordinary people of Withycombe, with the exception of those who had fought and died for their old masters, would have continued to live as before, although under their new lords their status may have declined somewhat. Saxon society included various classes, depending on whether they owned or rented land, or held none at all, and whether they were noble, free or enslaved. Naturally the Saxon victors would have had the pick of any existing farms and estates, while the 'Welsh', as they called the British, would have made up the majority of the slaves. Only gradually did a new homogeneous society grow up, neither British nor Saxon but a combination of the two peoples.

The arrival of the Saxons in Withycombe is revealed in some of the names of the farms that must have existed in that era, notably Gupworthy and Brownsworthy. Worthies were Anglo-Saxon farms containing a house surrounded by an area of farm land, fenced around according to the laws of King Ine, who was ruler of Wessex in the late-seventh century. This pattern can still be seen at Gupworthy Farm in the west of the parish. Brownsworthy no longer exists, but it once lay near Carhampton Cross, where fields called Browndry, Brownsery, etc. can still be found. The house today called Little Browndrey stands in one of these. Also of course the name of Withycombe (and for that matter Rodhuish) has its origins in the Anglo-Saxon language.

In the Withycombe of that period there would certainly have been a number of man-made features that can be seen today, such as many of the roads and tracks that run through or around the village. There would have been a manor farm in existence too and there is no reason to suspect that it would have stood anywhere else than on the site of the later principal manor farm, i.e. where Withycombe Farm now stands, contained within the triangle of land between West and Lower Streets. The manors of Combe and Gildencote would also have had their demesne farms. Judging by its name alone, it must be a possibility that the present Combe Farm is a direct descendant of the former. The whereabouts of

Gildencote's manor-house is unknown but there certainly was one. In 1327 Alicia de Gildenecote paid a tax in Carhampton, suggesting that part of the manor, probably including the house, may have been across the parish boundary. This is interesting because an old farmhouse at Oak in Carhampton, literally just across the road from the Withycombe fields now known as Gilcotts, was traditionally associated with those fields some 500 years ago. It is tempting to link the manor to Golsoncott in Roadwater, as did the authors of the *Domesday Gazetteer*, but the evidence suggests that this would be incorrect.

We have no clues regarding the existence of a church at Withycombe before the current building was erected in the Norman period, but it is likely that some facility existed, given that the West Saxons embraced Christianity, as had the Romans before them. It could be that the peasants had to be content with services held at the preaching crosses, at Brethren Cross to the north of the village and possibly also at Top Cross, next to the churchyard; or they may have had to visit the church at Carhampton, as some still do today. The manor-house may have had a private chapel, in which case this would have been close to – perhaps even on the site of – the later church.

The next major upheaval in village life occurred in 1066, when victory at the Battle of Hastings saw the Normans wrest England from the hands of the Anglo-Saxons. As with the coming of the Saxons, this would have had the greatest effect on the aristocratic possessors of the land, and less on the ordinary people of Withycombe. The Norman invaders, initially spread thinly throughout the land, sought security by building castles for themselves and so were concerned with garnering the income from existing estates. They retained their common soldiery within their strongholds for protection so that there were no sudden dramatic seizures of farms, houses, etc. as there had been when the Saxons took over. Thus Dunster Castle was built, from which its Norman lords ruled the lands around it. Only gradually, as they began to feel secure, did occupation of local houses and farms take place, inevitably beginning with the best of these.

To enable the Normans to maximise their income from the newly conquered land King William had the Domesday Book drawn up in 1086. This was intended to be a survey of the entire country, for the purpose of tax assessment. Withycombe had land for 10 ploughs, 2 of which belonged to the demesne (the principal farm of the manor, for the use and direct benefit of its lord), which had 6 serfs or slaves. The land for the other 8 ploughs was divided between 14 villeins and 7 bordars. These were basically farmers and smallholders respectively. There was 1 riding-horse, also 3 cattle, 10 pigs, 40 sheep and 30 goats, 10 acres of meadow, 550 acres of pasture and 96 acres of woodland. It had been held in the time of Edward the Confessor (whose death prompted the Norman

invasion) by one Alnod. Interestingly though, in 1086 it was held by another Saxon – Edmer – from his Norman overlord Geoffrey, Bishop of Coutances. Before 1066 Edmer had jointly held Aller, a smaller manor on the Carhampton side of Withycombe Hill. Withycombe's three hides of land in total, which had paid a geld of four pounds under King Edward, was now assessed to pay six.

The manors of Combe and Gildencote had both been given to Roger of Courseulles. At Combe there was land for only 1 plough, half of which made up the demesne, the other half being farmed by a single bordar. There was 1 pig, also 8 sheep and 4 goats, 16 acres of pasture and 18 acres of woodland. Worth only 5s.0d., it had been held by the Saxon Alric but in 1086 was directly in Roger's hands.

Gildencote, previously held by Edwin, had by this time been given to Alric. There was land for one and a half ploughs there, one of which was being farmed by 3 bordars. There were 2 cattle, 1 pig, 11 sheep and 11 goats and 6 acres of meadow, 50 acres of pasture and 15 acres of woodland. Previously worth 8s.0d., the Normans declared it to be worth 10s.0d.

If some of the acreages given in Domesday seem low (Rodhuish was only 13 acres in total!) this is mainly because uncultivated areas such as heathland were not included in the assessment because they had no intrinsic value.

Geoffrey of Coutances had been a soldier who fought bravely for William at Hastings and in subsequent battles and was rewarded with a host of manors, including 70 in Somerset alone. He died in 1093 and Withycombe passed to his nephew Robert de Moubrey, the Earl of Northumberland. He rebelled against the King and was stripped of his lands two years later. It is likely that this was when Withycombe was given to the first William de Mohun, the lord of Dunster Castle who already possessed much of the land in the vicinity.

He gave the manor of Withycombe to hold in fee (i.e. in return for knight's service) to a kinsman named Durand, who in 1086 already held some of William's other manors, including Brown (in Treborough) and Old Stowey. It was probably then or soon after that alterations were made to some of these manors, which included the creation of the new manor of Sandhill by cutting out an area of land in the north-east part of Withycombe and combining it with that at Stowey.

Durand's son William fitz Durand succeeded him, followed by his son Ralph (who styled himself as Ralph fitz William). In consideration of his marriage to Yolenta, the sister of William de Mohun IV, Ralph had the scutage (military service) due from the manor of Withycombe remitted.

Clearly this marriage to the sister of his feudal overlord brought considerable advantage to Ralph and it is likely that the building of the church at Withycombe was prompted by it. The de Mohuns at

Dunster were great benefactors of the Church, especially the Benedictine brotherhood, and the provision of a new Parish Church, situated next to his manor-house at Withycombe, would have been just the action to ensure his favour in the eyes of his wife's family. In 1194 Ralph granted a pension to the Benedictine Prior of Bath out of his church at Withycombe, and the Prior later restored the advowson – the right to appoint an incumbent – to him.

Ralph died around 1212, leaving three heirs: Lucy (relict of William Malet), Ilaria (wife of Richard of Combe) and Isabel (wife of Hugh Peverel). While the first two were his daughters, Isabel is more likely to have been a granddaughter, offspring of a known third daughter. A dispute and a lengthy court case ensued, which resulted in the division of the manor of Withycombe into thirds around 1238. Lucy Malet, the senior co-heiress, inherited the manor and the advowson of the church, which she held directly from the lord of Dunster. Ilaria and Isabel each held a third of the manor from Lucy.

Technically, Withycombe was still only one manor, comprising three parts; but it was effectively now three manors, each with its own demesne and Manor Court, and generally came to be treated as such. Only the valuable advowson clearly demonstrated the superiority of Lucy's holding. Each had its own distinct history from this point on.

We have a brief glimpse of the lives of the ordinary men of Withycombe dating from Lucy Malet's lordship in the court records of the time. In 1225 William de Hulle killed Ralph de Hulle in the 'vill [implying village] of Withicumbe' and fled. Their names suggest that they both lived at somewhere known as Hill – probably the area adjoining the Higher Rodhuish Road where the three of the farms named 'Hill' (Lower, Middle and Higher) are known to have stood – rather than that they were related, as many surnames at that time were not hereditary. William was outlawed and his chattels, declared to be worth 6s.4d., seized. Another murder was recorded in Withycombe during this period, in this case of one Robert Cory, for which there were no suspects.

In 1242 Lucy Malet herself was accused of unjustly dispossessing one Adam le Gras of his free tenement in Dunster and Withycombe, which consisted of a messuage with two acres of land. Adam thought that he had inherited the property from the previous tenant, a man named Elias, a priest. However, Lucy successfully asserted that because Elias was a bastard he could not legally have an heir; and so the property reverted to her as chief lady of the fee. Adam was found to be in the wrong and was declared 'in mercy', i.e. subject to a fine, but being a pauper had no means to pay.

When the manor of Withycombe was divided into three parts, Lucy Malet retained most of what was clearly the original demesne land adjoining Withycombe Farm, as well as much of the higher

ground in the west of the parish – Gupworthy, Higher Dumbledeer, etc. Also included were most of the properties that seem to have been built on the edge of glebe land, such as those on the east side of Mill Street. Withycombe Farm (with its private entrance to the churchyard – a clear indicator of its status) continued to be the manor farm. The little manors of Combe and part of Gildencote had probably been absorbed into Withycombe by this time: the area around the former was certainly later part of the superior third; and when the heirs of Ilaria's manor took in the fields associated with the latter (by 1325) an annual rent of 5s.0d. became payable to the superior manor as well, indicating that it had also become Withycombe property. Lucy's manor became known as Withycombe Wyke, supposedly as a result of an error made when a sixteenth-century scribe, consulting a list of manors, thought the name referred to a single manor instead of two in an alphabetical sequence.

Her sister Ilaria's manor seems to have consisted mostly of land in the north of the parish. It is impossible to be certain because Isabel's third had a relatively short existence before its lands were purchased by Ilaria's heirs, so it is difficult to ascertain which property originally belonged to which. It is likely that Ilaria's manor farm, now with its own demesne lands, was at Court Place; and it certainly became the demesne farm after the two sub-manors were combined. Isabel's manor may have been located in the south-west of the parish, extending perhaps as far east as Buckhill and Rattle Row. It certainly included the area known as Hill. The two combined manors later became known as Withycombe Hadley.

The creation of the three manors from one original had some interesting financial consequences. The mill had been built at some time between 1086 and 1238, and all three manors needed to use it, so all three paid a third of its annual manor rent, which was 10s.0d. in total. Thus each paid 3s.4d., so that after two of the manors were combined, the now larger manor paid 6s.8d. This continued until 1709, when Withycombe Wyke ceased to exist. We see a similar situation with the stream at Brethren Cross, where the people of Withycombe were obliged to maintain a 'bulwark' to direct the Withycombe Brook towards Marshwood in Carhampton, to supply the deer and the keeper of the de Mohun's park there with water. Each third part of the manor was obliged to play their role, so after the amalgamation of the two parts the enlarged manor of Withycombe Hadley had to contribute two-thirds of the labour and cost of maintenance, with Withycombe Wyke providing the other third.

This situation, whereby the superior manor was now half the size of the other, gradually led to an increased influence of the lords of Withycombe Hadley in village life. This was helped by the fact that by the end of the fourteenth century the

The effigy on the north side of the church, thought to represent Lucy, the mother of Withycombe's first known incumbent, Walter de Meriet.

superior manor had passed into the hands of various individuals who had no real connection to the village. There is no room here to go into full details regarding the history of these separate manors and a brief summary will have to suffice.

After Lucy Malet's death in 1258 her manor passed first to Simon de Meriet and then to Thomas of Timworth, both of whom had married her daughter, also called Lucy. It is thought that the two effigies in Withycombe's church represent Thomas and his wife. Lucy outlived her second husband and in 1307 conveyed the manor to her son Walter de Meriet, to whom she had earlier presented the living of her Church of St Nicholas, despite the fact that he had not been ordained! Nevertheless, he was clearly a highly religious man who rose to a high position in the Church (the King personally recommended him to the Pope) and accordingly he eschewed marriage and the prospect of an heir and left the manor to his nephew, another Simon de Meriet.

After the death of Simon's widow Margery in 1390, it passed through various distant hands before becoming part of the huge Beaumont estate. This was transferred after 1500 to various feoffees: Giles, Lord Daubenny, took on Withycombe. It passed to his son Sir Henry Daubenny, then fell to another Beaumont heir, James Basset. In 1560 he conveyed the manor to John Southcott and it remained in his family until 1650, when Edward Southcott got into trouble as a 'Popish recusant' and sold it on. The manor at this time was said to contain 20 messuages, a water-mill, a dovecot, 300 acres of land (arable), 100 of meadow, 300 of pasture, 60 of wood, 500 of furze and heath, and £3 of rent, at Withycombe and Dunster. It was purchased by Thomas Cridland, gentleman, and then passed in quick succession through several members of his family, and subsequently by marriage to Gifford, Tynte and Wyndham, all of whom died after short periods of tenure. Widow Jane Wyndham then married Colonel John Codrington of Gloucestershire, before dying herself.

John Codrington was the last owner of Withycombe Wyke. In 1709, being about to marry a second wife, he was forced to raise a large sum of money as his part of a bargain with his father concerning a marriage settlement, and so he sold the manor piecemeal, raising over £3,400 thereby.

Turning our attention now to Ilaria's sub-manor, this quickly passed into the hands of the notorious Fitzurse family. It is assumed that this came about because Ilaria was at some time married to John Fitzurse, nephew of the murderer of Thomas à Becket. The manor stayed in that family for four generations, mostly under successive lords named Ralph Fitzurse, before it was settled upon a daughter named Hawis, who married Hugh Durburgh of Heathfield in 1344.

James Durburgh had the manor settled upon him by his father Hugh in 1379. James died in 1416 and was briefly succeeded by his son John; then the latter's widow's remarriage to Alexander Anne led to a lengthy dispute over her inheritance. The manor of Withycombe was finally settled upon the pair of them for the nominal rent of a gillyflower, with the remainder passing to Ralph Durburgh. This was later altered so that Ralph's daughters, Joan Courtenay and Alice Hadley, would eventually inherit. Consequently John and Joan Courtenay were in possession from about 1436, then after their deaths the manor was settled upon Alice Hadley, her husband Alexander and their son John. It was from this time on that the manor became known as Withycombe Hadley.

John Hadley died around 1502, being succeeded by his son Richard. He was followed in 1524 by his son James, who died in 1539. His son Christopher Hadley did not live to succeed him, dying in the following year when Elizabeth, his father's third wife, was still in possession. On the death of Elizabeth Hadley the manor passed to Margaret, the granddaughter of James Hadley, who had married Thomas Luttrell. From this point on until its final dispersal in the last century the Luttrell family of Dunster Castle retained the manor of Withycombe Hadley, holding it from themselves as lords of the fee, via the lord of the superior manor of Withycombe Wyke until 1709, then afterwards directly.

Finally we come to Isabel's short-lived portion. After the death of Hugh Peverel she married Sir Nicholas Martin; and a marriage between her granddaughter Amy and his son Robert saw the manor pass to them. A document drawn up in 1286 by Sir Robert Martin, granting a messuage in his manor of Withycombe to Geoffrey Dobel, which his father Robert Dobel had held as a villein, shows that it was a complete and separate manor at this time, with its own Manor Court.

In 1304 Robert Martin granted the manor to his younger son Edmund, who is known to have lived in Withycombe. Edmund Martin, like any manorial

Since early times a number of the community's groups and organisations have traditionally been connected with the Church. A modern village society in action: the ladies of Withycombe's Women's Institute performing a mimed 'Nativity' at Washford in 1963.

Members of Withycombe's Women's Institute at Minehead Grammar School in medieval dress for a performance of 'Mistress Bottom's Dream' in 1962. Left to right: Ann Fielding, Mrs Cridge, Debbie Crossman, Miss Huntley, Mrs Crossman, Mrs Watts, Mrs Strong, Miss Poyser and Katherine Bird.

lord intending to live on his own demesne, had his own chapel, which in 1318 was granted an episcopal licence for a chaplain to celebrate there during the term of his life and that of his wife. However, it seems that Edmund and Isabel had no children of their own to whom they could leave their manor, so in 1329 they sold the reversion of it to Ralph and Maud Fitzurse, via an intermediary. They remained as tenants for life, in possession of lands at Withycombe, Watchet, Cutcombe and Luxborough, which they held for a nominal rent from Sir Ralph Fitzurse. These lands beyond the parish of Withycombe were no doubt those that were associated with the manor of Withycombe Hadley throughout the centuries that followed: several farms, cottages and a mill at Watchet; two tenements and woodland in Cutcombe, held for a long period by the family of Chapman; and a tenement at Drucombe, Luxborough.

By 1350 Edmund Martin was dead and his third of the old manor of Withycombe was amalgamated with that belonging to Ralph Fitzurse. However, that is not quite the end of the story. Edmund's nephew Robert Martin was not happy about this loss of the manor and had been pressing his suit at law since 1329. It failed, but a grant of land made by Ralph Fitzurse to Robert Martin in 1349 looks suspiciously like an attempt to appease the latter. This property was at Hill ('La Hulle'). In 1325 Edmund Martin had demised a tenement to Adam, son of Nicholas de Hulle, and Joan, daughter of Henry le Poare, which had previously been held in villeinage by Paul de Hulle. This property, in 1349 held in villeinage by Adam and William atte Hulle, was granted to Robert Martin for a rent of a pound of pepper and a pound of cumin, and he was granted exemption from any obligation to serve as tithingman.

While an account of Withycombe's history during the medieval period would be incomplete without mention of its various feudal lords, this history really starts to come to life when we encounter the true villagers such as the family 'atte Hulle'. Unlike the lords, of whom many would only have been irregular visitors to the parish at best, these people had held the property in villeinage for generations, and would certainly have lived there. The name, meaning 'at Hill', emphasises this, whereas 'of Hill' is more equivocal. The descendants of this family could include some of Withycombe's later residents such as the Hills, who were still farming in the area of Hill in the 1600s, and/or the Tuttles/Tuthills. This family appears briefly in the records of another violent incident that occurred in 1316, which also mentions one or two other villagers. On the night of 2 October three robbers, 'strangers and unknown', forced their way into the house of Richard le Elyman at Sandhill, tied him up and killed him with a blow to the head before making off with their booty. Richard Crop, a Withycombe villager, found the body, and Thomas

and Paul Uppehulle gave pledges to this. The latter is likely to have been the Paul de Hulle mentioned in Edmund Martin's document of 1325. At the inquest into the death the coroner was Sir Ralph Fitzurse, who was coincidentally also the lord of his family's third of the manor of Withycombe at that time. The jury was made up of the gentry of the district, with only Robert of Sandhill and Gilbert le Pestour likely to have been Withycombe residents. Thomas Uppehulle must have been one of the village's more successful farmers, as he contributed 12d. to the Lay Subsidy in 1327, the same amount as Alice of Sandhill and Gilbert le Pestour. The only people in the parish who paid more were Walter de Meriet and Edmund Martin (3s.0d. each), Ralph Fitzurse and William Barbican (2s.0d. each), and William Boghdone (15d.). The first three of these were the lords of the three sub-manors, the fourth was the vicar, while William Bowdon (whose name suggests his home within the parish) was at one time reeve to Ralph Fitzurse. Also named were William of Sandhill (paying 8d.), and Geoffrey Teori and Elena of Sandhill (7d. each).

Most of the population of Withycombe at that time would have been involved in farming, as was the case right up until the twentieth century; just about everyone would have been working for part of the time on their lord's estate, while those with their own farm or smallholding spent the rest of their time tending their own animals and crops. Although there is little record of it, there must have been a weaving tradition in the village, given that sheep rearing was the prime concern of the hill farmers. The field between the village and Great Wood Close has been called Rack Close since at least the early-seventeenth century, indicating that it was once used for drying cloth, and there was another with that name at Dumbledeer.

It would be wrong, however, to think of everyday life as purely unremitting labour. In many villages in the modern era various societies thrive (in Withycombe in 1927, for example, there were the Mothers' Union, the Girls' Friendly Society, the Clothing Club, a Nursing Association, the Women's Conservative League and even the Junior Imperial League!) and this is not a new phenomenon. Many of today's societies have their roots in groups set up centuries ago, and during the medieval period these were, more often than not, established in connection with the Parish Church as Church societies.

The medieval Parish Church was of course Catholic, and consequently the interior would have looked very different to today's rather austere appearance. The walls were plastered and possibly painted as well, while wooden items such as the rood-screen would have been brightly painted and/or gilded. Withycombe Church's late-medieval screen was still gilded (and the building's internal walls plastered) in the late-eighteenth century. As well as the main altar there would have been other images of the saints

Twentieth-century revels: the coronation of King George VI in 1937 saw extensive celebrations in the village, including this fancy-dress gathering in Bean Meadow. Those identified (left to right) *include: Reg Young and Bob Gould* (two boys looking at the camera), *Miss Maidment, Mrs Scudamore* ('Buy British...'), *Mary Cridge, Polly Davey* (nurse), *Gertrude Sully, Rhoda Wyburn* (flags), *Miss Edbrooke* (behind), *Linda Cridge, Rene Needs* (in white), *Mrs Rowberry, 'Timmy' Burnett* (behind), *Annie Gould, Fred Jones* (soldier, in front), *George 'Jolly Roger' Davey* (accordion and moustache), *Ted Davey* (behind), *Charlie Coles* (another accordion), *Carl Meddick, Ralph Pearse.*

Maypole dancing, organised by Mrs Read, was part of the festivities at the coronation celebrations. Ralph Pearse, Fred Hawkins and George Davey played the accompaniments.

with their own side altars, before which candles, tapers or mortars would be burned. There were often four of these 'lights' and this was the case at Withycombe. In the will of John How of Withycombe, dated 28 May 1530, the sum of 16d. was left for the four lights in the Parish Church. One of these would have been in front of the High Cross, called the 'dead-light' because it was burned in remembrance of the dead, while another was an image of the Virgin Mary, for which the manor of Withycombe Hadley contributed payment for 6lbs of tallow each year, but we do not know what the others were at Withycombe.

There would have been a fund or store associated with each of these, not just to pay for the candles, etc., but also for the paraphernalia of the several altars, such as embroidered cloths and adornments intended to enhance and glorify the images thereon. In addition there would have been funds for the upkeep of the building and other obligations and responsibilities within the community. The maintenance of any of these funds could have been the responsibility of a village society. At Morebath, a parish on the other side of Exmoor, for example, these included one made up of the young men and another of the maidens of the parish. Money-raising, then as now, was largely done by holding parish events, such as annual revels and the ever-popular church ales, where ale, brewed in the Church House, was sold.

All of this came to an end in the 1530s, when Henry VIII started the process by which Catholicism was replaced by the Church of England, and all 'Popish frippery' such as worship of the saints was banned. Withycombe's last fully Catholic priest was Robert Bullar, who (mercifully, one would think) died just before Henry's changes began to take effect. His replacement was John Bullar, probably a relation, who saw the village through the difficult years from 1535 to 1542, followed by John Skypwyth, who endured the switchback of the Catholic resurgence under Queen Mary between periods of anti-Catholic rule.

This was a time of great transition in Withycombe, as elsewhere, with fundamental changes taking place in the village. Prior to the Reformation everyday life was still rolling along on the lines suggested by Domesday: villein-land was still distinguished from that belonging to free and customary tenants, and the latter were still obliged to do daywork on the lord's demesne, although by 1500 this seems to have been reduced to a largely symbolic minimum of just one day in the autumn. Property rents within the village seem to have varied from year to year and included many additions to the basic manor rent, such as 'Goosdon, Standon and Mardon', 'cocks and hens' and Saint Peter's Pence. We know this because of the survival of some Withycombe Hadley rentals from Henry VII's time and a detailed survey of that manor made in the first half of the sixteenth century. Here

we begin to see the people of the parish with the modern type of surname, passed from generation to generation: William White, followed by his widow Alice for a tenement; Robert Willyns, then John Howe for Willyns' Tenement; John then Richard Trott for a cottage. Some properties are identifiable, even at this early date. We find William Woodward at Lower Dumbledeer, William Howe and Laurence Westcott at two of the Hill farms, while Robert and then John Thorne were paying for the mill and its water. The Thorne family was ever-present in the village throughout the next three centuries

Goosdon, Standon and Mardon were areas of hill pasture, likely to correspond with different parts of the common land on the high ground in the west of the parish. Goosdon was Goose Down, the eastern end of Withycombe Hill, nearest the village; Standon was Stane (Stone) Down, close to the 'druidical remains' by Higher Dumbledeer; and Mardon was possibly Mark Down (the name indicating its position next to the parish boundary), either at the western extremity of Withycombe Hill or just maybe on Black Hill. This theory is largely borne out by the fact that tenants paid only for those areas closest to their homes. Consequently most of the customary tenants, who tended to rent smallholdings in the village itself, paid only for Goosdon, whereas those with villein-land, many of whom rented the hill farms to the west and who had more animals to pasture, tended to pay for either Standon and Mardon, or Goosdon and Standon, depending on their location. William Stephens of Gupworthy, for example, paid for Standon and Mardon, as one might expect. The sum paid seems to have depended upon the amount of stock that the tenant owned. These payments were only made by tenants of property which lay within the parish of Withycombe, again as one would expect. The demesne farm at Court Place paid for 'two parts' of all three, implying that Withycombe Wyke paid the other part – this is the old division into thirds, suggesting that the system was in use when the manor was divided.

'Cocks and hens' seems to have been a local term for hen-rent, which in the early 1500s was set at $7^1/_2$d. and was paid by a handful of customary tenants. Saint Peter's Pence was a levy of a penny for the Church of Rome, which only some tenants had to pay. As well as the above, a number of tenants had to present goods with or instead of money. Three farms – two of the three Hill farms and Lower Dumbledeer – had to pay a bushel of rye every autumn. It is not clear how this custom originated but it was kept up until around 1700. The most bizarre items, however, were owed by the free tenants of the manor, i.e. those who held property in areas that had been granted separate status, such as Sandhill, or which had come to the manor as discrete entities, like Gildencote. Some paid in cumin, or wax (for candles), but several people, most connected with property at Gildencote, had to deliver a single red rose to the ash tree there on Midsummer Day! A small field in that part of the parish is still called Rose-Ash. These were clearly symbolic, intended merely as acknowledgements of obligation to the lord of the manor.

The Reformation obviously swept away any obligations to pay Saint Peter's Pence, but the lords of Withycombe Hadley went much further, creating an altogether simpler system. The complexities of cocks and hens, Goosdon, Standon and Mardon and daywork disappeared, as did many (but not all) of the token rents. Where rents had been constantly variable they became fixed, to the extent that many a farm, cottage or field can be identified between 1570 and 1750, or even later, by its rent alone. The system of payment for hill pasture seems to have survived in a new, simpler form, called 'goose money'. The larger farms paid 8d. annually, on top of their rent, smallholdings paid 4d., while one or two of intermediate size paid 6d. The name was surely a shortening of 'Goose Down money'. Whether animals continued to be pastured across Withycombe Hill or were now enclosed at the Goose Down end is a matter for conjecture, but the 1840 Tithe Map shows a single large enclosed field called Withycombe Hill Inclosure on Goose Down. The manor of Withycombe Wyke also adopted this system, its payments generally being set at 10d. Goose money, like the new manor rents, remained fixed whatever changes occurred to the property. No matter if a smallholding gave up its few acres of fields and became just a cottage and garden, it still had to pay its 4d. at Michaelmas.

It is likely that this modernisation was instigated by the Luttrell family after Thomas Luttrell's marriage to Margaret Hadley. With many manors and estates to manage they were meticulous record keepers and would have made the ordering of the complex Withycombe Hadley accounts a priority. Thanks to them we are able to trace the history of almost every property in the village from the time of the first Queen Elizabeth. In the following chapters we will attempt to do just that by taking a journey around the parish, visiting the various properties en route and meeting some of the people who have lived in them over the centuries. Commencing by the churchyard at Top Cross we will follow a figure-of-eight route that takes in all of the village's main highways.

Before we set off though, a brief glance at an event from Elizabeth I's reign that affected Withycombe in an age-old way: the threat of assault from the sea, as trouble flared on the high seas between Britain and Spain, beginning the conflict that would eventually lead to an attempted invasion by the Spanish Armada. As in centuries gone by, watchers were posted on Withycombe Hill to look out for enemy ships, the fire beacon there readied for instant ignition should a warning need to be flashed across the country. Local militia were mustered, armed and prepared to defend our shores.

In 1569, at the start of these troubles, eight able men of Withycombe stood ready to repel any invader: John Liddon, wielding his pike; Donat (probably the man whose real name – Covenant – gave scribes endless trouble) Harris, Robert Hill and David Thorne with simple bills; archers Thomas Wethey (Withey) and Richard Thorne; and gunners Robert Blandon and Lewes Allen. The tithingman's armour of corslet and almain rivet (flexible armour) was provided for their use, while other villagers produced three more pairs of almain rivets, seven bills and a handgun. Fortunately for them and the rest of us the Spanish Armada never made it as far as the Bristol Channel.

Looking towards Withycombe Hill from the field called Oakey, with the heart of the village laid out between. In the foreground is the Rectory, with the top of Lower Street behind, the Parish Church and Withycombe Farmhouse occupy the middle ground, while the houses of West Street stand further away.

Two

West Street (Top Cross to Culver Lane)

Top Cross lies at the heart of the village, at the junction of Lower, Mill and West Streets, next to the churchyard. Its name, obviously indicative of the meeting of roads, also suggests that a preaching cross might once have stood on the corner (the base of one can be found in the churchyard). Was it called 'Top' Cross to distinguish it from Brothers' or Brethren Cross at the bottom of Court Place Lane?

We will commence our tour of the parish at the little Church of St Nicholas (*above*). From architectural evidence the building is said to date from the thirteenth century, a period of great change in the village, when the three female heirs of Ralph fitz William split the manor into three parts. Ralph himself made reference to his church at Withycombe, and logic suggests that he was its most likely builder, although it may not have been completed until after his death in 1212. The earliest surviving external feature – a small lancet window on the south side – is said to date from 1230. Early photographs and paintings, however, show that this was not apparent from the outside until the twentieth century.

The building was constructed of rough rubble, said never to have been intended for exposure; instead it was plastered and periodically limewashed to give it an attractively bright appearance, especially when viewed from a distance. At least, that is the established view. A watercolour painting executed in 1843 by John Buckler appears to show exposed stonework: however, another by William Wheatley painted just two years later depicts it in its more familiar state, so it may be that Buckler used a certain amount of artistic licence. The churchwardens' accounts of 1782 include a large payment to John Jones for painting, plastering and limewashing the church, and notes made for Collinson's 1791 book describe the tower at least as being externally plastered – both of which suggest that the established view is the correct one.

The church is dedicated to St Nicholas, who was associated with travellers and merchants, as well as children and scholars. He was celebrated annually on 6 December. Inside, a couple of windows and the remains of a small doorway all date from the fourteenth century. The walls, which now show only the rough stonework, were once plastered. The splendid rood-screen is one of seven ornate fan-vaulted screens constructed locally by Flemish craftsmen during the period 1490–1520. The others were made for Bicknoller, Carhampton, Dunster, Exford, Minehead and Timberscombe. The example at Carhampton has been restored to its original, richly decorated condition, but that at Withycombe – once gilded – is now plain.

The font, the oldest item in the building, is Norman, thought to date from around 1180. Significantly it belongs to the era of Ralph fitz William. It has seen the christening of thousands of Withycombe babes, the author included.

There are two effigies in the body of the church, carved of Ham Hill stone. A female figure reposes below the north window, opposite the doorway into the church; the other, a male, is on the south side to the right of the door, oddly placed almost at ground level and partly hidden behind the pews. The woman is almost certainly Lucy de Meriet (daughter of Lucy Malet) who inherited the superior manor of Withycombe Wyke from her mother, and hence possessed the advowson of the church; and the man is thought to be her second husband, Thomas of Timworth, for a period Constable of Taunton Castle. Through his marriage to Lucy (c.1280) he also became possessed of the manor. His effigy is thought to be the oldest known example in England showing a man wearing a hat!

The embattled church tower is unusual in that its ground floor forms the porch. It contains four bells, which were re-hung in a new oak cage in 1903, with further improvements being made in 1955. The oldest bell is the treble, cast in 1619 by George Purdue of Taunton; then the third bell (William Purdue of Bristol, 1648); then the second (Thomas Wroth

John Buckler's 1843 painting of the church. While it clearly shows the building with exposed stonework, this may simply reflect his preferred style of drawing. However, it seems to be generally an accurate depiction, including such detail as the Verelst family grave at the base of the yew tree. The railings around it are long gone and the grave itself is now completely overhung by the tree's branches. (COURTESY OF SOMERSET ARCHAEOLOGICAL AND NATURAL HISTORY SOCIETY, PAINTING JOHN BUCKLER)

Left: *A photograph taken inside the Church of St Nicholas in the early 1960s, showing the ornate rood-screen.*

William Walter Wheatley's 1845 watercolour. More of a sketch than Buckler's piece, this nevertheless shows the church with its familiar façade. Moreover, the plaster seems weathered, making it unlikely that this had been newly done. The cottage shown in the background is surely a case of artistic licence, with an impression of the building across the road, belonging to smith James Case, being included to 'improve' the picture. (COURTESY OF SOMERSET ARCHAEOLOGICAL AND NATURAL HISTORY SOCIETY, PAINTING W.W. WHEATLEY)

of Wellington, 1719); and finally the tenor (William Evans of Chepstow, 1742).

The church's incumbents are listed in the porch, the names differing only slightly from those listed by F.W. Weaver who in turn drew on the Bishops' Registers. The list below was compiled following comparison of both sources.

The Rectors of Withycombe

1297	Walter de Meriet
1305	William de Milverton
1311	William Barbecan
1330	William Raspyn
1333	William Percehay or Pertehay
1334	Reginald de Buggewell or de Ruggewell
1349	John de Horton
1356	John Raspyn
?	Edward Gyst
1390	Ralph Modiforde
1391	Stephen Priour
1402	Richard Grenevyle
1406	John Hales
1416	William Comb
1418	Richard Hockeday
1419	George Feddys
1419	John Piers
1469	Stephen Clement MA
1505	John Hopwode or Heywode
1506	Robert Bullar MA
1535	John Bullar
1542	John Skypwyth
1565	Robert Watkyns
1571	Edward Croftes
1573	Thomas Jones MA
1581	John Bourne
1588	Laurence Uppington
1639	John Uppington MA
1670	Thomas Collard
1691	Andrew Verryard
1715	Benjamin Bulkley MA
1725	Samuel Rogers MA
1767	George Inman
1791	Thomas Bowman
1818	Arthur Charles Verelst
1844	Charles Cooke
1873	Robert Birtwhistle MA
1894	George William Govan
1931	Albert George Ford
1935	Ernest Williams
1945	Cyril Vine Camplin-Coggan
1952	Harold Montague Hyde-Lees
1963	Joseph Hamilton-Jones
1964	Robert Leslie Watson
1968	George May Hickman
1984	Robert Doré
1994	Michael Paul Grantham

Bridgwater photographer Robert Gillo visited Withycombe c.1870: this is a picture which he took of the Rectory. (COURTESY OF SOMERSET STUDIES LIBRARY)

One name that does not appear on the list is that of John Jenkins, who was described as 'minister' or 'rector' at the christening of many of his own children in the parish during the supposed incumbency of Andrew Verryard. Possibly some kind of informal exchange of benefices had taken place.

While Withycombe's church escaped the heavy-handed 'improvements' that afflicted many others in Victorian times, some major alterations were made during the early years of the First World War, which caused the building to be closed for some considerable time while the roof was replaced. Various doors have been either blocked up or opened at one time or another, especially one on the south side, at the chancel end, inside of which stands a colourful modern sculpture depicting St Nicholas, created by local artist Rachel Reckitt.

The houses on the other side of West Street are fronted by what was originally a length of causey stretching from Top Cross at least as far as the smithy and possibly even to the Culver Lane turning, but this has been disguised by alterations made in the modern era. However, nineteenth-century maps show it as it once was, lying alongside the highway, beyond the individual property boundaries.

The property at the Top Cross end of West Street had its original entrance on this causey, sharing it with its neighbour, The King's Arms. The messuage was an old and substantial house that belonged to the farm known as Milton's Tenement. Its surrounding grounds mostly overlooked Mill Street (reaching as far as Mill House), but the house and entrance were in West Street.

It paid an annual rent of 8s.4d. to the manor of Withycombe Hadley, indicating that it was in the small-farm bracket in terms of the value of its associated lands – little more than a large smallholding in that sense – but it did pay goose money at the highest rate of 8d., implying that it had its fair share of livestock. The earliest reference to it reveals that it

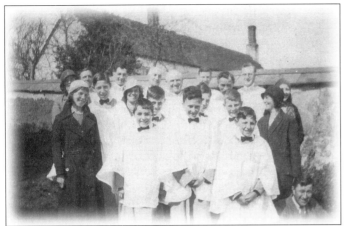

Left: *The choir, Easter 1931, in the churchyard with Withycombe Farmhouse in the background. Left to right, back: Olive Spracklan, Reg Young, Leonard Gould, James Andrews, Eli Burnell, George Maidment, Bill Nicholas, Mr Amherst (organist); middle: Joan Griffiths, Dennis Young, Rhoda Wyburn, George Hall, Reg Young junr, Harold Sully, Gertrude Sully, Winnie Nicholas; front: Charles Cridge, Fred Nicholas, Ray Young, Tom Lewis. This is one of the few old pictures to include Ray Young, probably because he was too busy for photographers to catch standing still! He has served the church and village in many capacities, and is always ready to assist those who need a helping hand. He was awarded an MBE for his service to the community in 2002.*

Workmen replacing roof timbers at the west end of the church, c.1914. The building was closed for worship for some time while these major repairs were undertaken.

Above: *The choir posing outside the church, c.1949.*
Left to right, back row: *Miss Coggan, Chris Bourne, Revd Camplin-Coggan, Leonard Gould;* middle: *Ann Prout, Edna Davey, Nora Cridge, Mavis Maidment, Janice Dibble, Trevor Cridge, Beatrice Nicholas;* front: *Derek Stevens, Bob Nicholas, Terry Jones.*

Left: *Gertrude Sully, Revd Hickman and Wendy Case in the church, 1972.*

Right: *Withycombe Church reopening in July 1913 following closure for repairs. Charles Hagley, with hand on hip, and Edgar Case are at the forefront, in their capacity as churchwardens, with the Revd Govan just behind. Charles had just put in the key for Prebendary Hancock.*

was in the hands of John Hiles from at least the late 1570s. John may have been the first of that family to settle in the village, making this their first Withycombe home. By 1604 widow Elnor Slade was in occupation. She was probably connected in some way to the Hiles family, as she also held a parcel of fields that were described as 'pt of Margaret Hiles' and which reverted to that family shortly afterwards.

Richard Hiles was the tenant in 1617. Then in 1678 it was widow Joane Hiles; she died in 1684, and two years later Francis Luttrell granted the lease to Elianor Milton, widow of Christopher. The 'messuage and tenement' was stated to consist of a dwelling-house and outhouses, court, garden and orchard of half an acre, with seven acres of land that included half an acre of meadow.

Elianor's son Christopher Milton was probably the man running the farm at this time, because he was named for the goose money payment in 1689, although his mother's name continued to appear on the reeve's list for it; and in 1693 'Elianor Milton's Estate' performed this duty. She died in 1696 and son Christopher was accordingly taken as the new tenant. Ten years later he too died, to be replaced as tenant by Robert Hole, yeoman of Carhampton. He leased the property 'late in the possession of Christopher Milton or his undertenants' on the lives of himself and children Robert and Joane.

There is no reason to believe that Robert Hole or any of his family ever occupied the property or even lived in Withycombe. Instead, he would have let it to undertenants. In the tithingman's list made in 1739, Robert Hole's estate was described as being 'opposite the churchyard', one of the few clues as to the whereabouts of this property. Hole's death was presented to the Manor Court in 1746 and another investor in property, William Oldman, was next to take on Milton's. He leased it in 1753 on the lives of his daughters Margaret Oldman, Catherine Prole and Joan Uppington, just a couple of months after he had taken the mill on the lives of two others (Mary and Jane Oldman). William must have been dead by 1769, because in that year his widow Margaret Oldman paid the Church Rate of 3d. 'for Hole's'. It is likely that the actual occupiers were William Uppington and his wife Joan (Oldman's daughter named on the lease), because William Uppington's name began to appear on the list of those obliged to do the tithingman's duty, and Milton's was one of those properties that traditionally returned a tithingman. Also, as will be seen below, his son John Uppington subsequently lived there.

A document of 1777 reveals that of the three lives named on the lease only Catherine Prole, aged 59, then survived. The property was still referred to as Milton's Tenement, said to include seven acres of land. However, in the following year it was described as a dwelling-house in the hands of widow Oldman – probably a truer picture of the situation at that time. Margaret Oldman appeared finally for Hole's in the Church Rate list of 1790, but the entry was overwritten 'John & Sam Hobbs'. These two had arrived in the village a few years earlier and had now acquired this and two other small farms. They amalgamated the land from all three, but selected the farmhouse belonging to Hoare's Tenement in Lower Street for their dwelling. The acquisition of the properties caused the Luttrells' bailiff to make a record of the complex situation, in which he noted that John Uppington had the house, garden and linney belonging to 'Oldman's or Milton's Tenement', which he presumably sublet from John and Samuel Hobbs.

Following John Uppington's period of residence, the house was found to be in dire need of repair. Consequently the Luttrells granted the occupiers disbursements towards the cost of improving it. Robert Cording lived there from 1810 to 1815 at least, and in the latter year he put in his claim for payment for the work done, which included:

George Cavill, for Sawing of Board:	*£0.7s.4d.*
Samuel Hobs, for Reed:	*£3.0s.0d.*
William Lovall, for Thatching:	*£1.0s.1d.*
James Case, for Ironwork:	*£0.7s.9d.*
Mr. Royal, for Laths:	*£0.2s.8d.*
James Hobs, for Carpenter's Work:	*£0.8s.0d.*
John Hobs, for Mason's Work:	*£0.11s.8d.*
Samuel Hobs, for Drawing Lime:	*£0.13s.4d.*
Mr. Pearce, for Lime:	*£0.14s.0d.*

The roof was thatched, part of the floor re-laid and much replastering was done. Note that the Hobbs family played a large part in the work, which is not surprising as they were the primary tenants. Mr Pearce was Nicholas Pearse of Whitehall, Old Cleeve, brother of William Pearse of Gupworthy Farm. The initial repairs done, Robert Cording quit the premises and it seems that James Chapman may have replaced him (see below).

Later James Hobbs the carpenter moved in with his wife Elizabeth (Blackwell), whom he had married in 1813 at Dunster. There was still apparently much work to be done, and soon James was presenting his landlord with another sheaf of bills for reimbursement. William Lovell was again called upon for thatching, but otherwise the work was exclusively done by the Hobbs family. James himself put up a new roof '22 long by 12 rafter', Mary was paid for lime and reed, Samuel for carriage of lime and bricks, and John for masonry work, including payments for the labour of (William) Burge, Richard Hobbs, and Richard and Thomas Milton. John's bill tells us that the work involved 'Building a new Shoop' – a shop, presumably.

In 1830 James Hobbs' house, etc. was valued at £1.5s.0d. A notice to further repair his premises, described as a cottage and orchard in Withycombe, which were 'ruinous and in decay', was sent by John

*A class photograph taken at Top Cross around 1901. Geoff Leversha
is on the left at the back.*

*A different class photographed at Top Cross around 1901. This was copied from a postcard sent on 11 March
1909 to Miss Olive Leversha upon the occasion of her birthday.*

Fownes Luttrell to James Hobbs in 1836, naming James Chapman as the previous occupant. It had been held since 1822 on the lives of James Hobbs, his wife Elizabeth and daughter Betsey.

The Tithe Map of 1840 shows the occupant of No.102 – a house, shop and garden – as George Burnell; and the census made in the following year also lists him, with his wife Mary and several children, between the entries for the house by the mill and the 'Old Kings Arms'. James Hobbs was not in the village. The explanation for George Burnell's presence in the Hobbs house lies with his wife: Mary was the sister of James Hobbs. James and Elizabeth Hobbs were back in the cottage in 1851, with James being referred to as a 'pauper carpenter', and they were still there in 1861, both in their seventies, with Elizabeth's sister Jane Blackwell staying with them.

By 1871 mason James Perkins and his family found themselves in the old house, but by this time it must have been obvious that they were fighting a losing battle against the crumbling fabric of the building. In letting him have the premises there may have been a plan for James to do a similar job of repair as the Hobbs family had performed earlier, but it came to nought. James was back in the family home of Smith's Cottage in 1881, with no sign of anyone at the house that once belonged to Milton's Tenement, either then or thereafter.

The first Ordnance Survey map of the village, produced in the 1880s, reveals that the house had gone by then, although an outbuilding that might have been the shop still stood, next to the road, more or less opposite what is now called Shell Cottage. Towards the end of the nineteenth century Henry Pearse took on much of the Hobbs' property, including Christopher's Farm and Milton's. The latter consisted of a garden and orchard, together with the outbuilding. Henry kept his cider press in it. His son Dick remembers that it was still thatched (William Lovell's work?) and recalls that traces of the house could still be seen well into the twentieth century. Parts of its walls remained above ground and the hearthstone survived. These remains and the 1840 Tithe Map reveal that the house stood quite close to The King's Arms – hence also to modern Foxwarren – and would have dominated the view of Top Cross. It was possibly Henry who made a new entrance to the plot by breaking out the retaining wall at the Top Cross junction and installing a gate there in order to simplify access. When it was sold by the Luttrells in 1951 it was described as 'a useful paddock', containing orchard, garden and fowl house. The tenants, still the Pearse family, purchased the lot. The author remembers the fowl house being used in the 1960s as the first home for day-old chicks, kept warm under electric light bulbs. The young birds would run around fearlessly in the fresh sawdust that covered the floor, scrambling over feet and cheeping constantly, until they had grown sufficiently to be transferred to the hen houses at Christopher's Farm. Since then the plot has been sold and a modern house built upon it.

Next to Milton's was the village inn, known throughout most of its history as The King's Arms. It stands no more, destroyed by fire at the dawn of the twentieth century, but overlooked the church for some 300 years at least prior to the disaster.

The earliest records suggest that it began life as a smallholding and was probably not opened as a hostelry until after the Civil War. Like all properties adjacent to the road in West Street (apart from the church), it belonged to the manor of Withycombe Hadley, to whose lord it paid an annual rent of 6s.8d., plus 4d. goose money at Michaelmas. The goose money payment is a reliable indication that it was originally a smallholding. In 1579 it is likely to have been the property held by Hugh Hampton, the same having Margaret Hampton as tenant a year or two earlier. Making the payment in the early 1600s was widow Joan Burrow. Subsequently it came into the hands of the Norris (alias Lieky) family. In 1655 it belonged to Thomas Norris, aged 50, and was described as a cottage, garden and orchard, late in the tenure of Daniell Norris, held by copy dating from 1639. It was granted in 1657 to Elizabeth Norris, the daughter of Thomas. This lease states that the cottage was then in the possession and tenure of Elizabeth Norris 'widdowe'. Thomas Norris rented the property until his death in 1681. It is not until 1689 that surviving rentals refer to it as 'ye Kings Arms'. In that year John Maunder was the tenant, having leased the property in 1682 when it was simply described as a cottage. Maunder had been a farmer in the village before moving to Stogumber, but had acquired property in Withycombe which he retained in order to provide income through subletting. The King's Arms was included.

Thus John Maunder seems to have been the man who turned the house into an inn. Why did he call it The King's Arms? Did this have anything to do with the attempted uprising in the West Country in 1685, when many Somerset men flocked to support the Duke of Monmouth, only to be decisively defeated at Sedgmoor? The King's men searched the towns and villages for the surviving rebels who, if caught, could expect summary justice from the ruthless Judge Jeffreys. Was Maunder's pub sign a visible statement of the village's – or his own – loyalty to the Crown?

In 1706 the Manor Court noted that Maunder's wife Elizabeth, on whose life the inn was held, had died; subsequently it passed to their son, also called John, who lived at Bicknoller. During this period the name of it was changed to The Queen's Arms – Queen Anne was on the throne – but this was a half-hearted attempt that was mostly ignored in the written records.

In 1718 the property was in demesne, Madam Luttrell paying the Church Rate of 1d. for The King's

Left: *Mary Hennessy, dressed in somewhat masculine fashion, in the doorway of Halswell, c.1918. On the far right is her groom Arthur James, beside him gardener Bill Gould.*

Below right: *Looking across to the churchyard from Halswell/Foxwarren.*

Below left: *Withycombe's famous artist John William North, who in the early years of the twentieth century lived at Halswell, the newly built replacement for The King's Arms.*

Members of Withycombe's sewing group posing on the lawn at Halswell (now Foxwarren) during the First World War. The Causey cottages behind still display thatched roofs.
Left to right, standing: a Belgian evacuee (name forgotten), Fanny Pearse, Lizzie Burnett, Lizzie Pearse, Polly Davey (daughter of Mrs Burnett); seated: Ann Willis, Lavinia Gould, Mrs Govan, Mrs Hennessy (the owner of Halswell), Mrs Maidment, Laura Boalsh.

Arms. Then in 1721 another Stogumber man, Edward Oatway, leased it, being admitted as a tenant of the manor for a dwelling-house, etc., known as The King's Arms. In the lease it was described as a 'messuage or dwelling-house together with outhouses, orchard, gardens, etc., late in the possession of John Maunders deceased.' Although still called The King's Arms, it seems that it had by this time reverted to being a private dwelling. A note survives among the Luttrell papers, sent by Edward Oatway to Madam Luttrell, in which he apologises for having to cancel a meeting with that lady (concerning the financial arrangements relating to his purchase of the lease) because his backer had to go to Bampton Fair!

Within a year of his being taken tenant Oatway was being presented at the Manor Court, for 'not repairing the staires going up to his Chambers belonging to the house wherein Henry Escott lives' which were 'much out of repair & dangerous for psons to goe upp.' This surely refers to The King's Arms, clearly in a poor condition at this time.

An Edward Oatway was buried at Withycombe in 1754 and William Oatway took over at The King's Arms. He was certainly a Withycombe man, what today we might call an entrepreneur, although the jurors at the Manor Court might have used a different term! He was presented in 1754 for cutting and carrying off turf from the Withycombe Hadley common for sale in other parishes; and again in the following year, this time for 'making an Incroachment on the Lords Wast in this manor by Inclosing part of it for a Potatoe Garden.' William would have been just the fellow to reopen The King's Arms as an alehouse or inn, and it seems as though he did precisely that.

Before each meeting of the Manor Court, a precept was issued, summoning the jurors to attend at a certain place and time. Some of these have survived from the 1750s. In 1755 the jurors were summoned to appear 'at the Dwelling-house of Wm Uppington'; in 1756 (Michaelmas) 'at the dwelling-house of Henry Mitchell' (Chester's Cottage at the foot of Rattle Row); and at Lady Day 1756 and both courts in 1757 'at the Sign of the Grey Hound'. However, from 1758 onwards all Manor Courts were held 'at the Sign of the King's Arms'.

William Oatway was buried 'by the parish' in 1783, to be replaced by Thomas Weetch. A survey made around this time describes the property as 'The King's Arms alehouse, garden and orchard.'

Thomas Weetch was the tenant in 1790, then Robert Weetch, together with wife Joanna, replaced him, being named for The King's Arms in the land tax assessment of 1795 (he being one of the two assessors), but by 1830 it had reverted once again to a smallholding, being known as 'Strong's Farm', in the possession of Richard Strong. It was valued at £18.10s.11d. The farm was still a going concern when the Tithe Map was drawn up in 1840. As well as the orchards adjoining his house, barton and gardens, he

had assembled a collection of eight fields, many of which were on the slopes of Withycombe Hill behind West Street. However, one year later he was simply Richard Strong, publican of what was now called the 'Old King's Arms'.

By 1851 Richard's widow Fanny was running the pub and she continued to do so into her eighties, assisted in her old age by son-in-law and daughter, Hugh and Fanny Griffiths. By 1866 Hugh was the man in charge, and the change of innkeeper brought a change of name when the hostelry enjoyed a brief interlude as The New Inn. The name failed to impress, however, and by 1871 it was again the Old King's Arms. Then by 1881 history had repeated itself: widow Fanny was the innkeeper, assisted by son-in-law and daughter, this time Thomas and Emma Smith.

Among a group in The Butcher's Arms, c.1920, are Tom Burnett (left) and Lizzie Burnett's brother Marky Blew (seated with the accordion).

VE night in that part of The Butcher's Arms, Carhampton, used by the Withycombe boys and known by them as 'The King's Arms'. Left to right: Jim Cridland, Fred Nicholas (peering over), Bill Griffiths, Les Martin, Dick Pearse, cockney Herbert Flint (barely visible), Sid Pateman, a man named Lamacraft from Dunster (behind), and a chap who worked as a cowman at Briddicott Farm (name forgotten).

Fanny continued as mine host until about 1889. In 1890 James Vickery (the name also appears as Vicary but will be standardised here for simplicity) of The Butcher's Arms in Carhampton took on The King's Arms as well, and he is named as the proprietor from then on. Of course, he could hardly be expected to personally run both establishments at the same time, so someone else actually minded the Withycombe bar. In 1891 a Brompton Ralph man, George Elliot, was the publican, and in the final years before The King's Arms met its fiery doom, Albert (Jack) Chilcott was in charge.

The building caught fire on a Thursday night in the week of Christmas 1901, when the Chilcott family were asleep in their beds. Fortunately they escaped unharmed, even managing to rescue most of the furniture from the flames, but the Dunster fire brigade arrived too late to save the inn itself. The cause of the blaze was never established. Sadly, the fire led to the end of the tradition of the village inn in Withycombe, and with its loss some aspects of community life were inevitably diminished. Subsequently a walk of about a mile to The Butcher's Arms was necessary in order to reach the nearest watering hole and many locals headed in that direction after a hard day's work. This became a tradition in itself: the Withycombe folk monopolised one of the bars there, dubbing it – The King's Arms!

A new house rapidly sprang up on the site of the old pub, and certain features of its interior suggest that it was intended to serve a similar purpose, although in an altogether grander style. It stands today as Foxwarren, but its earliest name was Halswell. Possibly its first and most illustrious occupant was the artist John William North (1842–1924), who had lived in West Somerset since 1860. He had married Selina Weetch, and they moved from Beggearnhuish to Withycombe in 1904. Despite earning the reputation of being one of the greatest watercolour painters of his day, by this time he had become obsessed with an ambition to create the perfect watercolour paper, and it was in this pursuit that he spent most of his later life.

Nevertheless he still found time to practise his art, and he made many sketches in and around the village. He painted the church and the ancient yew next to it, exhibited a picture entitled 'House and Orchard, Withycombe, Somerset' and it is known that he made a drawing of the houses and fields round about in winter white, entitled 'Snow'.

The Norths moved away at the start of the First World War, and the house was taken over by widow Mary Hennessy, who came down from Bath with her stepson Leonard. It was she who must have named the house Halswell, for that had been the name of her Bath residence. Mary played a leading role in village life, as the photograph of the sewing circle, taken on the lawn at Halswell, indicates. She was a Roman Catholic, and on Sunday mornings Henry Pearse

would drive her in his wagonette to the church of that denomination in Minehead, for which he was paid half a crown. Of course, she also employed her own servants, including Arthur James and Bill Gould, as groom and gardener respectively; and ill health meant that at least one nurse was always on hand. Mary Hennessy and Leonard were still at Halswell in 1920, but left soon after, moving to Minehead. She retained the ownership of the Withycombe house, not selling it until 1929, when it passed to Winifred Lloyd-Worth. Mary died in 1930 at Warden Court, Minehead. She left a legacy to the village in the form of Mary Hennessy's Charity, which was intended to provide coal for the poorer parishioners.

One of the first tenants of Halswell after Mary's departure was a Canadian gentleman by the name of Shutler. He had a particularly deep voice that used to scare the village children. On one occasion he walked to the market at nearby Washford and decided to purchase a shotgun. After fortifying himself for the return journey at one of the inns there, he set off for home. Alas, by the time he reached the village the effects of the drink had overpowered him and he found himself in the stream that runs down through the village, alongside the road. Undaunted, he sloped arms and marched on homewards through the water. He later claimed that he was the first warship to sail into Withycombe!

For some years in the 1920s at least, Halswell was used as a guest-house, preserving a little of the tradition of the site perhaps. In 1927 artist Herbert Alexander made a pilgrimage to North's old home and stayed there. In 1938, by which time its name had changed to Foxwarren, it was the home of the Reads: Percy, Winifred and Brenda. In 1959 it was auctioned at The Egremont Hotel, Williton. The notice of sale informs us that applications to view the property were to be made to Mr Frank Griffiths of Mill House (practically next door in Mill Street), the gardener.

At the time of writing it is the home of Peter and Jean Humber, who worked tirelessly to put together an exhibition of village history in the Memorial Hall in the 1990s, and who have helped with the collection of material for this volume. In the grounds of the house can still be seen outbuildings – stables, etc. – that once served the old inn.

The next house along the street, opposite the west gate of the churchyard, is an attractively thatched building that served for many years as the village Post Office. The author remembers venturing into its dimly lit interior to buy a stamp or two in the 1960s. An elderly lady dispensed the goods from behind a black metal grill, an incongruous sight in what seemed like someone's front room, because of course the place was far from being purpose-built. The first known occupant was George Escott, who held the copyhold in the late 1600s, and Escott's was the name by which it was known. He paid 5s.0d. annual rent plus 4d. goose money for it, indicating that it was originally a smallholding. Perhaps it was still serving such a purpose in George's time, because when son Henry took on the lease in 1707 his occupation was described as husbandman.

Henry took the lease on the lives of himself, wife Joan and their daughter of the same name. He continued to live there until his death in 1741, when one or other of the Joans replaced him. In 1752 Henry's son Richard Escott took over the property, naming sister Joan again in the lease of lives and also Robert Strickland, the eight-year-old son of his sister Mary and her husband James Strickland. Richard remained there for the next 40 or so years, still paying the ½d. Church Rate for the property in 1790. He died in 1795, after which Robert Strickland inherited the property, and then came a major renovation.

Probably soon after 1800, James Case, a blacksmith born at Old Cleeve, erected a new house, the former cottage and garden being replaced by house, smithy, garden and orchard, the latter being across Culver Lane (where some modern houses now stand). Throughout the rest of the nineteenth century the property was used by the Case family as a blacksmith's premises, James being replaced by sons George, then William. We have a description

By the Culver Lane junction with West Street is Eva Ellis, the postmistress. Young Adrian Slader is astride her horse, Fairy.

Procession into the church at Revd Camplin-Coggan's 1949 jubilee. The churchyard is overlooked by the ancient cottage once known as 'Escott's', here enjoying the position of village Post Office.

of George from February 1837 when, aged 15 and already a blacksmith, he was committed for a period to Wilton Gaol in Taunton whilst awaiting trial. He was 5ft, 5ins tall, with a fair complexion, hazel eyes and brown hair, and he had a scar across the fourth finger of his left hand. He was said to read well but write imperfectly. More details of his alleged crime can be found in the following chapter.

Then into the twentieth century, William's son Beadon Case, nicknamed 'Tipper', came into possession and after the First World War the house began to be used also as the Post Office. It retained this dual role between the wars, when Kate Ellis, whose husband Charles was a blacksmith, took over the running of the Post Office.

As a smithy the property was something of a social centre in the evenings for the young men of the village, especially when cart wheels were being constructed or repaired. Many hands were needed to manage the tricky operation of bonding – the fitting of the metal band around the rim – as the metal had to be fired so that it would expand and then shrink to a tight fit, and water swiftly applied to prevent the wood from burning. Jack Kent was a regular helper, George Maidment and Fred Nicholas two of the boys who enjoyed the spectacle.

Eva Ellis, Kate's daughter, later took over the running of the Post Office. She used to deliver mail to the outlying farms on her motor bike before ill health caused her to change to horseback! During the war young Adrian Slader and his mother came to lodge at the Post Office with Eva while the father was away in the Army – after the war was over they stayed on.

At the 1951 sale of Luttrell property the house was described as being built of stone and cob and rendered over, with a thatched roof. The ground floor included a living-room 'part used as a Post

Office, with single oven range and cupboard'. Outside were a brick and tiled penthouse and blacksmith's shop.

At approximately the time that James Case was setting up his smithy, two other little houses were erected close by. As a blacksmith frequently worked in conjunction with carpenters (the majority of his products, such as tools, wheels, etc., consisted of wooden and metal components in combination), it is likely that these were intended to be carpenters' premises. Carpenter Jonathon Griffiths was involved with a great deal of construction work – both renovation and new building – in the village, which seems to have been intended to provide homes for his descendants. It is likely that the two houses by the smithy were projects of his, as the first known occupants were James and Daniel Griffiths, together with their families. James was a labourer, but Daniel was a carpenter. The two 'houses and gardens' by the smithy were first recorded in 1830, when James' was valued at 14s. and Daniel's at 15s. The 1840 Tithe Map shows that these properties were situated close by the smithy, and names the two men as tenants. James remained in his dwelling for a further 20 years or more, but there was no sign of an occupant in 1871. The house did not survive much beyond this time.

Most of the Griffiths-built houses lasted for no more than a century and one suspects that wood featured prominently in their construction!

Daniel had married Joan Gay in 1823, and in 1842 she was left a widow at the little house. By 1871 her son William had replaced her. He had taken up tailoring, and his wife Elizabeth assisted, in 1881 describing herself as a seamstress. This house too apparently ceased to be used as a dwelling not long afterwards.

Beyond the old smithy and the buildings associated with it, Culver Lane peels off to the west, beginning its climb up to Withycombe Hill. Its name refers to the woodpigeon that once formed a significant part of the diet of local people, and it appears again in the nearby field named Culver Close. In years gone by many villagers would have trekked daily up this lane in order to work upon the common (permissible upon payment of an annual fee) or to tend the little gardens they had brought into cultivation around the edge of it. This latter practice tended to be done on an informal basis, without prior application to the lord of the manor for permission; but once he found out about it, a small rent was usually levied. We will pass by Culver Lane, however, and continue along West Street.

Looking down on the Lower Street area of Withycombe from the vicinity of Culver Lane, the path that winds up from the village on to Withycombe Hill. The row of council-houses, built in the 1920s, is visible across the field from Withycombe Wood.

Three

West Street (North from Culver Lane)

Situated beyond the point where Culver Lane joins West Street, and past some modern buildings, is an attractive pair of thatched cottages called Syringa and The Haven, which were created some 250 years ago out of a single dwelling known at the time of the conversion as Thorne's Tenement, an ancient property not to be confused with William Thorne's Tenement in Lower Street. Its high rent was 6s.4d. and it was one of only two manor properties that paid 6d. goose money.

The earliest definite reference to it is in a rental of 1604, where widow Margaret Hill was listed as paying 6s.4d. Within a few years Thomas Hill had replaced her, then from 1635 it was the home of John and Mary Thorne. The property was described as a tenement with eight acres of land. John was probably the man who was buried at Withycombe in 1670/71, and was succeeded by his relict Mary. She was listed for it in 1678 and was also on the appended reeve's list (all payers of goose money at the higher and middle rates were obliged to take a turn as reeve), as 'Mary Thorne wdw for Thos. Hills'.

Widow Mary Thorne was still there in 1694, when she appeared at the Withycombe Hadley Manor Court to give evidence on a matter of custom. Mary was said to be 82 at the time. She eventually died in 1697 but had already passed on her tenement to Thomas and Jane Thorne a year or two earlier. It is likely that they had been living there for some time, helping to run the little farm. However, the pair did not live to enjoy their inheritance, both predeceasing Mary. Thomas was buried in February 1695; widow Jane less than two months later. Their son Solomon Thorne (born 1675) was accordingly taken as the new tenant.

He remained there for the next 40 years, paying the usual rent and the Church Rate of 1d. due on the property. His estate was one of those obliged to provide the tithingman every 20 years or so, and he did the duty himself in 1733. Despite the fact that he was approaching his 60th year, he was clearly willing and able to perform the job himself as he did it again the following year (on behalf of Edward Thorne's estate at Higher Dumbledeer) and in the year after that (for Milton's Tenement). However, this was something of a swansong for him, as he had already taken steps to surrender his copyhold.

Solomon, together with wife Hannah, had christened several children at Withycombe between 1699 and 1714, yet it seems that he was left in his old age with no heir on whom to settle the property. Thus in 1731 he surrendered his messuage to the lord of the manor 'to the use of John Trevelyan, baronet' – the Luttrells' relation at Nettlecombe Court. John Hiles, Joseph Tuttle and John Hoare witnessed the agreement. Clearly Solomon continued as tenant for a time, but he had gone by 1735, when John Uppington the younger leased the property. In the lease, 'Thorne's Tenement' was described as consisting of house, outhouses, court, garden, orchard (half an acre) and three closes called the Crufts (two acres). John Uppington (1700–67) took out the lease on the lives of himself, wife Mary and son John junr. The rent was now set at 6s.8d.

With the acquisition of the tenancy John Uppington found himself liable for the tithingman's duty, and accordingly appears on a 1739 list 'for his estate in West Street' in place of Solomon Thorne. It may have been John Uppington who was responsible for the conversion of the house into two cottages around this time. The house originally had a central door and hallway, and the conversion was effected without disturbing this arrangement, so that the new dwellings now shared this common entrance. The result seems slightly comical (at least to modern eyes) and an inventory of goods belonging to perhaps the first tenants of the two cottages tends to reinforce this impression.

John Perkins and William Griffiths both found themselves unable to keep up with the rent on the property and in 1781 their household goods were seized and taken to Farmer Sully's down the road to be sold in lieu of payment. John Perkins' goods, taken for a debt of £3.17s.3d., consisted of:

2 pewter dishes & 1 plate, 3 Delf dishes & 1 plate, 6 small Parthen plates, 1 common Parthen dish, 1 side board & shelves, 5 Tea dishes & saucers & 1 sm Bason, 1 Pint & 1 pott [?] 2 porringers, 2 small jugs, 1 drinking glass, 1 pepper box, 1 water pitcher, 1 brass pott &

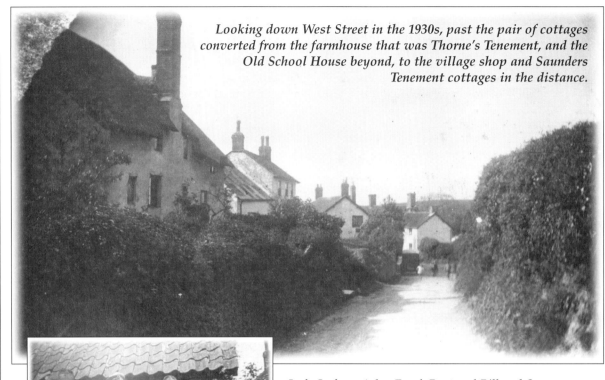

Looking down West Street in the 1930s, past the pair of cottages converted from the farmhouse that was Thorne's Tenement, and the Old School House beyond, to the village shop and Saunders Tenement cottages in the distance.

Left: Left to right: *Frank Burt and Bill and Sam Griffiths, standing behind Sam's wife Mary. Sam and Mary moved down from Dumbledeer to the West Street cottage now called 'Haven' (pictured) because of Mary's bad leg. Previously Bill had to walk up to Dumbledeer every night to help his mother upstairs (Sam being too frail and brother Walter being considered too rough!). Frank Burt was married to the daughter of Sam's brother Uriah Griffiths.*

The pair of cottages created from Thorne's Tenement as they looked in 1950, when Eli Burnell and H. Pugsley were in residence.

hangings, 2 spoons, 5 trenchers, 1 brass skimmer, 1 looking glass, 1 hour glass, 1 long [illeg.] form, 2 prongs, 1 hog scraper, 1 iron ting, 1 pair of sheepshears, 2 square tables, 2 chairs, 2 long crooks, 2 stools, 1 Frying pan, 1 pr of tongues, 1 iron candlestick, 1 flock fort [?], 1 prayer book (not remerced), 1 bedstead, 1 old feather bed, 2 blankets, an old Rugg [Jugg?], 2 Matts, 2 coffers, 1 blanket, 1 bolster & 2 small pillows.

William Griffiths' goods, taken for £2.16s.3d., comprised:

1 coffer, 2 Parthen dishes, 2 trenchers, 3 Tea dishes & saucers, 1 looking glass, 2 porringers, 2 spoons, 1 Tinder box, a parcel of old iron, 2 knifes, 1 fork, 2 pr of Seissoors, 1 Tin Pint, 1 Parthen jug, 1 iron candlestick, 1 stone saltstand, 1 padlock & 1 pr of pinchers, 1 chimney crook, 1 pair of Tongues, 2 woodden chairs, 1 butter pott, 1 iron pott & hangings, 1 baskett, 1 small stone Jarr & 1 long shelf, 1 bedstead & matt, 1 old feather bed, 1 bolster, 1 blankett & 1 jugg.

On one side John Perkins had the pepper box; on the other Bill Griffiths had the stone saltstand! Were these passed across the hallway at mealtimes? Similarly each household had one iron candlestick. Did they originally make up a pair that belonged to the old house?

Alternatively it could have been landlord Henry Fownes Luttrell who made the structural changes after the death of John Uppington in 1767. Certainly the property was in demesne in 1769, when Henry paid the Church Rate for it, so that leaves ample time during which he could have made alterations to the property.

We do not know when the Perkins and Griffiths families commenced their occupation of the cottages, but as both were probably married in the 1770s it is likely to have been around this period. Presumably their problems in 1781 led to their eviction because on Christmas Day in that year a new lease was granted to John Vickery and George Thorne. (At this time Perkins and Griffiths were still in possession, the seizure of goods, etc. not taking place until after the Christmas and New Year festivities.)

The new lease described 'Thorne's late Uppington's' as a dwelling-house converted into two small dwellings with garden and orchard (half an acre), then in the possession of John Perkins and William Griffiths as tenants to John Fownes Luttrell. As a note added to a manorial survey of this period indicates, 'the field [was] not granted' because the property had ceased to be a smallholding. The lease was taken on the lives of George Thorne (28), his wife Mary (27), and Ann Vickery (5), John's daughter. While John Vickery was stated to be from Carhampton, George Thorne was a Withycombe man, although not closely related to the earlier tenant, Solomon.

We now enter a period of some 40 years when little is known concerning the occupants of the two cottages. Vickery and Thorne continued to hold the lease, however. In 1821 John Vickery made an amendment, granting a moiety of the property to his daughter Jane, a spinster, for £10. Both were described as being of Withycombe; and a note pencilled on the 1781 lease notes that a heriot was due in 1832, upon the death of Ann James (presumably the Ann Vickery named on it) in Bristol, so the lease was still in force at this time.

However, from the rate list made in 1830, it would appear that the cottages were then in the possession of William Case (his cottage was valued at £1.2s.0d.) and William Cridland (his at £1). This is confirmed by the 1840 Tithe Map, where the occupiers of the two cottages are shown to be the same, as tenants of John Fownes Luttrell. The census made the following year also shows William Cridland, together with wife Mary and child Ann at one of the cottages. William Cridland, born c.1800 at Old Cleeve, lived for the rest of his life at the cottage, and was buried in Withycombe in 1884. His daughter Ann continued to live at home with him after her marriage to Thomas Toes/Tooze. The other cottage became the home of Thomas Court, and a similar situation developed here when his daughter Mary Ann, who had married Benjamin Boalsh (variously spelt), a navvy from Colyton in Devon, brought her family to live with him.

In 1891 Benjamin and Mary Ann, with daughters Laura and Isabella, were still in their cottage, with Thomas and Ann Toes across the hall. In that year the latter had George Case, aged 65, lodging with them. Ann Toes was widowed in 1895, while Ben Boalsh lost Mary Ann four years later, but otherwise in the years that followed little changed, with Benjamin Boalsh in the one cottage and Ann Toes in the other surviving into old age. In 1972 George Maidment of Wiveliscombe wrote to his old friend Fred Nicholas of Withycombe, reminiscing about their days as children growing up in the village around the turn of the century:

... old Crimea Veteran John Hard who lived with Ann Toes, the old Lady who used to mangle clothes etc for people about 1d per Day her mangle was an old Table type, a great Box full of large stones ran to & fro on rollers & pressing the clothes, next door lived bald Benny Balch who was a real navvy, came down I believe when the Railway was cut to Minehead...

'John Hard' was in fact Jesse Heard, originally from Luxborough, who made straw baskets and beehives and hawked them around the local villages on a tricycle. At one of the coronation celebrations (probably George V) races were held in the Bean Field at Court Place: Jesse joined in on his tricycle but a wheel caught in a rut and broke, throwing the old chap to the ground.

In 1920 both Benjamin Boalsh and Ann Toes still lived in West Street, with Benjamin at one of the two cottages. Ann probably still lived next door, although Eli and Emily Burnell were also in the street then, and they too lived there. Eli was a carter for Henry Pearse. Samuel and Mary Griffiths replaced Ben Boalsh after his death in 1933, having moved down to the village from Lower Dumbledeer.

The two cottages were included in the 1951 sale, where we see that very little had changed since their creation out of the old house nearly 200 years earlier. They were described together as semi-detached, of stone and cob with a thatched roof. Both still shared an entrance passage. Mr H. Pugsley and Eli Burnell were the tenants at that time. Later, Ray and Barbara Young made their home in one of the cottages, from where Ray ran his greengrocery business, delivering his produce door to door around the local area.

Beyond Thorne's Tenement is the Old School House, which was probably erected in the 1830s by Thomas Blackwell Leigh. However, the evidence suggests that it was a replacement for an earlier building, belonging to a property known as Harris' Tenement. This was quite a substantial small farm at one time, certainly more extensive than Thorne's next door. This is reflected in its higher rent (originally 11s.4d. plus 8d. goose money) and rates (10d.). Covenant Harris was the name of one or more tenants between the 1570s and 1630s. The last of them had died by 1649, by which time his relict, Jane Harris, had succeeded to the property, being named as the occupier when Richard Sully was granted the property by copy of court roll in that year.

Richard Sully and his wife Margaret began a dynasty in the village, which has continued to thrive into the modern era. They were relatively wealthy, although Richard was not quite of the class that was designated 'gentleman'. However, that he was close to it is shown by the successive marriages of his daughter Eleanor to two men who were definitely such, Henry Chester and Giles Daubenny. When she died in 1730 at the age of 88, Eleanor merited a burial and a memorial inscription inside the church.

Richard and Margaret also had sons named Richard and James, and daughters Margaret and Frances, but after Richard senr's death (by 1653) it was the youngest son James who inherited Harris' Tenement. Widow Margaret held an overland of her own at that time, two pieces of meadowland called Woodwall Meadows, consisting of three acres in the north of the parish next to Black Monkey Lane. Woodwall was an old name for the green woodpecker. William Withey (alias Wheddon) had held these from around 1590 and it is likely that Margaret was a relation of his. After Margaret's death in 1674 the meadows passed to James and they became part of his farm, their rent (6s.8d.) being added to that of Harris' Tenement so that the payment associated with it then became 18s.0d. plus goose money.

James Sully died in 1718 and was replaced by his sister Margaret Gimlett, a widow. When in 1726 she was called upon by the Manor Court of Withycombe Hadley to take her turn as reeve, she was described as a copy tenant and pound-keeper. This suggests that her farmyard was being used as the village pound at that time. As a rule (although not an infallible one), yards that were not in use were preferred for use as a pound, for obvious practical reasons, so it is likely that by this time Harris' Tenement was falling out of use. This theory is supported by the fact that in 1730 Margaret was presented at the Manor Court for her house being out of repair.

The following year Mrs Catherine Escott took over the property, referred to as 'Sully's late Gimblett's Tenement' on the lives of her children Benjamin and Susannah. It was said to consist of house, outhouses, barn, stable and two little orchards (one and a half acres), together with 20 acres of land and an overland called Woodwall Meadow. Almost immediately Benjamin, who had been christened in Carhampton in 1716, the son of Catherine and Giles Escott, found himself in charge. However, throughout his tenure one receives the impression of a property in terminal decline; and while a thorough survey of the manor made in 1777 makes 'late Sully's Tenement' sound like a typical small farm, an entry in a rent book made the next year simply refers to it as a dwelling-house. It is unlikely that Benjamin Escott lived there. He died in the year 1800 and was buried at Carhampton.

Even before this it would seem that the property had been passed on to a new owner, Robert Leigh of Carhampton. In a land tax assessment made in 1795 he was named as the tenant of John Fownes Luttrell's 'Benlocotts', which is surely a misread rendering of 'Ben Escott's'. Thomas Escott had been a witness at Robert Leigh's 1774 marriage to Hannah Blackwell, so clearly there existed a friendship between the Leighs and Escotts of Carhampton that may have led to the transfer. Robert and Hannah (of Aller Farm in Carhampton) were the parents of Thomas Blackwell Leigh.

Thomas Blackwell Leigh's new house is not referred to before the Tithe Map of 1840, where he is named as the occupier of a cottage and garden (No.111) with adjoining orchard, belonging to John Fownes Luttrell. The census of the following year shows that Thomas Leigh was a man of independent means, so it is possible that he built the house to enjoy in his old age (he and wife Betty were in their late sixties).

The smart new building and its wealthy owner proved too much of a temptation to one of the village lads. Eighteen-year-old James Davey, brother of the future miller Thomas Davey, lived in the house next door with parents George and Sarah. In January 1837 he was committed to the Assizes for breaking into the house of Thomas Leigh and stealing upwards of £10.

Detained in Wilton Gaol, he was described as 5ft, 6ins tall, of fresh complexion, with hazel eyes and brown hair. He had a scar over his left eye, could not read or write and was a labourer. James was found guilty and sentenced to 12 months' imprisonment, which included 12 weeks' solitary confinement. George Case, the young lad from the smithy, was charged with him for the same offence but was acquitted at the trial.

Thomas Leigh died in 1850, his will giving a hint of the precious objects that had tempted the young Davey: there were silver teaspoons, sugar tongs and a punch ladle, originally possessions of his wife. Generously, he bequeathed them back to her! Having no children of his own, he ordered his executors – one of whom was his friend Charles Hagley of Combe Farm – to liquidise his assets and share them amongst a number of nephews, nieces, etc.

The house was empty for a while, then it may have enjoyed a brief period of occupancy by Henry Pearse, who described himself as a farmer of 30 acres in the 1861 census. A son of William Pearse the tailor, Henry was the first of the village Pearses to venture into farming and he made a success of it, by 1881 working 180 acres in Bampton, Devon. The year 1871 saw Dunster butcher John Staddon and his wife in residence, and boarding with them was Elizabeth Leigh, 30, an unmarried annuitant. Perhaps this indicates that the Leigh family still retained an interest in the property at this time. Then in 1881 the family of china dealer Joseph Locker were the occupants, having moved up from Minehead.

At some time around the turn of the century the house was acquired for the use of the teachers at the village school, giving the property its current name. Accordingly schoolmistress Harriet Stamford was there in 1901, headmaster Archie Foote in 1920, Vera Maisey in 1938, etc. The Luttrells' grand sale of 1951 indicates that it was let to the Withycombe School Managers, the occupier at that time being Miss R.M. Case, one of the teachers. Called the Old School House, it was described as being built of stone and cob, rendered over, with a slate and asbestos roof. A grander house than most of its neighbours, it contained hall, two sitting-rooms, kitchen, larder, store, scullery and a large 'back house' with loft over; upstairs were three bedrooms.

Next to the Old School House is a substantial dwelling now called Simon's Steep, although for most of the twentieth century it served as one of the village shops. Although, as with Harris' Tenement, it is much altered, it has a pedigree going back to around 1600 at least. For much of its history it was known as Maud Stone's Cottage, and its manor rent of 4s. plus 4d. goose money tells us that it was originally a smallholding.

Maud, widow and relict of Giles Stone (a parishioner in 1641), held the cottage 'for her widowhood' in 1655, by right of an agreement made around

1625. It was said to have been previously in the tenure of Joane 'Chepman otherwise gage', and, sure enough, a rental of 1617 lists 'Johane Gage, widow' as a tenant paying 4s.0d. annually. Before Joan Gage's time it is probable that the cottage was rented by a family named Slade, with William Slade there in the 1570s and widow Joan Slade in 1604, but this is not certain. Maud Stone lived to a ripe old age and it was not until 1700 that George Thorne, already the tenant of both Little Sandhill and Pyle's Hill Tenement, took over the copyhold. However, trouble was brewing, and we will never know whether George was a conspirator or an unwitting agent.

There were constant complaints in the Manor Court against various tenants of the manor of Withycombe Wyke and others for taking liberties upon the common belonging to Withycombe Hadley. Typical was the following made against John Question of Gupworthy Farm and Mr William Orchard at Michaelmas 1697, presented for:

... freitinge [grazing] *on our Common and for takeinge heath and turfe from our waste, or Commons, they having no right thereunto,* ideo ad Domum misericordiam.

Both Question and Orchard were determined and persistent offenders, who no doubt felt hard done by as a result of these complaints. They possessed land that adjoined the Withycombe Hadley common. They were sheep farmers in the main and sheep will tend to wander... especially when encouraged to do so! But the law of the manor was clear: one had to be a tenant of the manor to use its common. So, in 1701 William Orchard decided to become just that. George Thorne surrendered the copyhold of Maud Stone's cottage to him, and now he was free to use the common just as he pleased.

The next court firmly disabused him of that misconception. Firstly he was informed that not even tenants were allowed to remove turf from the common to sell elsewhere; and secondly it spelled out precisely what he had been up to at his farm:

And likewise that he's no way intitled to any intercommoning, or right of common, on our Commons on the account of any Common that he hath adjoyning to our Common, for ye little plot that he calls by the name of his Common, was very lately inclosed by him, and taken to be part of his Tenement, called by ye name of Burket [Briddicott, in Carhampton].

Orchard nevertheless persisted with his plan to use the tenancy of the cottage to his advantage. He next tried to claim that being a tenant was alone sufficient to give him the right to turn his animals onto the common. The Michaelmas 1704 court made a firm statement of the law on this situation, not naming the offender but obviously aimed at him:

West Street, c.1905. The house that was the village shop throughout most of the last century is very different here, with its thatched roof and strange outbuilding (on the left), thrusting out into the road. Beyond, Tudor Cottage also has a good head of thatch. Among the children are the Maidments from this cottage, and the Daveys from next door.

Left: West Street pictured around 1920, when the sign above the shop read simply 'W.G. Eames'.

Right: This portrait was thought by George Maidment to be of a sister of his grandmother Eliza Ann Hobbs, the lady who first kept the West Street shop and was known as Eliza Cut-fig.

Below: West Street around the time of the First World War, with the village shop showing signs of the major changes that turned it from a thatched cottage into the more familiar structure.

Below right: Beatrice Taylor of Buckhill shops at The Cottage Stores in West Street before its closure. Mrs Mortimer is behind the counter.

... we present it to be the custom of our sayd Mannor that no tenant can stock on our Commons at his, or her will, or pleasure, but they ought to fret in proportion to their estates, and to be thereby stinted.

In other words, the 4d. goose money payable on the cottage only allowed a small number of animals to be 'fretted'. William Orchard continued to hold the tenancy and to be a constant offender to the court until 1714, when the cottage was returned into the lord's hands. The next tenant was Andrew Phillips, who leased the property in 1717 on the life of George Harrison. Andrew Phillips, described in the lease as a husbandman of Withycombe, was probably the son born to Robert and Mary Phillips at Carhampton in 1683. The property was described as a 'cottage house, garden and orchard', being 'late in the possession of George Thorne deceased' with 'or Daniel Norris als Lyckey' inserted. Perhaps Daniel Norris was Orchard's undertenant; or he could have occupied the premises while it was in demesne for repairs, many of the Norris family being carpenters.

Andrew Phillips lived there throughout his life, paying rent and Church Rates at regular intervals, and appearing from time to time at the Manor Court, but as a juror rather than a defendant. He was last named as a ratepayer in 1769. In 1777 the property was once again in demesne but in the following year the cottage house and garden was referred to as 'late Andrew Phillips', since Malachia Gould's'. Malachi was a name traditionally used by the Gould family since before the Civil War. This Malachi was the church sexton, a post which earned him the princely salary of 5s.0d. a year. He was buried by the parish in 1786. His widow continued after him but was clearly in dire financial straits. The lord of the manor paid the ½d. Church Rate in 1790 'for Andrew Phillips' in the possession of Malachia Gould's widow'. She was almost certainly the Joan Gould buried by the parish the following year. The facts tend to suggest that the building was in a poor condition at this time.

It is likely that the cottage spent some time in demesne and underwent some reconstruction, for when it was leased again in 1809 both the rent and the heriot due upon taking a new tenant had increased by 1d., and it was now described as

Ethel Sully (later Cridland) posing in West Street in the early 1900s. She is standing in front of the houses now called Simon's Steep and Tudor Cottage, the former of these still showing its thatch; and between the two buildings can be seen the brick structure protecting one of the street's water outlets.

cottage, garden and stable. The new tenant was 68-year-old George Davey, labourer, and the lease was taken on his own life and on that of his son, also called George, 27. George the father had lived there since the 1790s, for the land tax assessment of 1795 named him as the occupier of 'late golds'. He was described as a husbandman at his marriage in 1773 to Mary Gay (when he was called George Davis).

The Church Rate made in 1830 valued George Davey's house at £1.3s.0d. This would have been George the son named on the lease, who had married Sarah Sully in 1815 and whose occupation was 'colt breaker'. His widow Sarah was in possession of the house at the time of the Tithe Map, on which the property is No.112; and she was there in 1841, with daughter Mary.

George and Sarah's son Thomas, the baker and future miller, with wife Jane and family succeeded to the tenancy, but by 1871 they had moved to take over from John Ridler at the mill, and Richard Hobbs, mason, and his family were the new tenants of the West Street cottage. It is possible that Tom Davey, being a baker, first opened part of the premises as a shop: it is certain that Richard Hobbs continued to do so as his wife Eliza Ann became something of a legend as its keeper. In the days before large shop windows and effective lighting the old lady would have been forced to poke around in corners, abetted by a lighted candle, to find the items that her customers requested. It is not hard to imagine that one or two of them might have taken unfair advantage of the situation when her back was turned! She may well have treated the village children with some suspicion because of this: certainly she was not well liked by them, supposedly because of her legendary meanness. The story goes that once, when weighing out a quantity of raisins, then known as figs, she cut one in half to make up the exact weight! She was known ever after as Eliza Cut-fig.

Richard and Eliza died in the 1890s and were succeeded by their daughter Sarah Jane. Sarah had a daughter named Ethel who in 1901, aged 17, was one of the school's 'pupil-teachers'. Sarah subsequently married William 'Cocky' Eames and around the time of the First World War the building was modernised, losing its thatch and gaining a larger shop window. William and Sarah were Jehovah's Witnesses, or 'Bible Students' as they were known. Next-door

A portrait of Ethel Sully as a young woman.

Sister and brother Ethel and Edwin Sully.

Right: *Ethel Cridland cradles grandson Malcolm.*

Top left: *One of the seven village men who died in the First World War, Edwin Sully of the First Battalion Somerset Light Infantry was killed near Ypres on 3 July 1915.*

Far left: Left to right: *Arthur, Jane (née Harrison, mother), Charlie, with sister Ethel Sully behind, Sarah Harrison (née Heard, grandmother) and Albert Sully. Note the rabbit and ferrets held by the boys; father Bill was a keen rabbiter*

Ethel Cridland steps out of her West Street house to talk for a moment with her brother Charlie Sully, c.1950. Bounce the dog looks keen to be off. The village shop on the left was then 'The Cottage Stores'.

neighbour Winnie Maidment – Sarah's niece – was persuaded to share their beliefs. William Eames died in 1924 but Sarah continued to run 'Eames' Shop' into old age, assisted by daughter Ethel. Later came a family named Rayleigh, then a chap (his name forgotten) who did not have the best of luck at the shop. On his first day he suffered a burst water pipe, which caused much damage, and when he finally left the premises he reversed his car into poor Mrs Tubes, knocking her over. In more recent times, the shop was run by families named Sanderson and then Ridley, before finally closing and becoming just a dwelling-house once more.

Across the street is a row of three dwellings that were converted from a single messuage during the eighteenth century. The original property was known as Saunders Tenement. It had originally been a small farm, as the rent of 6s.8d. plus 8d. goose money indicates, held by first John then Hugh Martin in the 1570s. The latter continued there until his death in 1605. Richard Hiles 'for Saunders Tenement' was holding it 12 years later. The 1655 survey of Withycombe Hadley describes the property as being just a cottage with two gardens and two orchards, since about 1629 in the hands of Eleanor Hiles, the widow and relict of Richard Hiles. Another entry in this same survey mentions someone with the surname Martin (alias Sanders), which probably explains the Martin/Saunders connection here. John Hiles followed Eleanor as tenant and within a few years all of the Hiles properties in Withycombe were consolidated in his hands (or those of a son perhaps, with the same name). His main farm was in Lower Street, where the pound is located at the time of writing. However, it is quite possible that he or another family member actually lived in Saunders Tenement: in the list of properties eligible for tithingman's duty the house is described as his 'wester living'.

Early in the eighteenth century John left the village for pastures new and the entire Hiles estate in Withycombe Hadley came into the hands of James Newton, yeoman of Withycombe, except for Saunders Tenement. The 1753 lease specifically states:

... except one cottage or dwelling house with garden adjoining, which was formerly two gardens and two little orchards heretofore in possession of Eleanor Hiles, now leased to John Sully, husbandman.

At the same time that John Sully took out a lease on the cottage for the lives of himself, wife Betty and daughter Mary, an allowance or consideration was made, presumably for the conversion work done to the premises, for it was described as:

... all that cottage or dwelling house... formerly two dwellings but lately divided into three with large garden plott adjoining... formerly in the possession of

Eleanor Hiles widow long since deceased and since of John Hiles yeoman deceased.

Wife Elizabeth died in 1758 and John remarried the following year in Cutcombe, his new bride being Frances Hobbs, probably a relation of John and Samuel Hobbs who were to establish themselves in Withycombe some years later. John Sully died in 1777, leaving daughter Mary Hawkins as the sole surviving leaseholder, but in a Church Rate made in 1790 it was his widow Frances who paid the 2d. due for four cottages in West Street. She died two years later.

From the time of the conversion into several dwellings it is impossible to say who was actually living in the cottages as undertenants. It is not until the mid-nineteenth century that sources revealing such information became available.

By a strange coincidence the next lessee to be discovered was one John Saunders, sawyer, who had obviously renovated the cottages, because his lease of 1820 allowed him a consideration for work done on the premises. However, whoever drew up the lease did not understand the information given, as Saunders was credited with having done the initial conversion from a single dwelling, something that took place some 50 years before he was born!

There is some doubt as to whether there were three or four cottages in the row at this time. The 1830 Church Rate cites John Saunders and others for three cottages and a garden, but the 1840 Tithe Map shows the row apparently divided into four, in the occupation of Thomas Griffiths, John Saunders, George Lettey and James Burnell. John's was called a house, the others' cottages. The following year's census shows Thomas Griffiths and John Saunders there, but we cannot be certain about the identity of the other occupants. John was now described as a poulterer. However, at some time during the 1840s, the cottages definitely became a threesome and have not changed their look greatly since. This probably occurred when the middle cottage was opened as a dame-school (obviously requiring more space than the average cottage permitted), under the tutelage of John Saunders' daughter Hannah, who was married to John Gay. This was in place in 1851, flanked by Thomas Griffiths again and widow Miriam Case; and the situation remained little changed in 1871, when the dame-school was still in action, although Hannah Gay was now a widow. Thomas Griffiths remained her neighbour but Alfred Strong had replaced Miriam Case on the other side.

By 1881 only Mary Griffiths, the widow of Thomas, was still in place. The dame-school was no more and both Hannah Gay and Alf Strong were dead. Jonathon Griffiths was one of the new tenants, while shoemaker John Sully took the middle cottage shortly afterwards. This remained the situation until the turn of the century, when John Sully died and was replaced by son Bill. His daughter Ethel succeeded him after her marriage to steamroller driver Jack Cridland. This pair was in residence between the wars, with George 'Jolly Roger' Davey and wife on one side and Jack and Maria Davey on the other.

Of the three cottages, evidence suggests that the two furthest down West Street were created from the original farmhouse: the smaller one having been the kitchen, while the other is the conversion of two dwellings into the dame-school. The third cottage appears to have been a separate building, perhaps created from an outbuilding associated with the old farm.

Back across the street again, beyond Simon's Steep, is Tudor Cottage. Its name gives a fair indication of its age, as does its appearance. For much of its history it was known as Smith's Cottage. Its earliest known tenant was Walter Clement, who held it from the 1570s until at least 1604. It paid a high rent of 4s.0d. plus goose money of 4d., putting it on a par with Maud Stone's Cottage next door. Widow Agnes Clement had replaced Walter by 1617 and presumably it was after her death in 1629 that the cottage passed into the hands of the Smith family.

Henry Smith, born around 1609 and recorded as living in the village in 1641, claimed that the property had been granted to his brother Hugh Smith for life. This claim must have been accepted, for after Henry's death in 1674, his widow Sarah continued to pay the rent due on it. Sarah died in 1704 and it was established that the lord of the manor of Withycombe Hadley was due a heriot of one table board, although in lieu of this, 5s.0d. was deemed an acceptable alternative.

Another widow, Sarah Eyre, was the new tenant, though she may not have lived there herself, being referred to sometimes as 'of Rodhuish'. Then in 1723 yet another widow took over the tenancy of Smith's Cottage: this was Cecile (variously spelt) Question, relict of Augustine Question of the Gupworthy Farm family. She was another who was constantly offending against the customs of the manor, her principal 'crime' being the cutting of turf from the common and carrying it away to sell elsewhere. Tenants were allowed by ancient custom to cut turf for use as fuel, but there were always some who went further than custom allowed. Indeed, in taking on the cottage (and thus becoming a tenant of the manor) Cecile may have been trying to circumvent these rules, as others were doing at the time.

On Christmas Day 1740 Mr William Troyte, yeoman of Carhampton, leased Smith's house and garden, 'late in the possession of Sarah Eyre, since of Cecil Question widow', on the lives of three children: his daughter Ann (14), William Orchard (15) and Robert Leigh (6). It fell to Ann and, through her, to husband Robert Jones. He paid the ¼d. Church Rate for the property in 1769. A survey made in 1777 shows that the rent had been reduced to 1s.4d., and

the heriot to 1s.0d., the whole being valued at £1.10s.0d. This is a large and highly unusual reduction.

Ann died in 1781, terminating Troyte's lease, Robert Jones followed in 1790, and in that year landlord John Fownes Luttrell himself paid the Church Rate for 'late Robert Jones'. William Burge may have lived there for a while before Jonathon Griffiths purchased a new lease in 1796. As mentioned earlier Jonathon was a carpenter who seems to have had a sideline in taking on properties in need of renovation and doing them up for the benefit of his children. This one was for daughter Mary and her husband William Perkins (both 28); grandson William Griffiths (5) was also named on the lease of lives.

Smith's Cottage became the Perkins family home for the next 100 years or so. William paid the Church Rate in 1830, when the property was revalued (downwards again) at 16s.0d.; and he was named as the tenant of No.113 on the Tithe Map of 1840, which shows that this property is the modern Tudor Cottage.

In 1841 and 1851 William, a widower, was still there, although head of the household was John Perkin. John was not William's son, but his son-in-law, having married William's daughter Hannah Perkins in 1829. John, a stonemason, lived at the cottage into old age, son James moving in with him by 1881 and becoming head of the household by 1891. John was then aged 85. Incidentally, in 1867 the Manor Court – which was still in operation – decided that it was John's turn to perform one of those onerous parish duties, and so they appointed him (for the following year) as aletaster – a tough job, but someone had to do it!

If the nineteenth was the century of the Perkins family at Smith's Cottage, the first half of the twentieth belonged to the Maidments. Son George's memories of his childhood in the village have already been referred to. He was at school in the village at the turn of the century and was of the generation unlucky enough to reach maturity at the time of the First World War. Like many local men he joined the Somerset Light Infantry. Luck was with George though: when the bullet with his name on it found him in the Middle East, near Jerusalem, it was stopped by his mess tin, which was preserved ever after as a memento.

Safely back home again, one of his first jobs was helping his father strip the thatch from the Causey cottages. The father, Harry Maidment, was a colourful character who held strong political views. He would paint slogans on the side wall of his house so that they would catch the eye of anyone travelling up West Street into the village, especially at election time. The Cridge boys, who lived close by, remembered that he once adorned the wall with a huge swastika! Unsurprisingly, he was also the man in charge of Withycombe's Junior Imperial League.

A photograph contributed by G. Maidment. On the back is written: 'A few of No 4 Platoon at Ambala 1915.
Standing: *Fred Carever* [?], *Bicknoller, Joe Hunt, Williton with Cork Helmet, Ray Farrar, Williton, G. Maidment,*
Withycombe, G. [?] *Leucha* [?], *Milverton;* sitting: *W. Venn, Williton, J. Parkins, E. Somerset, W. Thrush,*
Dunster, & some Barrack Room boys.'

He was a big man who proved an awkward customer even after his death: the only way the pallbearers could remove the coffin from his little house was by manoeuvring it first through a window and then a hedge before attaining the road.

In 1920 Harry, Henry (son George was christened 'Henry George') and Amelia Maidment were listed as living in West Street. Harry's wife Amelia was a daughter of Richard and Eliza Ann Hobbs, making her the sister of Sarah Jane Eames in the shop next door. Later, in 1938, Roland John Maidment and wife Kathleen were the occupants; and it was still in the family in 1951, when the little cottage was included in the sale of Luttrell properties. It was described as being built of stone and cob, rendered over, with a thatched roof. Downstairs was just a hall, living-room and back kitchen, while upstairs comprised two bedrooms and a landing. Mrs Maidment was the occupant.

Past Smith's is the relatively modern Merton House. It was built in the early-twentieth century, it is thought, by Edgar Case of Withycombe Farm for his mother, Lydia. It was originally named Kraal, presumably in connection with another of her sons who had emigrated to South Africa. A story concerning this lady provides us with a cameo of the isolation from the modern world of village life at this time. One day an airship was spotted flying up the

Bristol Channel. Edgar hurried over to his mother's house and took the venerable lady up the hill behind it in order for her to get a good view of the event. They watched the dirigible's progress for some time before returning to the house, where Edgar asked his mother what she thought of it. She pondered for a while before finally declaring: 'I don't believe it!' Lydia died in 1921, aged 92. Later the house came into the possession of the Holland family, who were there in 1938.

The site of the property is shown on nineteenth-century maps as vacant, but somewhere nearby – possibly on it – was Hugh Norman's Cottage, a Withycombe Wyke property. When John Codrington sold off his manor of Withycombe Wyke in 1709, Hugh Norman, carpenter, purchased his own cottage for £8 plus 1 guinea. It was described as lying on the north side of the garden of Sarah Smith, widow, and being 'bounden on the East with the highway [and] containing the $^1/_8$th part of an Acre'. This fits quite well with the site. If the identification is correct, then this must be where properties on this side of West Street ceased to fall within the purview of Withycombe Hadley. Hugh Norman had held the tenancy from at least 1700, when it was leased on his own life and those of his children Henry and Rebecca. Hugh had married Rebecca Smith in 1678, and here we see the forging of his link to the property, for before him the house had been in the possession of George Smith. Doubtless George was related to the family next door. When the house ceased to exist is not known, but the only possible reference to it so far discovered is in a land tax list of 1795, where Thomas Milton is mentioned as the occupier of a house owned by 'Mr Norman'.

Opposite Merton House is Sully's Farmhouse, now a pair of cottages, with a modern house built on the site of its barton. Although the name of Sully's Farm is very appropriate, as will be seen, it was generally referred to in former times as Farmer's Tenement. In the 1570s it was rented by Nicholas Perkins, who paid a manor rent of 7s.2d. plus 8d. goose money. The rent was later increased by 2d., probably due to an accounting error. By the early-seventeenth century it was home to Thomas Sully (alias Farmer), from whom it took its name. There was a Peter Sully (alias Farmer) living in Withycombe in the middle years of that century.

The house bears the legend '1624 H.H.' high on its southern wall. The initials belong to Henry Hoare, who had the present house built at that time. Seven acres of land were associated with it and, through a separate lease belonging to Henry, another four closes plus fifteen more acres came to be associated with

it. Around 1649 James Blake took over the property. He was still there in 1678, when at the same time William Shenton held the additional land, paying 10s.0d. for 'an overland late Jas Blake's'. In April 1691 James Blake was presented for his houses being in need of repair, but he died and was buried in September of that year. His wife Grace took over the copyhold upon payment of one feather bed as heriot, but she did not outlive her husband for long, dying herself in April 1693. Soon afterwards the new tenant, farmer Hugh Blackwell, formalised the leases on both parts of the property. In 1695 he took on the tenement and three years later, following the death of Joane Shenton, reclaimed the overland acreage. Both leases were on the lives of himself and William Blackwell. Henceforth the rent for the property was 17s.4d. plus 8d. goose money.

Hugh Blackwell was still being named in 1718, when he paid the 10$\frac{1}{2}$d. Church Rate for the farm, but his son William had officially succeeded him in 1717, when the pair underwent a particular ceremony at the Manor Court. Hugh gave over all rights to his estates in Withycombe to his son by symbolically handing him a ceremonial rod. In 1729 William did his duty as tithingman 'for his own estate' and John Hoare's 1739 list of those liable to do the duty of

Right: *Three of Bob Gould's daughters, thought to be* (left to right) *Violet, Rhoda and Olive, posing outside the cottage that was once Sully's Farmhouse in West Street, some time in the 1920s.*

Below: *Withycombe boy made good! Jim Harrison, son of Robert and Sarah, looking very smart in a Knightsbridge photographer's studio. Not so long before (1881) he had been a farm servant for Thomas and Mary Hagley up at Combe Farm.*

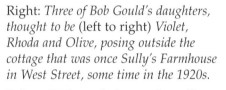

Above: *Harry, a son of Robert and Sarah Harrison, who worked up at Styles Farm. He died aged only 37 and is buried at Withycombe.*

Left: *Before taking over from widow Sarah Giles at Withycombe Farm, Robert Case took on Sully's Farm in West Street. This (1890s?) photograph shows sheep-shearing in one of the farm buildings there. The shearer on the right is, appropriately, William Sully. Although he was by trade a shoemaker like father John, William was regularly called upon at shearing time because of his skill with the hand-cranked mechanical clippers.*

tithingman included William Blackwell 'for his estate in West Street'. However, soon after this he must have died, leaving the estate to his widow, Mary. At the Manor Court of Easter 1747 John Brewer was presented for diverting the course of a waterway belonging to 'widow blackwill's estate', at Marshall Meadow. Perhaps as some kind of reparation, this same John Brewer was presented at the Michaelmas court later in the same year to do duty as tithingman next on behalf of 'Mrs Blackwill's Estate'. Widow Blackwell sublet the farm to an undertenant, quite possibly John Sully. He took a lease on it in 1771 and thus began the era which led to the property becoming known as 'Sully's Farm', but it was not an easy start. Clearly it was in a poor state of repair. The lease was only taken on after the Luttrells agreed to take care of necessary repairs and to take responsibility for any taxes due during its 14-year period. Consequently in 1777 it was 'in demesne for repairs' and all rate payments up to 1791 fell due to the lord of the manor.

The fullest description of the property, made in 1777, describes it as:

... house, barn, stable, linney & court; plus garden & orchard (1 acre), meadow (3 acres), the 4 acre field above, Worthy adjoining the field above (4 acres), Shuthay (2 acres), Churchill field towards Burcott (1 acre), Brownsery lying towards Bowerhayes (2 acres), and Marshall Mead (3 acres).

John Sully died in that year, to be replaced by Thomas Sully. He played a leading role in village life, the churchwardens frequently having their meetings at his house. By 1822 another John replaced Thomas and in 1830 he paid the Church Rate for Sully's Farm, when it was valued at £35.2s.4d. The 1841 census shows him and his wife Susannah living there but in 1851 the farmer (and 'Malster') Richard Taylor Copp of Carhampton and his family were in residence, at 'West Street Farm'. He was employing six men and one boy, and the farm was said to comprise 165 acres.

By 1861 Robert Case, born at Old Cleeve, had arrived. The farm's acreage was now reduced to 96, and only four men and a boy were employed. By 1871 though, things were looking up. Robert and wife Lydia were still there, at 'Sully's Farm', with an extensive family; and both the acreage and number of workers had doubled. Not long afterwards they made the short move to Withycombe Farm and the Sully lands went with them. From 1872 Sully's Farmhouse was that in name only, becoming a pair of cottages. The identification of their earliest occupants is speculative, but Robert and Sarah Harrison may have been one of the first, as well as Alfred Stevens, before his move to Lower Street. Richard 'Dicky' Farmer was almost certainly there from their creation until his sad demise in 1914.

Coming within the reach of memory, in the 1920s Bob Gould and his son Arthur occupied Sully's; also there were Walter and Mary Cridge. After the First World War Walter settled in Withycombe following his marriage to Mary Nicholas. Their sons Harry and Charlie were both keen members of Withycombe's football team. In 1938, Walter and Mary still occupied one of the cottages, with Henry and Nora Windsor in the other. The house and some of the farm's outbuildings still stand in 2003.

One more historic property remains in West Street, before the highway turns and slopes away to eventually become Withycombe Lane: this is Scout Cottage, beside Merton House. In 1795 it was Thomas Ridler's Cottage. Thomas was both owner and occupier, as was his son William who succeeded him in 1818. The fact that the Ridlers owned the property makes it virtually certain that it had previously belonged to the manor of Withycombe Wyke, but so far it has not been possible to identify its earlier occupants. There is some evidence to suggest that Scout Cottage was originally two adjoining dwellings, the other part perhaps being Hugh Norman's Cottage mentioned above.

Although not a large building, it was certainly split into two for much of the nineteenth century, initially to accommodate the unmarried William Ridler and his widowed mother Mary in one part, with William's sister Mary, her husband John Davey and their children in the other. This link between the Ridler and Davey families may explain why John Ridler at the mill took on young Tom Davey as his apprentice.

By the 1860s both William Ridler and his mother had died, leaving John and Mary Davey in possession of the West Street property. Like his brother George, John was a horse breaker for part of his life. The building continued to be used, on and off, as two dwellings, with various children and grandchildren (some of whom were Dyers and Bowdens) living there over the next 30 years or so. Finally, however, it came to their grandson John, known as 'Noble' Davey. George Maidment recalled him as a shepherd for the Case family of Withycombe Farm and remembered him cutting the hair of men and boys of the village with sheep-shears!

Photographs of this part of the village taken around the turn of the century show the cottage as attractively thatched, and with a door opening onto West Street. The family subsequently moved to High Park in Rodhuish, although their sons George and John junr remained nearby, living with their families in two of the Saunders Tenement cottages.

Around 1910 Waring Finch of Rodhuish introduced the Scouting movement to the village and the cottage was used as a sort of clubhouse, earning the premises its modern appellation. On one occasion a lad named Bill Lochey infuriated Waring Finch so much that he ripped up the lad's Scout hat and ran it up the flagpole that had been fixed to the chimney!

43

The Scout troop at Washford Farm, after a Cleeve Abbey service. Left to right, back: Fred Nicholas, C. Gould, ?, ? Smith, L. Leversha, ? Smith, Leonard Gould, ? Webber, ? Moggridge, George Maidment; front: *C. Chilcott, ? Chilcott, R. Chilcott, Geoff Leversha, W. Gould, W. Nicholas, ? Chilcott, ?. Fred Nicholas and his friend George Maidment are wearing their Territorial uniforms, a grim reminder of the approaching war.*

Camps were held at Higher Nothams and at Blue Anchor, but the older boys had to return home before nightfall because they had to start work at 7a.m. the next day.

After the First World War a family named Chapman lived briefly at Scout Cottage. Later it became the home of Albert and Ethel Scudamore, who arrived in around 1930. In 1951 there was a gas explosion inside the cottage, the blast severe enough to lift the roof, which put Ethel in hospital for three months. Quick-thinking Hetty Cridland wrapped her in a blanket to douse the flames.

One old, long-vanished property should be mentioned at this point because, although not in West Street, it could be reached by a lane that led up onto the hill above from its starting point just past Scout Cottage, where

Scout Cottage showing some signs of the damage caused by the gas explosion.

some garages are sited today. This was Bere's (occasionally written 'Bear's'), a smallholding belonging to the manor of Withycombe Wyke. The name comes from an old word for a type of barley. Now the area has been subsumed into larger fields, etc., but in 1840 a cluster of small plots marked its location: there was Bere Wood (part of which was associated with the mill), Great Bere, and most significantly Bere Croft, with a garden plot close by. In 1656 a grant was made by John Cridland of one close of pasture called Beare's (2½ acres) and herbage of Beare's Wood to Daniel, Joane and William Leigh. William was 65 in 1709, by which time the other two were deceased. In 1707 he had contributed 10d. to the rate made for highway repairs, an amount comparable to others who possessed substantial smallholdings, such as Solomon Thorne at Thorne's Tenement. At the sale of the manor of Withycombe Wyke in 1709 William Leigh's leasehold property remained unsold. It was described as a decayed dwelling-house with three acres of ground and herbage of two or three acres of wood, worth £3, with an annual rent of 2s.0d.

William paid the Church Rate of 1d. for his property in 1718, then little more is known until 1769, when John Birth paid the same amount 'for Bears'. The Birth family also held other fields in the area, known as the Perrys (Higher, Middle and Lower). Robert Birth paid the rate in 1790, and was named as the owner five years later, when Thomas Milton was the occupier. On this occasion the property was called 'Widlaks' (Widlake's). By 1840 its associated fields had passed into the hands of the Hobbs family.

It is likely that West Street used to end near the path to Bere's, becoming Withycombe Lane as the highway turns and drops quite steeply away towards Carhampton. Nowadays it continues a little further to include a few modern dwellings, one of which is a bungalow from which a number of members of Withycombe's Sully family ran a small farm during the previous century.

Four

Withycombe Lane

As one moves northwards down Withycombe Lane, nowadays one cannot escape the feeling of leaving the village for the countryside, as houses give way to leafy lanes and quiet fields. In the warmer months the uplifting song of the skylark fills the air from Crooksfield to Browndry. Yet there was not always such a marked transition from village to fields, as several houses once stood by the highway in Withycombe Lane.

An important feature of the highways in Withycombe has always been the causey or causeway, a cobbled pathway raised several feet above the road surface, the ancient West Country equivalent of the pavement. Everyone who knows the village is familiar with the extensive surviving causey near Top Cross and one or two other small sections around the village. However, despite the fact that there are or were fields here called Causey Close (where the village boys once used to play football) at this point, not many will have suspected that a length of causey once ran at least part of the way down Withycombe Lane.

The Withycombe Hadley Manor Court first mentions 'the High Casway between Simon Case's and John William's' as being out of repair in 1743. Both men lived in Withycombe Lane, by Crooksfield, as will be seen below. From this point on there was a constant stream of complaints about this causey and others in the parish. In 1752 the surveyors of the highways, John Uppington and Thomas Tutball, were admonished for not putting posts on 'the High Casway' and elsewhere 'to prevent horses and Bullocks going on these Dangerous places'. By 1756 things were going from bad to worse. Again the Manor Court presented 'the High Casway Leading from Withycombe to Carhampton to be out of Repair and very Dangerous... to be repaired by ye Surveyors of ye Highways...'. The complaints continued year after year, however, and one doubts that the repairs were ever made.

A little way down the road a lane branches off westwards a short distance to a house now called Orchard Croft. It is the direct descendant of an old house on the site, which was known for upwards of 250 years as the Church House.

During this period it was owned by the Church, through agreements made by the churchwardens, and leased to various occupants who paid rent for it directly to the Church. The Church House should not be confused with the Poor House, which was situated on the Causey in Lower Street. Both were owned by the churchwardens but whereas the Poor House was used as a home for the parish poor, the Church House was simply intended to generate income for the Church, helping (among other things) to maintain those unfortunate enough to find themselves in the Poor House.

Neither did the Church House stand alone in earlier times: a smaller house – Mary Western's – adjoined it, and the earliest document so far discovered refers to this. This too was owned by the Church. Like all property on the west side of Withycombe Lane, it lay within the territory of the manor of Withycombe Wyke, and so in 1670 it was John Cridland who granted it to Mary Collard, widow. Even then it was described as belonging to the Church and it was let at an annual rent of 3s.4d., for the life of Thomasin Collard, a girl of about ten. This transfer may simply have been a formal renewal of the property's assignment from the lord of the manor to the Church: it is unlikely to have been a coincidence that 1670 was the year that Thomas Collard became Withycombe's rector.

The occupier was in fact Mary Western, who was in constant trouble with the Manor Court of Withycombe Hadley throughout the 1690s for selling heath from 'our' common (she being a Wyke and not a Hadley tenant). At some point the little cottage was divided into two, so that by 1709 one finds Mary Western in one half and Hugh Moore (alias Knowle) in the other, both paying 1s.8d. – half each of the agreed rent.

Returning to the Church House itself, the 1709 survey made prior to the sale of the manor refers to an agreement made in 1701 whereby John Hiles, J. Sully, John Question and others (churchwardens, etc.) took possession of the Church House, with two bits of garden ground plus the little house and garden adjoining 'for ye poore of ye parish', at an annual rent of 5s.0d. At the sale neither Church

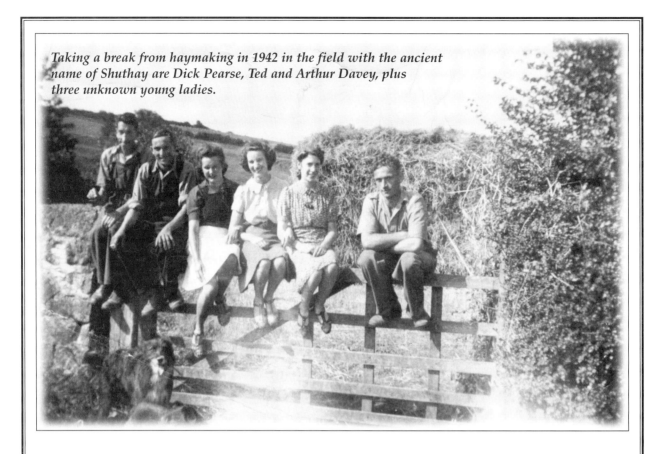

Taking a break from haymaking in 1942 in the field with the ancient name of Shuthay are Dick Pearse, Ted and Arthur Davey, plus three unknown young ladies.

Pausing from their work of cutting cattle cabbages in Withycombe Farm's Crooksfield, c.1930, are (left to right): Mary Cridge, Nora Windsor, Rhoda Gould (kneeling), Ada Irish and another (unknown). Note the young lad behind Mary Cridge.

House nor the little cottage were sold. A note survives which records the rents paid by the unsold Withycombe Wyke properties in the year 1718. Mr Hiles, representing the churchwardens, paid 5s.0d. for the Church House, and 1s.8d. 'for ye pte of ye house wch was Mary Westernes'. Hugh Moore paid 4s.8d. for two houses, his other house being held for 3s.0d. This is the last we hear of the little cottage.

In 1737 John Armstrong married Joan Gould, and it was probably around this time that he took on the Church House. He made his home there for the rest of his life, becoming so associated with it that it was still being referred to as 'Armstrong's' 70 years after his death. His wife seems to have died in 1760 but John continued, paying the Church Rent of £1.5s.0d. up to 1783. Repairs to the Church House were then deemed necessary and carpenter Jonathon Griffiths was called in. Perhaps he liked the look of the place because, following years of anonymous payments of £1.5s.0d. by someone for 'late Armstrong's', in 1822 his name appeared next to it. He must have made considerable improvements, because he paid £1.10s.0d. for just half a year.

Then in 1831 another long-term tenant moved in. This was Thomas Hurford, who had married Jane Vickery in the village in 1822. He appeared as the tenant of No.195 on the Tithe Map, a house and garden, the owners being listed as the churchwardens. He can be found there in every census up to and including 1871, where he was described as a widower of 80 years, the address being given as 'Church Land'. James and Elizabeth Parsons succeeded Thomas in 1873. James died around 1890.

In the twentieth century, the year 1920 saw George and Ann Willis junr at Church Cottage; while in 1938 William, Mary Jane and Emily Quantock lived there. William and Mary Jane gave their address as Church Cottage, while Emily preferred the grander title of Quantock Lodge, although all three are believed to have lived in the same house!

Just past the driveway to Orchard Croft, on the other side of Withycombe Lane, is a small triangular piece of overgrown garden, surrounded by trees that once hedged the plot. A gate leads into it from the short lane that connects Crooksfield to the highway. It has been a garden for about two centuries but for another century and a half before that it was a cottage and garden, known as Clement's Cottage, an example of the type of property 'erected upon the lord's waste' at the side of the road. This method of construction was one of a limited number of ways that a totally new dwelling could arise within the parish.

The property was newly erected around 1652, when the Luttrells leased it to its builder, John Clement, for an annual rent of 16d. A list of Luttrell copyholds made three years later betrays some irritation at the building's sudden appearance, for the copy was allowed only with a strict injunction upon the copyholder not to build any more houses there!

John continued to reside there until his death around the close of the century, to be followed by son James Clement for a brief period; then in 1717 Simon Case, thatcher of Withycombe, took up the lease. Although Clement did not die until late 1715 or early 1716, Simon Case was probably living at the cottage from at least 1711, for the latter was in constant trouble with the Manor Court from that date for 'making soyle in the highway opposite his house and for taking soyle away into another Lord's lands'; and this continued long after his purchase of the tenancy. It was a good thing that the cottage was in a fairly isolated position (although the Church House must have been a bit too close for comfort on a warm day) because the term 'soyle' meant dung!

Simon seems to have been the first member of the Case family to settle in the village. He probably married three times and his descendants included James Case, the 15-year-old 'killed by accident of a cart wheel' in 1770, and blind William Case, who lived in the village throughout much of the nineteenth century. The cottage and two gardens were leased upon the life of Simon's daughter Grace, who subsequently married John Williams. We have already noted that in 1743 the state of the Causey between Simon Case's and John William's houses was brought to the attention of the Manor Court. Perhaps this reflects a short period when the property was divided into two parts, as only the one house is thought to have existed here, with both men known to have lived in it.

In 1777 widow Grace Williams was living there, but the cottage was not to survive for much longer. It is not mentioned in records after this date and a note apparently made in the early 1800s records that the house was down. The Tithe Map of 1840 shows just a garden in the tenancy of William Ridler, who was handily placed up the road at Scout Cottage.

An interesting feature on the western side of the road, stretching from the lane leading to the Church House or thereabouts all the way to the Hill Lane turning, is the medieval open field that is still recognisable. This was once divided into narrow strips, at right angles to the road. Originally there would probably have been about a dozen such strips. Over the centuries many have been consolidated into larger fields and hedged around; but one has survived in its original size. It was called Tinker's Close in 1840 (earlier Tinker's Bridge Close), lying not far from the narrow lane with a stream alongside which used to lead to Marshall Meadow. The little field is a historical gem. The aforementioned stream, known as Willing's Water, was a valuable resource which was always a temptation to those who farmed nearby. It must have been especially galling for Withycombe Wyke tenants to watch it running away under Tinker's Bridge towards Withycombe Hadley's meadows. Consequently many found themselves presented at the latter's court for 'diverting Willing's water': such were George Gould in 1702, and John

Hoare and John Slocombe in 1714, who turned it into 'the wester field' and thereby caused 'great damage' to the tenants of the manor. Was 'the wester field' the name of the open field, one wonders?

By 1700, many of the fields in this area, including most of the remnants of the open field, had been acquired by the Hiles family. From 1650 John and Joane Hiles, together with John Chester, had held an overland in Withycombe Wyke consisting of 'Cawsey Close, two closes called Buskes and another called Broome Close'. A new agreement made in 1670 named only Joane Hiles for the same fields, but a cottage had since been built on one of the Buskes.

The site of Joane Hiles' Cottage has not been absolutely determined but it must have been close to Tinker's Close. In 1840 the adjoining fields were named Buss and Buss Meadow, either of which could have been the site of the cottage. Also it is likely to have been close to the nearby streamlet, as this would have been the handiest source of fresh water. At the 1709 sale of the manor John Hiles purchased his overland for £60 plus 2 guineas, but little more is heard of the cottage, which could not have been the most substantial of structures. When John Hiles left the village some years later and James Newton took over most of his property, there was no mention of it in the relevant lease.

The end piece of the open field to the north, a roughly triangular area defined by the angle made by the junction of Withycombe and Hill Lanes, is another area that almost certainly once contained a farmstead. There is no specific record of a building there, but the field did have its own lease; and in the 1709 sale it was referred to as Dullinghead Tenement. John Maunder of Hedford's (modern Christopher's) Farm had leased it in 1697 and over time it became integrated into that property. Before this it had been in the possession of Elinor Milton, widow. There was an annual rent of 1s.0d. and significantly a Church Rate of ¹/₂d., which implies that there had been a dwelling on the site.

The field in itself is an interesting one, as it confirms the existence of the open field. Several variations on its name have been noted, the closest to its original form probably being Durland Head. The 'headland' was an introduction made towards the end of the Anglo-Saxon period, being the end piece of an open field, which was reserved in order for the

team of oxen pulling the plough to have room to turn around. By 1840 the field's original name had been completely forgotten and it was then known by the name 'Browndry', in common with several other fields, mostly to the north. One of these fields was 'Little Browndry' on the other side of Withycombe Lane, and upon this a house was built during the period between the wars, which bears that name. In 1938 it was the home of two ladies, Eva Ellias and Marjorie Sanderson.

Past this point the lane falls away steeply towards Carhampton, and it is here, where the rough track that is Hill Lane curves away westwards, that we first encounter the parish boundary. Ancient parish boundaries tend to follow roads or paths of some description, in part because of the tradition of beating the bounds, when a perambulation of the parish took place, primarily to instil in the younger men of the parish an

Celebrating the golden jubilee of the Carhampton and Withycombe branch of the British Legion in 1977 are founder members Mary Cridge and Gertrude Sully, flanked by 'Old Contemptibles' Bill Gould and Fred Nicholas.

understanding of precisely where its limits were. Such boundary tracks, especially where they have been used as a major roadway, are frequently deeply cut below the level of the ground on either side, worn away by the constant passage of people, animals and vehicles; and we can see this phenomenon here as we pass by the Hill Lane turning and continue down to the old boundary junction at Carhampton Cross.

Modern boundary changes mean that we are well and truly in Carhampton from Little Browndry onwards, but the land on the east side of Withycombe Lane right down to the junction was part of Withycombe until the middle of the last century. Of course, even in centuries gone by, the inhabitants of this corner of the parish would have used the local shops, inns, etc. and in many respects would have regarded themselves as Carhampton people; but it was to the parish of Withycombe that they paid Church and Poor Rates and other taxes, and to which they looked for aid when in need.

Stretching all the way from the Hill Lane turning to Carhampton Cross, on the eastern side of the road, is a field called Knowle, which was described as a meadow in 1840. At its northern end is a small close which now contains just a few farm buildings; but for a long time it was home to a Withycombe Wyke tenement known as Knowle's. It was named after the Moore family (alias Knowles) that lived in Withycombe in the seventeenth and eighteenth centuries, owning several properties in both of the manors. This was the most extensive of them, paying an annual rent of 7s.7¹/₂d. John Moore (or Knowles – both surnames were used interchangeably, often in the same document) had held the property by copy since at least 1689. In 1709 the three lives on which it was held were John senr (aged 50), John junr (his son, 19) and George Moore (deceased). John purchased his 'home estate' at the sale of the manor, paying £59 plus 1 guinea for it. In the event it was actually conveyed to Withycombe farmer James Sully, with whom John Moore had come to some financial arrangement.

The 1709 conveyance from John Codrington described the property as 'all that copyhold messuage, tenement, dwelling-house and curtilage called Allercott Tenement in Withycombe.' It had been formerly in the tenure or occupation of Margaret Allercott, widow, deceased, and was 'now in the occupation of John Moore alias Knowle'. Margaret was buried at Carhampton in 1686, which fits with John Moore's subsequent admission to the tenancy. Before her 1669 marriage to William Allercott she had been a Willway, probably a daughter of Thomas and Mary of Carhampton.

Thus we can reasonably assume that the tenement was in the hands of the Allercott family throughout most of the 1600s, prior to the arrival of the Moores. Allercotts can be found in the parish registers of Withycombe throughout this period, the earliest being a John Allercott at the beginning of the century, and there is no record of them being associated with any other property there. Also it is unlikely that it would have been called Allercott Tenement unless that family had been associated with it for a considerable time.

John Moore continued there until at least 1732 but in 1739 a list of properties obliged to provide a tithingman has 'John Moore for his estate now Mr James Newton'. Documents in Chancery throw more light on the situation.

The Moores' acquisition of the farm, arrived at with the help of James Sully's loan, had placed a heavy financial obligation upon them. They had made matters worse by purchasing the tenancy of six additional pieces of land: the two Crofts, Churchill and Down Close in Withycombe, and two closes called Park Hearnes situated next to Marshwood Park in Carhampton. Two further loans had been taken, amounting to over £126 in total, from Francis Grimes of Carhampton, in order to pay what was owed. All was well until Grimes died in 1721 and his widow Elizabeth called in the debt. John Moore, unable to find the money, was forced to assign all of the property on which these loans were secured to Elizabeth. She transferred it to other members of her family – the Sharyers of Carhampton – who in turn sold it to James Newton. The latter is unlikely to have lived at Knowle's, being a successful yeoman farmer and an investor in property. His is the name that appears in connection with 'Moors' in the Church Rate collected in 1769. The property paid 3d., and perhaps it should be noted that there were actually two properties called Moors, both paying 3d., on the lists of ratepayers. The other was in Lower Street, on the site of the Memorial Hall, but Newton definitely held this one.

Around 1780 we find the first evidence of who was occupying the house, in an undated tithing list, which included 'James Gay for Knowles'. James was the occupier from at least the time of his marriage in 1780 to Sarah 'Perken'. He was described at his marriage as a husbandman, implying that Knowle's was still a smallholding at that time.

The Revd James Newton (son of James Newton) paid the 1790 Church Rate, and Revd William Newton paid it in 1830, when 'Knowles' Farm' was valued at £16.5s.5d. In 1840 the Revd William was listed as both owner and occupier of the property, although the latter claim is surely an error. The Tithe

Leversha's haymaking operation.

A Court Place Farm tractor at work with Bill Griffiths on the back.

Apportionment reveals that the house now comprised two dwellings, and as well as barn, barton and garden, seven fields were associated with the property. These included Down Close and Churchill, and the adjoining meadow called Knowle.

Meanwhile, the parish registers of Withycombe and Carhampton continue to reveal the real occupants. William Gay had been born to James in 1782, and from 1814, following his marriage to Jane Hobbs the previous year, he was the man 'of Knowle' presenting his children for baptism. Caution needs to be exercised with the Carhampton registers, however, as there was another Knowle Farm in that parish (occupied in 1814 by yeoman John Snook).

In 1841 elderly couple John and Mary Perkins occupied one dwelling. It was John's brother William who had taken on Smith's Cottage in West Street; and his son, also John, who had married William's daughter Hannah and gone to live there as well. By the 1850s John and Jane Morse had replaced the Perkins. Jane stayed on after her husband died and from then until the 1890s she shared her home with Harriet Escott. Jane worked as a washerwoman and cook to make ends meet, while Harriet was a dressmaker.

William and Jane Gay had the other house, which by 1851 had been further subdivided so that James and Ann Bryant had part of it. Both William and Jane lived to a considerable age and it was only after Jane's death in the 1870s that the Bryants were able to make use of all four rooms available. Next door Jane Morse and Harriet had to make do with three. This pair of dwellings disappeared many years ago, probably before 1901, with just the few outbuildings now marking the site.

We have now reached the end of the parish in this direction, but one further Withycombe property remains to be discussed. It is the neighbour of Knowle's, which still stands just around the corner from Withycombe Lane. Now just a cottage and garden in Carhampton, standing close to the busy A39 road as it swoops down the incline into that village

Court Place workers using the big elevator to build the hayrick.

from the east, Staddon's Tenement was an old farm of some 12 acres. It has survived (although of course much altered and periodically rebuilt to varying degrees) since Elizabethan times, and it was peculiar in that it paid rent to both Withycombe Hadley and Withycombe Wyke. This could be taken as a sign of its antiquity (as with the mill) but one suspects that the situation here is rather different: the rent was not split according to the usual proportion, but rather this was applied to its acreage (four and eight acres). It did not pay goose money to the manor, which is unusual for a smallholding of its size, probably indicating that it did not depasture any animals on the enclosed areas upon Withycombe Common. This may have been for purely practical reasons, given its location.

In the 1570s it was rented by William Hancock, but by 1604 the tenant was William Mylett (or Millet), and in 1617 widow Jane Myllett. The Myllets were a Carhampton family, their names appearing in the registers there during the 1600s. After Jane the property belonged to a family called Hancock (alias Stevens). Prior to 1644 it was in the hands of Joane, who was probably the widowed mother of Hugh, and it is likely that even before this date Hugh was the man in charge. His name appears in the 1641 Protestation Rolls for Withycombe and in the same year he also paid a Lay Subsidy of 2s.0d., an amount in keeping with a property of 12 acres. A 1655 survey of Withycombe Hadley mentions him as the copyhold tenant of a tenement 'late in the tenure of Joane Steavens', including eight acres (with 'noe meadow'), and granted to John Frankes (29), son of Robert Frankes, for life. A 1709 survey of Withycombe Wyke, referring back to a lease of 1656, names Hugh (deceased by 1709), John Staddon (the 65-year-old son of Robert Staddon) and John Hancock (60) as the lives for two closes named Browneserries containing four acres, which included a barn and an orchard. As mentioned previously, several fields around Staddon's Tenement were known by the name of Brownsery or Browndry.

In 1670 Hugh Hancock (alias Stevens) was Overseer of the Poor, putting his name to the list of Hearth Tax exemptions for that year. He died in 1678 and was buried at Withycombe. In that same year Elizabeth Stevens (alias Hancock) paid the rent of 10s.0d. to the manor of Withycombe Hadley for its part of the property. She died in the six months prior to the Michaelmas court of 1692, whereupon John Staddon was taken as the next tenant upon payment of a sheep (the property's 'best goods') as heriot. John had married Joan Stevens in 1672.

The sale of John Codrington's manor in 1709 saw Staddon's remain unsold. It was noted that John Staddon, aged about 65, held four acres of ground for his own life, part of which was a small overland, worth £3.10s.0d. for an annual rent of 2s.0d. This was later purchased by Madam Luttrell. Shortly after

An old Fordson tractor belonging to Court Place Farm and with Bill Griffiths on the back reaps a field to the north of the old Minehead–Williton road, just in the parish of Carhampton. Withycombe Wood and village are in the background.

this, William Withycombe of Dunster picked up the lease. From this we learn that the Withycombe Wyke part of the property was definitely more than just the two fields: it consisted of part of a house called Staddon's, including an orchard or garden, plus two fields called Long Close and Easter Close (four acres). In 1712 he also leased 'Stodden's Tenement', which was then said to consist of a house, outhouses, court, garden, orchard and eight acres of land in Withycombe Hadley, on the lives of his sons Robert, James and John Withycombe.

In 1723 some dramatic event took place in the village, which resulted in Richard Hill doing the tithingman's duty on behalf of Giles Daubenny, apprehending a pair of criminals. They were incarcerated temporarily at John Staddon's house, for which he was reimbursed the sum of £1.2s.10d. 'for the kiping of two felins'. Four men were deemed necessary to escort the prisoners to gaol, requiring a further payment of £2.5s.0d.

With William Withycombe's two acquisitions, both parts of the property were now consolidated, as noted in a lease of 1753. In this, William Withycombe of Timberscombe, aged 36, leasing Stodden's Tenement on his own life and on those of son James

and daughter Elizabeth, noted that the property had been previously leased as one third and two thirds, i.e. four acres plus eight acres. The rent was now 12s. It is unlikely that this William Withycombe or the earlier one ever occupied Staddon's: they should be regarded more as landlords of the property. This is supported by a survey of the manor in 1777, when the tenant was said to be 'William Withycombe now Jones', although the aforementioned lease was still in effect, implying that Jones was the undertenant in occupation. This survey describes the property as 'Staddon's Tenement near Carhampton Pound', consisting of 13 acres; and as being held on the lives of William (60), James (28 – with 'deceased' added later) and Elizabeth Withycombe (32). Around that time Staddon's was also described as 'a ruinous old dwelling-house near Carhampton Pound'.

James Withycombe paid the $3^1/_2$d. Church Rate for Staddon's in 1790, but by 1830 John Sully had added the property to his holdings. At that time Staddon's Farm was said to be worth £12.3s.5d. As a consequence of Sully's takeover, Staddon's lost its status as a farm, its fields being taken into the new tenant's estate. The 1840 Tithe Map shows it as No.189, a cottage and gardens, in the tenancy of John Sully, with four 'Browndry' fields also in his possession.

Throughout the nineteenth century the Tucker family was in occupation. In 1841, gardener Thomas Tucker and his wife Elizabeth, both in their sixties, lived there. Thomas had been heavily involved with the replanting of Withycombe Wood in the 1820s, being responsible for employing labourers to do the work. He was given money by Mr Veitch (who supplied the trees), which he used in turn to pay the workers at a rate of 1s.4d. per day. William Ridler did much of the work, with some assistance from James Bass, Thomas and William Cridland. Robert Cording had earlier been employed to clear the site of thistles and other weeds.

By 1851 the house had been divided in order to accommodate two households, although both were of the same family. Betsy Tucker, now a widow of 72, occupied one part with two of her sons, while son Thomas lived in the other with wife Mary and three children. Ten years later this family were in sole occupation, although brother John was described as a boarder. Thomas described himself as a seedsman. After he died, his son Robert Tucker and his family replaced him, and continued to occupy the house into the twentieth century.

James Henry Cridland lived at Bay Cottage (as it is still called in 2003) in 1927, while Bill and Alice Cridland were its occupants in 1938. It was included in the 1951 sale of Luttrell's holdings as 'a pleasant detached cottage in Withycombe Parish, but situate near Carhampton Cross' let to Mr W. Cridland. It was built of stone and cob, rendered over, and had a thatched and part-iron roof. Outside a lean-to stable still survived.

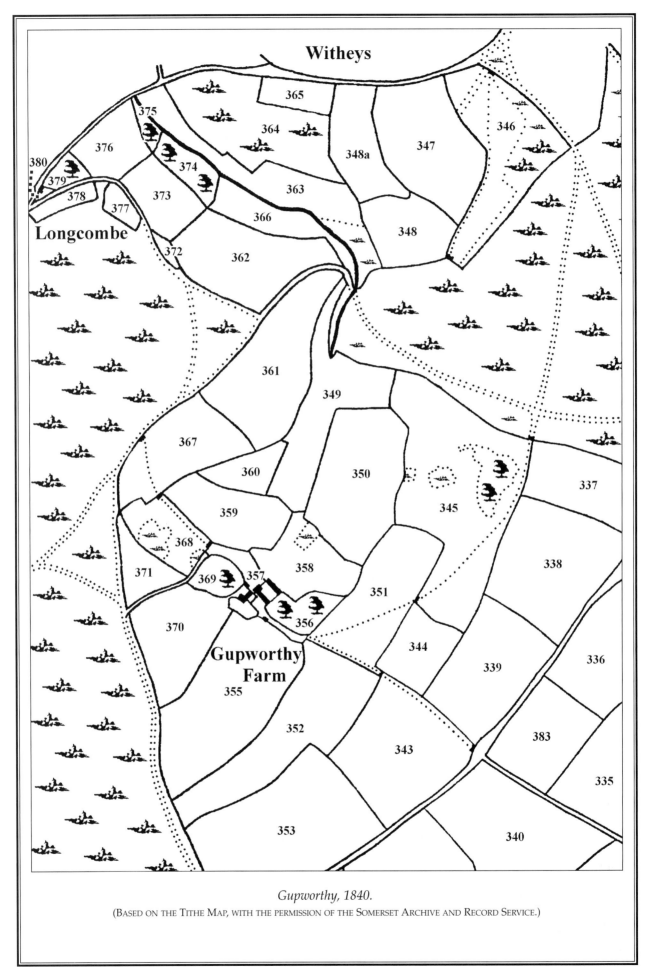

Gupworthy, 1840.
(BASED ON THE TITHE MAP, WITH THE PERMISSION OF THE SOMERSET ARCHIVE AND RECORD SERVICE.)

Five

Hill Lane to Gupworthy Farm

Turning back up Withycombe Lane now, after a few hundred yards we take the rough track that continues to mark the boundary between our village and Carhampton. This is Hill Lane, which winds steadily upwards, hugging the northern side of Withycombe Hill. Various fields, some of which have long been Church land, lie beyond the hedge on the Withycombe side, while Briddicott Farm, towards which a lane eventually branches off from the boundary track, occupies a position just south of Carhampton village on the other. Briddicott's position – with the handily placed lane leading directly on to Withycombe Hill – has frequently tempted its occupiers to breach the bounds of parish and manorial law. Already mentioned were William Orchard's attempts to use Withycombe Hadley's common land for grazing, and a generation later William Withycombe (or his tenant) was in more trouble at the same court. The court first presented:

... that a Bound stone which stood on Withycombe Hill near the fire Beacon on ye north west side thereof between ye common belonging to this Manor & an estate called Bredicott belonging to Mr Wm Withycombe hath been latley removed out of itts place by a Person un known & putt into Mr Withycombe's wall.

If this pointed accusation was judiciously phrased, the second presentment that followed immediately on from the first left little doubt as to the identity of the culprit. In this 'the said Mr Wm Withycombe' was presented for:

... opening a Qualley [quarry] on the Common be longing to this mannor and carring away from therr (having no Right So to do) Several thousand Seams of Stones for making of a wall on his said Estate called Bradicott which is not a parsel of this mannor but his own land.

Possibly William Withycombe claimed the right to quarry stone as his due as tenant of Staddon's Tenement, which he also held at this time; but the Manor Court was having none of it.

Beyond the Briddicott Lane turning a plantation of trees now occupies the Withycombe side of Hill Lane, on the site of fields that included the significant Sarah's Land. Originally called Sareland (or Sare Land), this had traditionally been associated with Lower Dumbledeer, since at least the reign of Henry VII. The field must have held some special significance because it was invariably mentioned specifically in rentals, etc., with a rent of 4s.0d. payable on it.

Eventually the lane emerges on to the hilltop, on that part of the common which some believe was once known as Stone Down, presumably from the prehistoric remains that have now disappeared. Nearby is the fire beacon, the focus of which has become increasingly ceremonial over time, being used as a site for celebrations such as the turn of a new century or the jubilee of a reigning monarch. One such was Queen Victoria's golden jubilee, held in June 1887 to celebrate her 50 years on the throne. However, the event turned into a local tragedy. An old cannon was dragged up to the gathering with the intention of delivering a respectful salute to Her Majesty. One lady – Maria Gould from Oak – was nervous of the weapon and so was invited to stand behind it, which was presumed to be the safest place. This proved not to be the case: the breech of the ancient gun exploded, killing the poor woman instantly. Also killed was Ernest Case, son of Robert of Withycombe Farm. Dreadful as this disaster was, it could have been even worse: Maria was holding her three-month-old niece at the time but miraculously the infant escaped serious injury.

In 2003 the site of the beacon is quite overgrown, but it was there that many gathered to see in the year 2000, with fireworks and a little champagne, despite the mud being a foot deep on the trackways leading up the hill. Happily there were no serious injuries on that occasion.

The boundary track runs westwards along the ridge of Withycombe Hill, heading towards the encampment of Bat's Castle, but as one approaches the important intersection at Withycombe Hill Gate few will be aware that the scrubby heath nearby was once the site of a long-forgotten farm known as Witheys.

Its lands abutted the parish boundary as it turns south towards Longcombe, and stretched as far as the lower land between Gupworthy Farm and Withycombe Hill. The fields can be identified on the 1840 Tithe Map as Outer Close (No.346), Broom Close (No.347), Moor (No.348), Barn Close (No.348a), Southern Close (No.362), Meadow (No.363), Brake (No.364) – in earlier times called Splatt, Carrot Close (No.365) and South Close (No.366). No buildings remained on the property at that date, but the little rectangular field called Carrot Close must have been the site of the farmhouse and barton. Its size and shape indicate as much, as does the presence of an adjoining Barn Close; and a track leads directly away from it to the north-west. Charles Hagley held this overland property from Thomas Dyke Acland in 1840, as part of his Combe Farm estate, into which it had been subsumed at some time prior to 1700.

The 1709 survey of the manor of Withycombe Wyke, to which it belonged, stated that a tenement called Wythes, containing 28 acres of arable land, meadow and pasture, was leased to Andrew Newton (who also held Combe Farm) for the lives of himself and Giles Newton, after the death of Dorothy Vellacott, for a rent of 7s.1d. in 1695. This indicates that Dorothy Vellacott, who held other farmland in the parish, was probably the previous tenant. She was the widow of John Vellacott and had previously been a member of another local landed family, the Blakes. And some time before that it must have belonged to the Withey (alias Wheddon) family, who had been prominent in the parish until the mid-seventeenth century.

It was purchased in the 1709 sale by Robert Siderfin (Andrew Newton's financial backer) as part of the Combe Farm estate, when it was described as an overland belonging thereto.

As a consquence of its situation high on Withycombe Hill, with its poor, stony soil; and being linked only by steep, narrow tracks to civilisation, it should come as no surprise that the farm was virtually abandoned more than 300 years ago. Indeed one might wonder why anybody would contemplate creating one there in the first place. There are a couple of reasons why they might, one historical, the other practical. Firstly, the site may reflect the farm's origin as part of a larger, very ancient community in the general area, dating back to the Iron Age. Secondly, the stream that trickles between two of its fields would have served not only as a supply for the householder, but also to create that valuable commodity – meadowland. Its value to the farmer in days gone by cannot be overestimated. Surveys from the seventeenth century and earlier invariably state the acreage of meadowland, or state 'no meadow' where there was none. In the Domesday Book, of Withycombe's 670 acres only ten were said to have been meadow. Whether this figure is accurate or not, meadowland was always at a premium, and the

four-acre meadow alone would have made Witheys a viable property, if a difficult one on which to live.

Although little more than a parcel of fields after 1700, the identity of Witheys has been maintained down through the years. As late as 1920 William Bond of Dunster qualified to vote in local government elections at Withycombe on the basis of his ownership of land in the parish, namely 'The Withies'; and until recently 'Withes Brake' and 'Withes Alders' were marked on maps.

Another similar property was Longcombe, the neighbour of Witheys to the south. It survived as a working farm for much longer, although its earlier history is even more obscure. Like Witheys, it relied on the little brook flowing down from the spring at Gupworthy Farm. There was also a Carhampton property called Longcombe, just over the parish boundary. Both were brought together under William Pearse (later of Gupworthy Farm) around 1800. Matters are further complicated by the fact that the Withycombe portion of the farm included Church land, held in the names of the churchwardens.

Longcombe Farm in Withycombe nestled in the valley bottom at the low point of Longcombe Lane, at an important junction of some ancient trackways. The house lay between Longcombe Lane and the track that curves away eastwards towards Gupworthy Farm. The house and garden were still inhabited in 1840, when they were recorded on the Tithe Map as No.380. A visitor to the site now may find it difficult to imagine how it was: shrouded by trees, the position is dark and dank, and the buildings are long gone. Belonging to the farm were Little Orchard (No.372), Higher Churchland (No.373), Higher Churchland Orchard (No.374), Lower Churchland Orchard (No.375), Lower Churchland (No.376) and Longcombe Orchard (No.379). William Pearse was the tenant then, holding it from the churchwardens.

From its position in the parish, Longcombe must have originally belonged to the superior manor of Withycombe Wyke, but there is no specific mention of it in the documentation surrounding the 1709 sale of that manor. Most likely it was then, as later, included as part of 'John Question's Tenement', i.e. Gupworthy Farm, and was little more than a convenient home for some of its workers. What evidence survives suggests that it was the Gould family that filled this role. John Gould of Longcombe was mentioned in a list of manorial tenants made in 1743. In September 1767 Thomas Weetch of Withycombe, yeoman, took on the tenancy of 'Lancombe', which consisted of a dwelling-house, orchard and two pieces of ground of six acres, via an indenture signed by the then churchwardens, Thomas Escott of Sandhill, gentleman, and John Price, blacksmith. It was taken for the lives of Thomas, wife Ann and son Robert. This was the family who were later to acquire the tenancy of The King's Arms, and it is possible that they were occupying Gupworthy Farm at this time. The previous occupier of Longcombe was stated to have been John Gould, deceased – no doubt the man who was buried at Withycombe in May of that same year.

As it was Church property, Longcombe seems to have been exempt from Church Rates, instead paying an annual Church Rent. Longcombe paid by far the highest Church Rent in Withycombe, Thomas Weetch paying £6.6s.0d. in 1771. He continued to pay for Longcombe until at least 1791, then, after a period when the tenant was unnamed, William Pearse took over, being first specifically named for Longcombe in 1822. It is not until 1841 that we discover who was actually living at Longcombe, and it is surely significant that it was another family of Goulds, that of James and his wife Honor. James had been a shoemaker when he had married Honor Rawle in Carhampton in 1831, but was now a labourer. It has not been possible to prove a direct relationship between James and the earlier John Gould, but it is at least a possibility that Longcombe remained a family home throughout this period. This western end of the parish had certainly been a Gould stronghold for a long time, with another family group living at Bowden.

By 1851 James had died, leaving his pauper widow to manage on her own. Fortunately, several of their children were old enough to help out, and she continued to live as a widow with her family at Longcombe until at least 1871. Shortly afterwards though Honor moved to Rodhuish to live with grandson Daniel Gould and it was probably then that the house was abandoned.

The boundary track continues southwards beyond the site of Longcombe Farm, following the line of the combe, and climbs inexorably, with the woodland known as Withycombe Scruffets to the east, and Black Hill beyond. Some in the parish still remember that villagers had the right to collect firewood from Scruffets: this is a quite amazing example of the persistence of old customs, for this was fire-bote, the right of tenants to freely take firewood for their own use from certain areas. The antiquity of this custom is perhaps best illustrated by the fact that the Manor Court of Withycombe Hadley found it necessary to clarify the tradition as long ago as 1681 (implying that some had forgotten the rules concerning this and similar practices even then), when the court presented that it was the custom of the manor 'to take house boot, plow boot & fire boot without any Leave of any Bayliffe or Reeve…'. Housebote and plowbote were the rights to take wood for the repair of buildings and tools respectively. Such were generally part of the rights of common, and so it is likely to be no coincidence that east of Scruffets is an area shown on modern maps as Withycombe Common. However, records clearly indicate that this area was not the common belonging to the tenants of Withycombe Hadley, who instead used a large part of

Withycombe Hill, the implication is that it must have been that belonging to the manor of Withycombe Wyke.

This also makes sense because it is close to the main farms that belonged to Withycombe Wyke, such as Gupworthy, Bowden, etc. Conversely it is too far from the farms of Withycombe Hadley to be of much practical use to them. In recent centuries the area came to be associated exclusively with Gupworthy Farm, which used it as a sheepwalk.

To the east of Withycombe Common lies Rodhuish Common, the boundary between the two being marked by a line of stones which runs roughly northwards towards Red Girts, the source of Withycombe's brook. The boundary here has clearly been arranged so that this water source is accessible to the users of both commons.

All of this land on or near the slopes of Black Hill is rough ground, suitable only for the grazing of sheep. To the north of this lies the principal property in this area of the parish, the second most important in the manor of Withycombe Wyke: Gupworthy Farm. Its origins in the Anglo-Saxon period have already been mentioned. The map of this end of the parish shows the probable extent of its lands since it was first created: it is limited on at least three sides by trackways so enjoys natural boundaries. Of course, the farm has included other fields at various times. In 1840, for example, William Pearse's fields also included the Gilcotts, all of Longcombe and Black Hill. However, those named below are likely to have formed the original nucleus of the holding, except that those on the north side have been extended in that direction as more of the hill has been brought into cultivation, always an ongoing process. Even today one is perhaps more likely to see wild red deer than farm animals on those northernmost 'pastures'.

In 1840 these fields were Lower Masley (No.337), Higher Masley (No.338), Burrow Close (No.339), Lydeard (No.343), Little Wood Close (No.344), Gupworthy Moor (No.345), Middle Meadow (No.349), Waterleats (No.350), Broom Close (No.351), Long Close (No.352), Stapling (No.353), Gurch Close (No.355), Hayrick Orchard (No.356), house, barton, etc. (No.357), Hayrick Meadow (No.358), Pond Meadow (No.359), Moor Meadow (No.360), Lower Roals (No.361), Higher Roals (No.367), The Moor (No.368), Little Orchard (No.369), Three Corner Close (No.370) and Little Hill Piece (No.371).

From the names of some of these fields – Hayrick Meadow, Pond Meadow, etc. – it is not difficult to see why a farm grew up at that location. The house is sited next to a natural spring, the outflow from which runs away northwards, providing water to create valuable meadowland.

As Gupworthy Farm was a part of Withycombe Wyke we do not know much about its tenants until around 1700, but a little information from earlier periods has survived. In the early- to mid-sixteenth century 'William Stephens of Gupworthy' was listed as making payments to Withycombe Hadley for certain property there.

In 1621 an indenture was made between Sir Nicholas Halswell on one side, and George Hooper and his wife Joan on the other, conveying Gupworthy to the Hoopers. Then in 1639 the will of George Hooper was proved, which passed the farm to George's son-in-law, John Question. It is probable that neither the Hoopers nor this first John Question resided at Gupworthy, instead preferring to let the farm to others (the Questions' home was at Dunster). There are no Questions recorded in Withycombe in 1641, for example. The first sign that there were Questions living in Withycombe was in 1688, when Augustine was christened, the first of several children of 'Mr John' and wife Mary Question. Clearly coincident with this was a grant of copyhold, dated 1689, of 'John Question's Tenement' to John (born c.1660) and his sons John junr (born c.1687) and Augustine, who died young. The rent for Gupworthy was 7s.7½d., paid by John Question in 1709. This is rather less than one might expect for a property of its size, in fact exactly the same as was paid for Maunder's and Knowle's Tenements, which were both less extensive. The 1709 sale of the manor saw Withycombe Farm and John Question's Tenement purchased together by Madam Whitlocke for the large sum of £1,850 – more than half of the total sum raised by the sale.

In 1718 John Question paid the Church Rate of 1s.7d. due for Gupworthy. This clearly demonstrates that the property was much more extensive than is apparent from the manor rent. The amount puts it on a par with the much expanded Combe and Hiles Farms; Maunder's and Knowle's only paid 3d.!

Indentures of lease and release were again drawn up in 1723 prior to the marriage of John Question (the son of John and Mary) and Joan Jeane (?). In 1724 the pair christened a son John in Withycombe. However, this is the last evidence we have of the Question family living in the parish, and this may be connected with a legal judgement made against them in 1723. This was an 'exemplification of a recovery' made by William Blackford, Edward Dyke, Charles Prowse and Richard Jeane (?) against Thomas Dyke (referred to as 'tenant') and John and Mary Question. This illustrates the complex situation regarding the ownership of the property that had developed through multiple marriage settlements, etc. over a long period.

Mr John Short was the next man to take possession of Gupworthy, although once again we can be certain that he never occupied the farm himself. Nevertheless, his name appears for 'Guppery', paying the Church Rate in 1769 and also the Church Rent of 1s.3d. from 1771 onwards. John Short continued to be responsible for such payments until the late 1780s, when presumably he died,

because the list of people paying the Church Rate for 1790 includes 'the executors of Mr John Short for Guppery'. The next owner was Sylvanus Jones and it is thanks to him that at last we have some idea of who was actually occupying the farm since the departure of the Questions. In 1788 he drew up a covenant, promising Gupworthy to Joshua Veysey for 21 years for an annual rent of £66. Veysey had been tenant at Court Place Farm since 1773, but was about to give it up. The rent of Gupworthy was only about a third of that of Court Place, making it much more affordable, and Veysey was to occupy it during the twilight of his life. However, what is most interesting is that the document describes Gupworthy as consisting of about 100 acres and being 'late in possession of Thomas Weetch as tenant, now of Charles Hurford as tenant.' Both the Hurford and Weetch families are known to have farmed in the general area during that period. We have noted that Thomas Weetch took an interest in Longcombe from 1767; and Charles and Sarah Hurford christened many children 1788–1811, son John later farming at Higher Dumbledeer.

By 1791 Jones had died and Gupworthy was sold to Mr Luttrell. He arranged for the sale of the farm to be held at The Luttrell Arms, Dunster, on 9 July. The farm was described as consisting of a good farmhouse, barns, stables and convenient outhouses, 110 acres of arable, meadow and pasture, and 9 acres of wood. This sale necessitated a valuation. The document is headed 'A Valuation of Gupworthy late Shorts, sold to Mr Luttrell in reversion after the death of Mrs Jones late Short', and contains the following information:

House, courts, linneys, barns, orchards and gardens were valued at £2; Pond Mead, Middle Mead, Spear Mead and Hayrick Mead at £10; Three Corner Close, Wood Mead, Barn Close, Lower Marshley, Burrow Close, Wood Close, Lydeard and Higher Rowhill at £28.2s.6d.; Hill Close and Lower Rowhill at £6.16s.0d.; Higher Marshley at £5.5s.0d.; Stapleland Field and Long Close at £10.10s.0d.; Waterleat and Gods Close at £6.18s.0d.; Aller plott at 15s.; and Wood or Wood Stile Close at £1, making a grand total of £71.6s.6d.

The names of the fields are roughly the same as those named some 50 years later in the Tithe Apportionment. The name of Stapleland (later Stapling) Field refers to the place where fleeces were sold. The field adjoins Stapling Lane and another field of the same name lies on the other side of it, so clearly this was an important area for the hill farmers who lived and worked at the western end of the parish. Gods Close must be the same as the strangely named Gurch Close. Was this last close Gupworthy's Church land and, if so, should the latter have been Church Close?

After Joshua Veysey's death at the turn of the century William Pearse, from the family that farmed at Binham, Old Cleeve, took over at Gupworthy. His period of tenure (and that of his sons after him) was to see the acreage of fields associated with the property almost triple. He was no doubt helped in this by the fact that his friends and relations by marriage, the Hagleys, also previously from Old Cleeve, took over Combe Farm at the same time; by 1840 almost the entire western end of the parish had the appearance of one huge estate, shared between the two families.

The Church Rate made in 1830 only gives a valuation for Gupworthy and Longcombe Churchland together, of £57.18s.11d. William also held the Gilcotts, valued at £30.2s.5d. These are the same lands, together with Black Hill, that he would hold ten years later.

William and wife Ann (Hagley), in their seventies, were still living at Gupworthy in 1841, together with sons William and Thomas, both over 35. A battery of servants, young men and women, lived in. After William's death in 1847 his sons took joint charge of the farm, running it together until Thomas' death in 1869. In 1871 there was no one living at Gupworthy as a new house was under construction. However, William remained for a time, being listed as the farmer at Gupworthy in trade directories until 1875. Shortly after this he took a rather belated decision to marry and moved to a smaller farm at Elworthy.

In 1881 the 298 acres at Gupworthy were in the hands of John and Elizabeth Hagley. Their young children John, Alice, William and Elizabeth were with them, as well as dairymaid Elizabeth Coles and servants Ann Hurford, and Daniel and Frank Griffiths. Unfortunately the faulty 1891 census for Withycombe contains no obvious candidate for the tenant of Gupworthy, and after 1883 (when John Hagley was named) the farm ceases to appear in trade directories, so it is not easy to know what was going on after this date; but after members of this Hagley family emigrated to America the farm's land was probably taken in by another Withycombe farmer – thought to be Robert Case – and the house used by a worker who would act as a sort of farm bailiff. This seems to have been the situation in 1901, when Robert Jones, described as a cattleman, was at Gupworthy with his family.

During the 1920s James and Emma Griffiths lived there. Around this time a new windmill powered certain farm machinery. Whenever the wind sprang up, workmen would leave their tasks and set it in motion! By 1938 the Bakers, Amos and Elsie, lived at Gupworthy. While they were there a terrible tragedy occurred when, one day, their two young daughters drowned in the pond near the house. The distraught mother ran all the way to Briddicott, which was also held by the family at the time, to get help. Today Gupworthy is still very much a working hill farm.

This was 'our farm back in England' to William Hagley after his family emigrated to America.
It may be the old house at Briddicott (Carhampton) which was destroyed by fire, as William's parents held this in
addition to Gupworthy in the 1880s. The occasion is the visit by the local Friendly Society on their
annual perambulation.

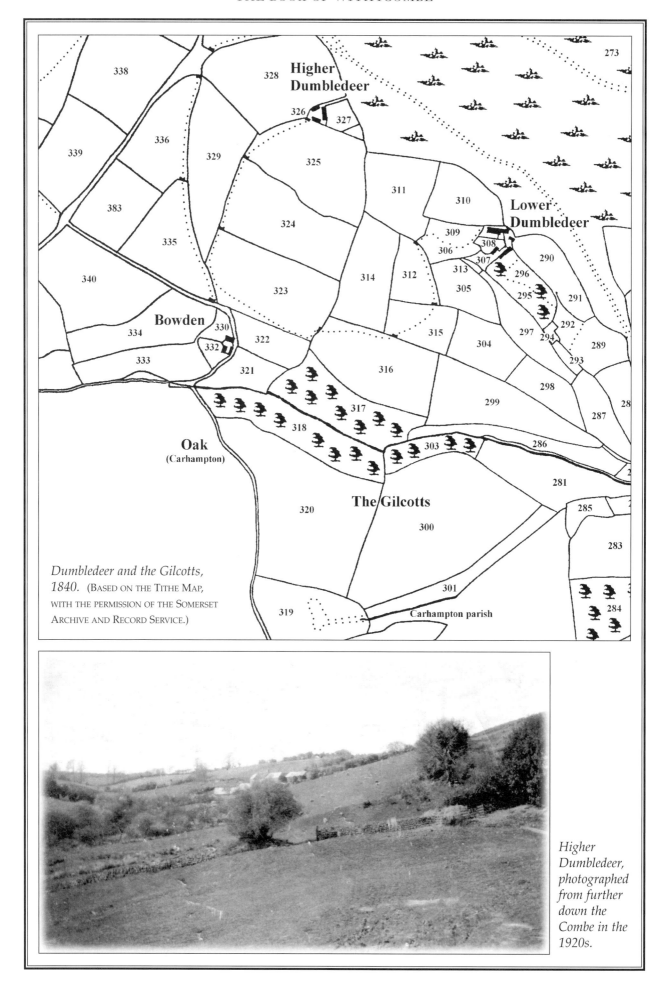

Dumbledeer and the Gilcotts, 1840. (Based on the Tithe Map, with the permission of the Somerset Archive and Record Service.)

Higher Dumbledeer, photographed from further down the Combe in the 1920s.

Six

Stapling Lane to Hill Bridge

To the east of Stapling Lane, which marks the traditional limit of Gupworthy territory, is an area with a complex history. Several small Withycombe Wyke properties once lay hereabouts, most of which were in the process of breaking up and being absorbed into larger tenements 300 years ago. Nearby are the Gilcotts, originally part of the manor of Gildencote, and at Hill we are in the general area of the Martins' third part of the Withycombe manor, about which little is known.

Of the small, now lost properties, most seem to have been acquired by Hugh Blackwell at the sale of Withycombe Wyke, for the purpose of adding to the lands farmed from his West Street holding, Farmer's Tenement. He paid £200 and 1 guinea for Stone's, Bradford's and Slade's Tenements, which he had leased in 1701. All three appear to have been functioning in the 1640s, but by 1701 seem to have been just a parcel of fields.

The precise location of these three tenements is not known, but the probability is that they lay close by Stapling Lane, on its east side, and that their fields eventually came to be associated with Bowden and Higher Dumbledeer. (They were simply too inaccessible from Farmer's Tenement to stay associated with it in the long term.) In the case of Bradford's there is evidence for this on the 1840 Tithe Map, where the fields called Lower and Higher Bradford, No.340 and No.342 respectively, can be seen in just such a position close by Bowden, although belonging to Higher Dumbledeer. These two last-named properties still survive, and it is to them that we turn next.

Bowden sits next to the narrow lane which leads away eastwards from Stapling Lane, at a point where it loops before plunging steeply down towards the little vale containing the young Withycombe Brook. Its antiquity is reflected in the name of one Willelmo Boghdone (William Bowdon), mentioned in an earlier chapter as an important man in the village around 1327.

However, it is not until the 1709 sale of the manor that we learn much about Bowden's history. It was a leasehold property, held by Samuel Kent since at least 1700 for a rent of 3s.6d. per annum. A further 10d. was due as goose money. It was held on his life (he was said to be 50 in 1709), and those of his son

Samuel junr (11) and daughter Mary (10), and was purchased for him at the sale by Mr Robert Siderfin. The latter acted also for Andrew Newton in the sale of Combe Farm, and we only have a combined price paid for the two properties, of £520 and 2 guineas. This connection between Bowden and Combe Farms in terms of absolute ownership has persisted into modern times. Apparently Samuel Kent never paid off Robert Siderfin (if that was ever his intention), effectively remaining his tenant or that of subsequent owners of the property. Samuel was described as a yeoman of Timberscombe, and there are no indications that he ever made personal use of the farm.

Thus we have three layers of possession with regard to Bowden. At the top we have the owners, gentlemen farmers in general, who were essentially its financiers. By the end of the 1700s the ownership of Bowden had passed into the hands of Thomas Dyke Acland, a major landowner in West Somerset. The middle layer consists of the official tenants. Their names appeared on tax and rate lists for Bowden, and they were responsible for parish duties associated with the property. Samuel Kent's name continued to appear throughout most of the eighteenth century. However, by the 1780s Bowden was being referred to as 'late Samuel Kent's' and Thomas Dyke Acland was contacted regarding payments due until a new tenant could be found. Tenants in the ensuing years included Mr John Newton (1822), Mr Thomas Wrentmore (1830, when the new rate valued Bowden at £22.17s.3d.) and Charles Hagley of Combe (1840). None of these lived at Bowden themselves. It is the third layer, comprising the under-tenants, that is of most interest, for it includes the people who actually occupied the property. The first resident of Bowden in this era that we know about was John Gould, who was described as 'of Bowden' in 1758, to distinguish him from another man of the same name. He died in either 1762 or 1770, and it is not known who lived next at Bowden, although if John left a widow she would have had the right to continue living there for her lifetime. However, we do know that soon after his 1810 marriage to Elizabeth Cording, labourer James Pearse came to live there; and, because he was always described as

Higher Dumbledeer, looking towards Black Hill.

Higher Dumbledeer, c.1968, when it was the home of Mr and Mrs Chorley for a brief period.

simply a labourer, it is clear that Bowden had ceased to be a true farm by this time. The house was being used as a residence while the owner of some nearby property was working its fields.

The Tithe Map lists the fields associated with Bowden (the house etc. being Nos 330 and 331) around this period as Lower Park (No.321), Higher Park (No.322), Orchard (No.332), Clift (No.333), Lilys Field (No.334), Hither West Field (No.335), Yonder West Field (No.336), Meadow (No.341), Stapling (No.354), Goosemoor (No.382) and Higher West Field (No.383), which together form a contiguous whole. It is quite likely that, apart from Goosemoor, these are the fields that belonged to Bowden for many centuries, perhaps since it was first built.

James Pearse was one of two brothers who moved to Withycombe around this time from Carhampton. Brother William was a tailor, like their father John. John Pearse had arrived in Carhampton from Winsford and set up his tailoring business near the church, where he soon fell foul of the authorities for allowing his premises to be used by supporters of John Wesley for their services. He had a large number of sons, whose descendants included the Pearse tailors in many nearby parishes as well as the highly skilled stonemasons of Minehead. Between them, James and William were responsible for all of the Pearses who have lived in the village of Withycombe (they were not related to the Gupworthy family) from the early-nineteenth century up to the present day.

James and Betty lived at Bowden until at least 1825, before moving down to Mill Street. They were replaced by labourer John Gould – yes, again! – and wife Mary who, since their 1823 marriage, had moved from place to place in the general area before finally settling at Bowden around 1836. Was this John Gould a descendant of the family who had lived there earlier? As his baptism at Carhampton in 1799 does not even give his mother's name (he was 'base-born'), we cannot say for sure, but there must be a fair chance that he was.

Certainly Bowden became a definite Gould home again from this point onwards, John and Mary residing there together into their seventies, their grandson – yet another John Gould – moving in with them by 1861, when he was just a boy, and later assuming the role of head of the household. By 1881 he had a wife, Harriet, and four children. His grandfather had died but Mary, aged 81, still lived with the family.

In 1891, it is likely that John and Harriet were still at Bowden, although the faulty census does not give their address. By 1901 the pair had moved to Pinns Cottages at Rodhuish and William Furse and his family were at Bowden. However, Bowden continued to be a home for the Goulds, Frederick and wife Rose residing there between the wars. It is still inhabited in 2003.

To the north of Bowden is another Withycombe Wyke property that has managed to survive into the new millennium. This is Higher Dumbledeer, at one time apparently known as Lower Bowden or Edward Thorne's Tenement.

The first we know of it is that it was granted to Edward Thorne (aged 70 in 1709) in 1691. Described as a messuage or tenement with orchard, garden and 20 acres of land, valued at £20, it was let by copy at a rent of 7s.2d. plus 10d. goose money. The copyhold was altered in 1700 to include Mary and Elizabeth Thorne. We also know that the previous tenant had been widow Catharine Stevens.

Edward purchased his estate when the manor was sold, for the sum of £104 and 1 guinea. A document of conveyance was accordingly drawn up, naming the grantee as James Thorne, yeoman of Withycombe, and describing the property as 20 acres at Dumbledeer called Lower Bowden's Tenement.

Edward Thorne definitely occupied Higher Dumbledeer himself, being presented to the Manor Court of Withycombe Hadley on several occasions between 1712 and 1724 for making a garden on the common. It is hardly surprising that he was tempted to offend in this way, seeing that the house is situated immediately next to the common land. Edward paid the property's Church Rate of $7\frac{1}{2}$d. and other taxes as required, and he was named 'for his estate in Higher Dumbledeer' on the tithingman's list of 1739. Judging by the timespan involved here it seems likely that more than one individual of the same name lived successively at the farm: one was buried in Withycombe churchyard in 1730.

It is possible that the Stennings family inhabited the property during the middle part of the century. Christopher 'Stenins' was nominated to be tithing-man for 1752, a year scheduled for the tenant of Higher Dumbledeer to perform the duty. There is also a field (belonging to Lower Dumbledeer in 1840 but close to the Higher property) called 'Stennings'. Christopher was buried at Withycombe in 1765.

The next we hear of Higher Dumbledeer is in 1769, when Mary Blackwell paid the $7\frac{1}{2}$d. Church Rate for it, and again in 1790, when her executors made the same payment. These executors also paid the rates due for Bradford's and Slade's, which, as noted above, the Blackwell family acquired many years earlier. This may imply that the property known as Stone's had been absorbed into Higher Dumbledeer, but the situation is complex and unclear. A tithing office list made in the 1780s includes Mr John Stenner for Higher Dumbledeer, but there is considerable confusion in the records at this time: he was also named in connection with Lower Dumbledeer, which was then itself divided into two parts.

What is certain is that Mary Blackwell did not live at Higher Dumbledeer, although it is just possible that John Stenner did. Later documents declare that after Edward Thorne, Higher Dumbledeer was occupied by his daughter Elizabeth Thorne, or her

Tom Wyburn thatching the top of a hayrick in the traditional way for his boss Charlie Hagley.

Left: *Tom and Mary Ann Wyburn, c.1930.*

Right: *Tom Wyburn's 1941 bill for the Michaelmas quarter's rent, payable at Mrs Eames' house in West Street. Dunster Castle estate was collecting rent in exactly the same way as it had been doing for hundreds of years.*

Left: *This time a 1945 receipt. 24 June was the Feast of the Nativity of John the Baptist, another quarter-day.*

Right: *Cyril and Edna Wyburn.*

Below: *This is thought to be Cyril Wyburn, with a pair of working horses, c.1930 – Cyril worked at Higher Rodhuish for the Thomas family.*

undertenants, and then by George Milton. George had married Jane Bryant in 1792 and may have taken Dumbledeer around that time, but in 1815 he sold off all of his goods and stock 'at Dumbledeer'. A valuation of £212 had been put upon them prior to the sale. The list of items included one sow and seven pigs (£5), one slip jug (£1.5s.0d.), seven lambs (£4.4s.0d.), etc. Around this period, which was clearly one of upheaval, the house was let briefly to labourer Robert Warren and his wife Mary; and Mary Newton was named as being responsible for the 1830 Church Rate, where the farm was valued at £27.1s.10d., but it was not long before farmer John Hurford moved into the property.

Meanwhile, the ownership of Higher Dumbledeer changed several times, invariably from one consortium to another, the documents of conveyance often showing signs of confusion between the different farms at Dumbledeer. When the 1840 Tithe Map was drawn up no less than four owners were named: Charles Rowcliffe, Thomas Blackwell Leigh, Richard Radford and John Thorne. The tenant was John Hurford. Higher Dumbledeer was shown as comprising house, barn, barton and gardens (Nos. 326 and 327), Higher Eight Acres (No.323), Lower Eight Acres (No.324), Meadow (No.325), Barn Close (No.328) and Six Acres (No.329), plus the two Bradfords over by Bowden which were clearly not part of the original property.

The census compiled in the following year reveals John Hurford as the man in charge at Higher Dumbledeer, described as a farmer, over 60 years of age. Three servants were living with him: Sarah Pugsley, 40, who probably kept house for him, and two teenage boys, George Vickery and John Hurford, the latter no doubt a relative. The Vickery and Hurford families were close friends as well as neighbours. John and Ann Vickery lived at Lower Dumbledeer at this time, and the elder John Hurford had been a witness at their wedding, also John's brother Thomas, who lived at Armstrong's Cottage in the village, was married to Jane Vickery.

From 1851, with John Hurford gone, we begin to see Higher Dumbledeer being occupied by agricultural labourers. As far as we can tell, James Willis of Rodhuish, with his wife Mary, was the first of these. However, by 1861 a Devon man, John Price, had moved in for a long stay and may still have been there with his wife Peggy in 1891.

Moving into the twentieth century, we find the Wyburn family in residence. Tom and his wife Mary Ann lived there from the turn of the century until at least 1946, when Tom died. He worked at Combe Farm. Mary Ann also brought several Webber children from her first marriage to the village with her. Reg Young came to live at Dumbledeer for a while after marrying Tom and Mary Ann's daughter Mildred, while guardsman William Garrett, who worked as a chef in Minehead, did the same prior to

the Second World War after marrying Gladys Wyburn. As a boy during the war, Ron Blundell of Minehead visited his godparents Sid and Rhoda Wyburn at the house and remembers standing in the large open fireplace and looking up at the stars. This was the fireplace concerned with an old Dumbledeer tradition wherein, every Good Friday, the man of the house would go out and cut a holly bush, attach a rope to it and take it up onto the roof. He would then lower the rope down the chimney and the children would haul on it, pulling the bush, together with a great shower of soot, down into the room – no doubt an effective, if quite mad, way of cleaning a chimney!

Ron also remembers an old barn on the north side of the house, which contained that essential piece of equipment, the cider press. The house at Higher Dumbledeer is still inhabited in 2003.

Children of Reg and Mildred Young, c.1923.

The Wyburns at Higher Dumbledeer, c.1940. Tom is on the left with his wife Mary Ann towards the centre. Arthur Hooper has his arm around her.

Skirting the edge of Withycombe Hadley's common land, the track from Higher Dumbledeer leads down from the hill to Combe Farm, passing Lower Dumbledeer on the way. The ancient farm that once stood here has now gone, which is a shame because it was historically an interesting and unusual property. To begin with, it belonged to Withycombe Hadley, when the logic of its position suggests that it should have been part of Withycombe Wyke. It was one of three properties that made an annual payment to the manor, in addition to its rent (10s. plus 8d. goose money) of a bushel of rye. This suggests that an unusual agreement existed between the farm and its landlords, dating from very early times, perhaps linked to a grant made between the manors. Was this a Martin property?

Whatever the case, we are able to trace the farm's history further back than any other in the parish, with the exception of the demesne farms, in part because of its long association with the field on the other side of the common called Sarah's Land or Sareland. It was held during the reign of King Henry VII, and probably before, by William Woodward. He is mentioned in several rentals dated from the 1490s to 1507 as paying 6s.8d. for a tenement, 4s.0d. for Sareland, and a bushel of rye. This was at a time when rents were unstable and liable to change from year to year, yet the total amount is already suggestive of that payable for Lower Dumbledeer in later years.

William Woodward was listed again, as a customary tenant, in the extensive Withycombe Hadley survey made a little later. He paid 6s.8d. for a tenement, 1d. Peter's Pence, 4s. for '1 parcel of land called Sareland', one bushel of rye at Martinmas and 12d. for hill pasture of Goosdon. The property is not named in any of these early sources but the combination of the bushel of rye and the field called Sareland makes it almost certainly Lower Dumbledeer. We know that a tenement was in existence here in medieval times because, as will be seen below, a survey of 1655 mentions an old house and a new house on the site.

After William Woodward, the next we hear of the property is just prior to 1579, when its tenant was Barbera Lyden (following pikeman John Liddon, perhaps?) but by 1579 Richard Barrow had taken over. He was also named in 1604 and then in 1617 he and John Kempe together paid the 10s.0d. rent plus a bushel of rye for it.

In 1623 Malachi Gould took over. We have already seen that the Gould family were something of a fixture on the farms at the hilly, western end of the parish, inhabiting the area for many centuries. Families would move back and forth across parish boundaries from generation to generation, but it is fair to say that the Gould family is one of the oldest established in Withycombe, the unusual name Malachi often traditionally recurring. In 1655 old

Malachi was named as holding one parcel of a tenement, 'to witt' the new house and one chamber in the old house, plus garden, two little orchards, two closes called Sareland of about five acres, a close called Bartletts, another called bromecliffe and a meadow of just under an acre. The other part was held by his son, Malachi junr, and this consisted of the old house (the chamber above the entry excepted – that was his father's), the north end of the barn, the stall and hopyard, and a field named Hill Close of two acres.

Malachi senr was buried in Withycombe in 1673, leaving his widow Joane and son Malachi in charge of the farm. They paid the rent jointly in 1678, with 'Malachias Gould and his mother' being named on the reeve's list. Young Malachi and his wife Jane christened several children in the village during the period after the Civil War but he died in 1687, in the same year as his mother. His widow Jane took over upon payment of the heriot due, which was a pig.

The following year William Hill, yeoman of Withycombe, took on a moiety (half) of the tenement 'in possession of Jane Gould, widow', and by the year after that had become responsible for the whole. He took his turn as reeve in 1703, but shortly afterwards surrendered his lease, assigning it to William Barrow, a merchant of Minehead. Was he a descendant of Richard Barrow, the earlier tenant? William's lease was taken on the lives of his wife Joane and one David Priest. Perhaps though, given the later history of Lower Dumbledeer, this was actually David Price.

A rental of 1709, in which William Barrow was listed as paying the rent due for the property, refers to his 'new tenement' and expresses the supposition that the additional payment of a bushel of rye was now 'extinct'. Barrow died in 1716, leaving his widow as the official tenant. She was listed for Lower Dumbledeer on the tithingman's list of 1739, but a few years before this David Price had taken over from her at Lower Dumbledeer. The Manor Court had already imposed a fine upon him for not coming to be admitted as a tenant of the manor in 1736. The same court also noted the death of Thomas Hill, who had been one of the lives for 'David Price's estate at Withycombe'. No doubt he was a relative of William Hill, the presence of his name on Price's lease perhaps a condition of Hill's earlier surrender to Barrow.

David Price held the property until his death, in or before 1755, when his widow Susannah of Minehead took out a lease on both moieties for the lives of her children William, Susannah and David. The eldest child, William, was probably the Revd William Price who eventually succeeded to the tenancy. His name first appeared in connection with payents of the Church Rate of 7^1/$_2$d. due for Lower Dumbledeer in 1769, although Susannah's name continued to appear for several years after this. She was still being named in a rent book of 1778 for '2 moietys of Dumbledeer late Barrows... viz. a dwelling-house.'

We can be certain that none of the tenants from William Barrow onwards lived at Lower Dumbledeer. Most of them were clearly inhabitants of Minehead. So the question arises: who were the occupants? Given the complexity of the situation at this time regarding the several properties at Dumbledeer, mentioned above, it is impossible to say with certainty. We have noted that John Stennor was linked with Higher and Lower Dumbledeer in the period around 1790. His family lived in the parish then; and when he married Susanna Tuttle in 1763 he was described as a husband-man, implying that he was farming (albeit in a small way) somewhere in the parish.

At this time we see Lower Dumbledeer divided into 'Thorne's' and 'Barrow's'. The exact nature of this split is unknown, with much of the evidence contradictory, but it may be that Thorne's consisted of some of the fields and perhaps farm buildings – the name indicating that these were being used by the occupants of

Some of Sam Griffiths' descendants photographed outside his old house, c.1960.

Higher Dumbledeer or Edward Thorne's; while Barrow's was the house and garden. This may have been a temporary arrangement made to suit John Stennor's situation as occupant of both properties.

Coming into the nineteenth century we are on firmer ground, with James Bryant (of Briddicott in Carhampton) being named as tenant from 1822, when he paid the Church Rent of 8d. In 1830 he paid the new Church Rate, when Lower Dumbledeer was valued at £33.19s.8d., and he was the tenant of John Fownes Luttrell in 1840, when the Tithe Map was compiled. On this, Lower Dumbledeer was shown to comprise house, barn, barton and gardens (Nos 307, 308 and 313), Sarah's Land (No.270), South Meadow (No.287) and Long Orchard (No.293) together, Lower Meadow (No.288), Higher Meadow Moor (Nos 289 and 292), together, Clift (No.290) and Labourland (No.291) together, Alder plots (Nos 294 and 295), Orchard (No.296), Waterleats (No.297), Dock Land (No.298), Lower Plain Close (No.304), Fore Pieces (No.305), Little Meadow (No.306) and Rack Close (No.309) together, Hill Close (No.310), Stennings (No.311), Little Broom Close (No.312), Great Broom Close (No.314), and Higher Plain Close (No.315). The presence of so many meadows (Rack Close and Long Orchard were also meadowland) and the Alder plots are a clear indication that a good water-supply, provided by a stream running from Higher

Dumbledeer down to Combe Farm, was the key to Lower Dumbledeer's importance.

John Vickery/Vicary was living in the house at Lower Dumbledeer at this time. He was certainly there in 1825 and had probably moved in shortly after his marriage to Ann Cavill in Carhampton four years before that. The 1841 census reveals that there was definitely only one dwelling at Lower Dumbledeer then, housing John and his family. John was an agricultural labourer, baptised in 1796, the son of William and Betty Vicary of Withycombe.

John and Ann remained together at Dumbledeer into their old age, but by 1871 Peter Lock, another agricultural labourer, and his wife Jane had replaced them. Jane was left a widow in 1878 but in 1882 Samuel Griffiths wed her daughter Mary Ann, and moved into the property. Samuel and his boys worked as labourers at Combe Farm for many years, and they are remembered in the village for the great misfortune they experienced during the First World War. No less than three of Samuel's boys – Richard, Edward and Ernest – were killed whilst fighting with the Somerset Light Infantry. One of them fell as he stood alongside another brother, Bill, who survived. Their sacrifice is marked by plaques in the church and in the Memorial Hall, which was built in part to honour their names and those of the other Withycombe men who lost their lives in that conflict. It is said that when yet another of Samuel's sons, Frank, was called up, Mr Luttrell successfully intervened to excuse the lad, on the grounds that the family had already done more than enough for their country.

Samuel and Mary continued to inhabit Lower Dumbledeer after the war, but moved down to the village in their old age. A gypsy family, Chris and Maud Carter, lived there for a while afterwards. He rode a bicycle around the area, offering to grind scissors and mend china. Later they also moved into the village, and in 1938 James and Mary Ann Gartside were listed as the occupants of Lower Dumbledeer.

During the Second World War a Mr and Mrs Gibbins moved there, having come down from Croydon to escape the bombing. They left around 1946. One or two other families lived there for a while in the years following the war, including one named Westcott, and the last occupants were members of the Price family. The house was finally abandoned in the late 1950s.

Above: *Carter Walt Griffiths* (holding the horse) *and brother Frank, with Charles Hagley of Combe Farm between them.*

Left: *Great-granddaughter of Sam Griffiths visiting his old home at Lower Dumbledeer.*

Above: *The long-lived Samuel Griffiths.*

Right: *A rare picture of Lower Dumbledeer. Feeding the fowls in 1941 is Mrs Gibbins, newly arrived from Croydon with her husband, the pair having moved to avoid the bombing in the London area.*

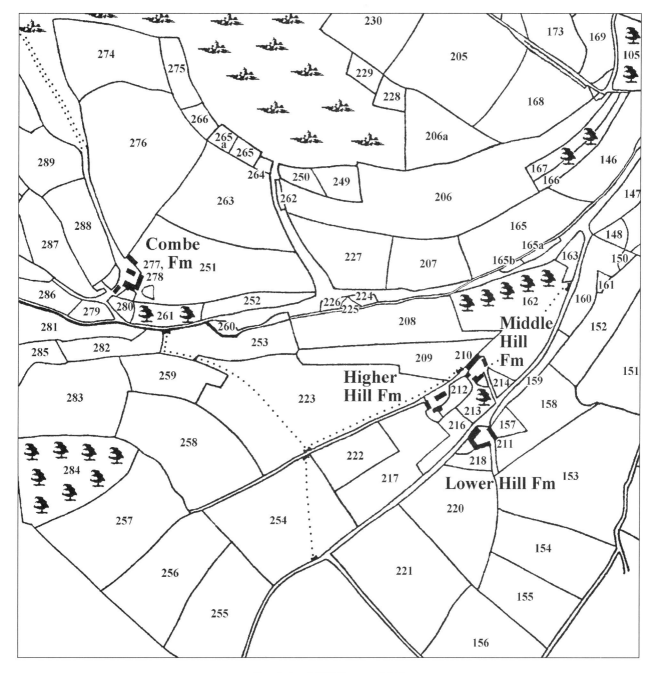

Combe and Hill Farms, 1840.
(BASED ON THE TITHE MAP, WITH THE PERMISSION OF THE SOMERSET ARCHIVE AND RECORD SERVICE.)

The track from Dumbledeer leads on down to Combe Lane where, not unnaturally, we find Combe Farm. However, before further mention is made of that property, we should explore another long-lost tenement called Shearingland or Shearland. This was another of those small farms absorbed by Combe Farm at an early date and nothing is known of its separate history. We can deduce, however, that the house was probably close by Combe Farm and that the land associated with it lay close to the Withycombe Brook as it runs down the combe from Oak. In this area is a field of what was once coppice woodland called Shere or Share Wood, which was part of the combined Combe/Shearingland estate in 1709. Its name clearly suggests a relationship with

the latter tenement. It is thought that its name ultimately derives from 'shear' rather than 'share', for surely this is the logical location for the annual shearing of the flocks belonging to the hill farms in the area. The sheep were dipped – driven through and briefly submerged in deep water, much as they are today – in order to wash the fleece before shearing, and the brook could easily be dammed in this part of the combe for the purpose. It is likely that an area was permanently set up for this operation, with sluices to control the water-level, such as can still be seen just below another combe in Alcombe, Minehead. Within living memory the Withycombe Brook was definitely used in this way, although further downstream at Hill Bridge.

Left to right: *Charlie Hagley with one of his dogs, possibly Andy; the young Max Dunscombe – who was a keen motorcyclist and a welcome visitor to Combe Farm – especially to Charlie Hagley's sheepdogs; and Charlie again.*

Right: *Charlie Hagley tending to the sheep at Combe Farm.*

Below: *Taken at Combe Farm by C. North (of the watercolourist's family?) in June 1919, this snapshot shows Annie Hagley and B.A. Mitchell.*

Inset, below: *Charlie Hagley having fun at Combe Farm, with sister Annie behind and two others.*

This image: *Combe Farm.*

The plaster frieze, restored to something like its original appearance, above the reopened fireplace in Combe Farmhouse. It was probably put in by Gregory Blake as an icon to fecundity, exemplifying his hopes for the success of farm and family, after he moved to Combe from Carhampton at around 1629.

Combe Farm's known history begins after the Civil War, with the 1663 marriage of John Newton to Elizabeth Hoore and the subsequent birth of their sons Andrew and Giles in the 1670s. However, we have a tantalising clue about slightly earlier times in the form of plasterwork above a fireplace inside the farmhouse. It is in the primitive English style that is seen at its best in the work of two Dorset plasterers named Abbot, who are known to have worked in West Somerset for the Luttrells, amongst others. It appears to be slightly cruder work than that done by the Abbots, and does not bear their signatures, but it is almost contemporary with them and important, as very few examples of this genre have survived. The work bears the date 1629 and some initials, which include GB and possibly AB or TB (the initial is strangely drawn), which could be a reference to the names of Combe Farm's occupants at that time. Was it made for Gregory Blake and his wife Tamsen, who from 1629 christened children in Carhampton? A John Blake held land in this part of the parish in the 1580s; and it was probably the same Gregory Blake who lost a previous wife named Alice in 1621. Could the strange initial be a cross between an A and a T, a reference to both of his wives? Two more sets of initials – IB and DB – also appear, and are likely to belong to their eldest surviving children at that time.

There is evidence that tends to support this theory in the lease of Witheys – a property associated with Combe Farm; this linked the Newtons as new tenants to Dorothy Vellacott, formerly Blake, the old tenant. This link may have existed with all parts of the Newtons' property. Do the DB initials belong to Dorothy?

John Newton 'of Sampford Brett' was buried in the village in March 1695 and it is unlikely to have been a coincidence that Andrew and Giles Newton were granted the Combe Farm estate in July of that year. Two grants were made, one for Witheys, the other for 'two tenements called Combe and Shearingland'. Shere Wood was added in 1701, granted to Andrew only. Giles had probably died in the interim period, certainly being noted as deceased by 1709, and only Andrew was presented at the 1699 Manor Court of Withycombe Hadley for diverting the water running to the mill.

In 1707, when a special rate was levied for the purpose of putting Withycombe's roads in order, Andrew Newton's payment was 17s.11d., one of the highest, indicating the size and value of his estate. Only the demesne farms and the vicar paid more. Andrew signed the document as one of the surveyors of the highways for that year.

As mentioned previously, the sale of Combe Farm in 1709 saw Robert Siderfin's purchase of the same. John Codrington's subsequent grant and release to Siderfin names the fields associated with 'Coombe and Shereland Farme' as long meadow, waterleat meadow (three acres), Oak(e) ball (nine acres), Gratton (five acres), Michellsyard(?) (seven acres), Downe Close (three acres) and one grove or coppice called Shere Wood (four acres). Andrew Newton remained in possession. He paid the Church Rate of 1s.9^1/$_2$d. due from Combe Farm in 1718 and was named on the tithing list of 1739 for 'Combe' (he had taken his turn as tithingman in 1730, the same year that he was presented at the Manor Court for the cutting and carrying away of turf from the common for sale elsewhere).

Andrew Newton was buried in 1748, three years after his wife Susanna. Son Robert, born in 1702, took over the farm. He was named as tithingman for 1749 'for Coombe estate which he occupies'. He was master at Combe Farm for most of the remainder of the eighteenth century, being probably the Robert Newton of Rodhuish who was buried at Withycombe in 1795.

The ownership of the property from Siderfin onwards went the same way as Bowden, eventually coming to rest in the hands of Thomas Dyke Acland; and, after Robert Newton, its official tenants also began to mirror those at the property upstream. Thus in 1830 we find Thomas Wrentmore responsible for the new Church Rate at Combe Farm, which was valued at £29.7s.2d.

One of Robert Newton's sons (he had married Joan Towell of Rodhuish in 1756) is likely to have succeeded him at Combe Farm. A. Thomas and later a John Newton attended parish meetings before and after Robert's death. However, by the late 1830s the Newtons' time at Combe had come to an end and we enter the era of the Hagleys, who – like their friends the Pearses at Gupworthy – had moved to Withycombe from Old Cleeve. The family had occupied Bilbrook Farm in that parish and had leased nearby fields in Withycombe during that time, but it was surely the influence of the Gupworthy Pearses that led them to Combe Farm. The man responsible

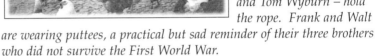

Above: *Combe Farm shearers, 1941. Left to right, inside: Charles Harding, Frank Burt, L. Sutton, Les Martin; outside: Ralph Sutton, Jack Baker (Gupworthy), Arthur Hooper.*

Above left: *Charlie Hagley supervising the farrier at work while three Combe Farm workers – from the left: Frank and Walt Griffiths and Tom Wyburn – hold the rope. Frank and Walt are wearing puttees, a practical but sad reminder of their three brothers who did not survive the First World War.*

Above: *This picture shows Charlie and sister Annie Hagley feeding the fowls.*

Left: *Thomas Hagley's widow posing with daughter Annie. The latter, despite being christened Elizabeth Ann, was always known as Annie.*

The wedding of Blanche Vickery, before the First World War. Her friend Annie Hagley is standing second from the right, while one of West Somerset's early photographers, Fred Vickery of Luxborough, stands behind his cousin the bride.

Above:
Outside Combe Farm, the boy is Stephen Chorley, whose mother lived there during part of the Second World War.

Charlie Hagley with his dog Shep, 'commonly called Daniels' according to some writing on the back, May 1919.

Above: *Annie Hagley and her friend Blanche Mitchell (it is believed) with a 1920s version of chicken in a basket.*

Right: *Charlie and Annie Hagley with their relation Max Dunscombe and his wife Nell, posing beside the footpath leading to Lower Dumbledeer.*

Above: *Charlie Hagley of Combe Farm, probably on the back of Jessy and accompanied by his dog Andy.*

Left: *Charlie Hagley posing proudly with his cattle at Combe Farm.*

Annie and Charlie Hagley listening to a crystal radio set, c.1924. Max Dunscombe, who built it, took the photograph.

Above: *This early 1900s group outside Combe Farm includes Charles, Annie and Thomas Hagley* (adults at the back, left to right), *with their widowed mother Mary. The identity of the two youths is unknown.*

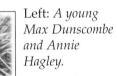

Left: *A young Max Dunscombe and Annie Hagley.*

Below left: *Charlie takes the reins as the Hagleys set off on an outing, perhaps to church.*

Opposite page: *Thomas and Charlie Hagley look on as William Sully shears the sheep at Combe Farm in the early 1900s. Bill's son Charlie Sully is turning the handle to power the clippers, while younger son Arthur stands in the shadows.*

for the move was Charles Hagley, who had married Mary Pearse, the daughter of William of Gupworthy. It was a marriage between cousins because Mary's mother Ann was also one of the Old Cleeve Hagleys. Firm evidence that the Hagleys had moved into the parish can be seen in the baptism of William, son of Charles Hagley, farmer of Combe, in 1835.

Charles was named in the 1840 Tithe Apportionment as the occupier under Thomas Dyke Acland of land that comprised the Combe, Bowden and Witheys estates. The fields associated with Combe (Nos 277 and 278 being the house, barns, barton and gardens) were Bere Close (No.248), Barn Close (No.251), Long-gut Meadow (No.252), Combe Orchard (No.261) and House Orchard (No.280) together, Gratton (No.263), Ball (No.274), Oak(e) Ball (No.276), Orchard (No.279), Waterleats (No.286), Middle Eddish (No.299) and Nicholl Gate (No.316).

Charles and Mary Hagley ran Combe Farm, increasingly helped by their sons William, Thomas and John, until 1867 when Thomas with his wife Mary (Crockford) took over following his father's death. Thomas was made a churchwarden in 1874 and he continued in that post until his death in 1890, when his widow Mary became tenant of Combe in his place. She was helped by sons Charles and Thomas, and daughter Annie, all three of whom were approaching adulthood. Charlie, as the eldest, eventually became the man in charge, but all three siblings worked the property together. They were a close-knit family, apparently choosing to remain unmarried in order to stay together.

During the 1890s, while widow Mary was still alive, the family of a Hagley relative who had emigrated to Grenada in the West Indies came to stay at Combe Farm in order for the children to have an English education. The children were black, like their Grenadan mother, and must have made an unusual sight in the isolated world of Exmoor as they trekked daily over the hills to a private school in Dunster (probably the one in Manor Road, Alcombe, meaning a round trip of some eight miles). There is a charming picture of all of these Hagleys at a family gathering in Alcombe in *The Book of Minehead with Alcombe*.

Thomas died in 1922, leaving Charlie and Annie to carry on alone. However, they had plenty of help, as the bigger farms always did. Most of the agricultural labourers who lived in the now defunct tenements like Bowden and the Dumbledeers would have been employed at either Gupworthy or Combe. During the 1920s Tom Wyburn and those Griffiths boys who had survived the First World War worked for Charlie Hagley. Withycombe man Dick Pearse remembers them well, having been called upon as a lad to help them out one day.

Charlie and Dick's father Henry Pearse were friends, having served together as churchwardens for a time. An occasion arose when illness left Charlie shorthanded, and so Henry helpfully volunteered 'the boy' and Dick readily headed up to Combe Farm for his first 'proper' job. He was already well practised at driving a horse and cart, what with Henry being a carter and a farmer, but was a little disconcerted to discover that Charlie wanted him to drive a cart with a pair of horses, something he had never done before. Happily all went well and the boy went home proudly when the work was done, but not before Walt Griffiths had passed on some sage advice to the lad. 'If you want to be a carter, you have to smoke a pipe,' he announced solemnly. Walt was himself a carter, seldom seen without his own implement. Ever keen to heed the voice of experience, Dick took the carter's advice, although to this day he is not sure of the reasoning behind it; to keep the flies off, perhaps?

Charlie and Annie Hagley retired to a cottage in Carhampton at the start of the Second World War. Margaret Chorley, who lived at Combe Farm during that conflict, recalled that at the bottom of the garden were an ancient mulberry tree (good for jam) and a bergamot pear, welcome sources of treats in a time of rationing and shortages. Both of these still survive. She remembers standing at the kitchen table in the farmhouse and hearing the explosion when a fishing boat came too close to a mine just off Minehead, and also the memorable day when fighter planes pursued a German aircraft over the village and up the combe, bringing it down near Porlock.

Arthur Hooper was the farmer there for much of the latter half of the last century. In recent years the present tenants have done much to restore many of the old house's original features, to its great benefit.

From Combe Farm the lane follows the brook down to Hill Bridge, passing narrow pieces of land, some used as paddocks, which were once gardens cut out of the waste at the side of the highway. These little areas were an invaluable resource to many villagers, to a degree that is perhaps forgotten in our affluent age. Occasionally gypsies would be allowed to set up camp on one or other of these small pieces of land. In the mid-1880s Thomas and Britannia Holland gave their address as Combe Lane when baptising children in the Parish Church. As on one such occasion Thomas gave his profession as 'travelling basket maker' it is likely that they were making use of the withies that grew nearby.

Something of a mystery. The man beside the cart is said to be Frank Burt of Oak, but neither the house nor its occupants have been identified.

We have reached Hill Bridge by travelling down the combe from Bowden, but there is an alternative route via Oak Lane and the Higher Rodhuish Road, which takes in some interesting and very ancient properties on the way. The first of these is Gildencote. Known in more recent times (that is to say, the last 500 years or so) as the Gilcotts, this is an extensive area of land that was part of the ancient manor of Gildencote to the south of the Withycombe Brook.

The name Gildencote, presumably from the Old English gylden cote, meaning golden house, must refer to a building of some significance that once stood in this area. Most likely this was a church or chapel, as such buildings could be elaborately decorated, to the extent of gilding if their patrons were sufficiently wealthy. Edmund Martin had a chapel in Withycombe in 1318, which passed to the Fitzurses. Is it coincidence that the Fitzurses' manor then became responsible for payments relating to worship at Gildencote? Tapers had to be provided to burn before the image of Our Lady, as well as fat to burn on the night of double feasts, and an annual payment of 2s.6d. was made to the Prior of Dunster for bread and wine used at Masses there.

We have noted that the manor-house associated with Gildencote seems to have been situated in Carhampton, possibly in the vicinity of Oak. William Houndell, described as one of the 'heirs of Oak', was the principal holder of land at Gildencote around 1500. During this period the area was divided into closes named Gylcote Downe, Middle, Little and Nether Gylcote, and Gylcote Mead. Houndell paid 6s.8d. annually for the first named of these. At the same time, Robert Hurford held Nether Gylcote and William Gore had the meadow.

In the Elizabethan period Gildencote passed first to George Escott (in 1565), then to John Hill (1590). In 1617 Sir Richard Hill, knight and friend of the Luttrells, took on the land, paying 13s.4d. for what

was referred to as Over Gilcottes. After him came the Blundell family, John senr and John junr in 1641, followed by widow Phillip (occasionally used as a feminine name at that time) Blundell. In 1655 she was paying the 13s.4d. for Over Gilcotts, which was described as four closes of land comprising 29 acres, and she continued to do so until her death in 1686. Immediately Robert Thorne, yeoman, was taken tenant for the same. His lease shows that all of the land in the area of Gildencote was encompassed, including part of Sheare Wood and all of a 'parcel of waste ground in nature of a Common called Rodehuish Hill,' of some 24 acres.

A Withycombe Hadley account made in the 1690s, when Robert Thorne paid his usual 13s.4d. rent, includes a reminder that the lord of the superior manor of Withycombe Wyke was still due his annual payment of 5s.0d. for the Gilcotts. Robert died in 1701 and no more is heard of the 13s.4d. rent, the land returning to demesne for a long period.

Oak Lane terminates at Rodhuish Cross, from where the Higher Rodhuish Road heads back downhill to Withycombe village. Taking this road in the old days, one would not be in Withycombe until passing the Beast Way, a narrow track connecting this road to Sandrocks Lane. The track, now a bridleway, defined the old parish boundary here.

The fields on either side of the Higher Rodhuish Road used to belong to the three Hill farms, but no houses are to be found until almost regaining the village. All three properties lay close together at this point, two up a track to the west of the road and the third, almost opposite, up another on the east side. Of these, only Higher Hill's house (one of the two to the west) still stands. First, however, we will consider the property on the east side of the road, which was Lower Hill Farm.

Known in the 1700s as Pyle's Hill Tenement, Lower Hill Farm was the most logical in its structure, all of its fields surrounding it in a solid block. The farm is shown on the Tithe Map as No.211, with its fields named as Great Furze Hill (No.151), Little Furze Hill (No.152), Great Eddish (No.153), Marl Pit (No.154), Marl Close (No.155), Barn Orchard (No.157), Little Eddish (No.158), Rap Orchard (No.159), Croft (No.160), Park Orchard (No.218) and New Park (No.220). A feature of interest is the field called Croft. Both its name and the fact that two small gardens survived within it suggest that a dwelling once stood on the site. The name 'Eddish' is an old word for pasturage, although the same fields are occasionally called 'Arrish', which means stubble field. 'Marl' is a particularly limy clay, often used as a type of manure.

The farm belonged to the manor of Withycombe Hadley, to which the tenant paid 8s.0d. rent annually, together with 8d. goose money and a bushel of rye. Around 1500 Lower Hill must have been in the hands of either William Howe or Lawrence Westcott: it is likely that one held Lower, the other Higher Hill, and they shared Buckhill Mead (later associated with Higher Hill) equally between them. When 'Jone Hundell', possibly the widow of William Houndell, the 'heir of Oak', made her will in 1533, Lawrence Westcott was the principal beneficiary.

Between the 1570s and 1617 John Hedford held the property, along with Buckhill fields next to Rattle Row. Probably not long afterwards the farm passed to one Thomas Standfast. He signed the Protestation Rolls in 1640/41, and had a daughter named Phillip. In 1654 the farm, with its 30 acres, passed to Phillip's husband Robert Pyle, who granted the property to their son Robert Pyle junr. Thus the name 'Pyle's Hill' became associated with the property.

It is likely that the farm then passed to Francis Pyle for, in a rental of 1678, George Thorne was the tenant of 'Francis Pyle's Tenement', and on the reeve's list (accompanying the rental but clearly copied from a slightly earlier document) George Thorne was named for 'Robert Pyle's Tenement'. One year after George Thorne's death in 1704 his daughter Mary married John Tudball, and the latter's name appeared on subsequent rentals for the farm. In the 1708 rental the reeve added a note indicating that he supposed that the yearly payment of a bushel of rye due from Tudball was now extinct.

John Tudball remained in possession until his death in 1750, paying rent and rates (10¹/₂d.) annually and performing the duties required of the tenant of one of the village's major small farms as and when he was called upon. After his death Thomas Tudball took over briefly and was immediately in trouble with the Manor Court. He was first presented at Easter 1751 for 'diverting of the water of the antient Mill Cause', on the information of Robert Oldman, then again at the Michaelmas court for his dwelling-house being out of repair. Apparently Thomas did little to rectify matters concerning the condition of his farmhouse because when a second John Tudball took charge of the property a few years later he was similarly taken to task for it being in a 'very ruinous' state.

John Tudball renewed his lease of 'late Pyle's Hill Tenement' in 1770, on his own life (he was then 58) and those of his sons Amos (22) and John (18). The document contains a good description of the Lower Hill premises. The house comprised kitchen, passage, hall, cellar, dairy and four chambers, and outside were a barn with ox stall, stable, linhay, court and garden. With some minor name changes the fields (35 acres in all) were the same as those already described.

A few years later the property was in demesne for some much-needed repairs, but the family remained as tenants, John still being there in 1790; and in 1830 son Amos paid the Church Rate for Lower Hill Farm, when it was valued at £27.6s.8d. Amos seems to have been the last of the Tudballs at Lower Hill, for by 1840 the property had been added to the estates of

James Leversha, the newly arrived tenant of Court Place. The following year's census shows two families living there, clearly as cottage tenants rather than as farmers. These were Richard Taylor, an agricultural labourer, with his wife Ann and four children, also William and Maria Gage. Indeed it is likely that the Lower Hill house had being used in this way for many years prior to this, because when William and Maria baptised a child at Withycombe in 1817 they were even then described as being 'of Hill'.

In 1851 Richard and Elizabeth Vickery (also Vicary) were at 1 Lower Hill Farm House, with John and Elizabeth Gage at 2. The Vickerys were still there ten years later, but the Gages had been supplanted by Robert and Ann Winter. Both Vickerys and Winters remained at Lower Hill in 1871 but the building was abandoned soon after.

Across the road is the site of Higher Hill or Robinson's Tenement. It was unusual in the way that its fields were intermingled with those of Middle Hill Tenement, and in the way that the farmhouse and barton abutted those of the latter. Also strange is the fact that the farm could only be reached directly by a track through Middle Hill's farmyard! All of these facts lend weight to the theory that the two farms were originally one.

Higher Hill Farm is shown on the Tithe Map as Nos 212 and 216, with its associated fields comprising Buckhill Meadow (No.147), Part of Baby's Pulpit (No.163), Clift Meadow (No.208), Orchard (No.215), Croft (No.217), Oat Eddish (No.223), Broom Close (No.256), Wood Close (No.257), Middle Close (No.258) and Bridge Meadow (No.282). The field names are mostly self-explanatory, with the exception of the intriguingly named Baby's Pulpit, which lies in the triangle of land formed by the junction of Combe Lane with the Higher Rodhuish Road. It contains a small but charming waterfall. It is tempting to speculate that this was some ancient preaching site, but the origin of the name may be more prosaic. Higher Hill can be seen to be a more valuable property than Lower Hill because of the presence of no less than three meadows. This is reflected in its manor rent of £1.1s.1d., plus 8d. goose money and a bushel of rye, which it paid to Withycombe Hadley.

We have already mentioned that, during the first half of the sixteenth century, Higher Hill was held by either William Howe or Lawrence Westcott. In the early-Elizabethan era it is possible that its tenant was John Howe, whose rent of £1.4s.0d. may have included the Higher Hill payment. However, the first definite tenants that we know about were Christopher Milton 'and his mother', who held it from at least 1604 onwards. Christopher's will of 1628 has been preserved but no clear mention of Higher Hill Tenement is apparent. In 1655 the tenant was Charles Prowse, the property being at this time described as 'one messuage or tenement containing 40 acres and one mead called Buckhill Mead', held on a 99-year lease of lives of David Robinson and George Prowse. Neither Prowse nor Robinson actually lived in Withycombe (Robinson was an Exeter man), so they would have sublet the property to undertenants at this time. We have no way of knowing who these undertenants were, but it is a possibility that the Milton family continued there, as they were then still living somewhere in the village. Charles Prowse, 'gentleman', remained in charge at Higher Hill until at least 1684, when he was named as being due to perform the office of reeve in the following year. However, by 1689 he had been replaced by David Robinson, who continued as tenant until at least 1718, when he paid the Church Rate of 1s.4^{1}/$_{2}$d. for the property. John Withycombe took over the tenancy officially in a 1722 lease, but he may have farmed there for some time previously.

The intermingled fields must have led to many practical problems, not least of which was the question of who owned what hedge, gate, etc. Thus on 3 November 1709 a 'view' was made of the hedges between 'Bastone and Withycombe Hills' (i.e. Middle and Higher Hill Tenements) by John Bastone, Hugh Norman, Robert Davis, Arthur Edwards and Thomas Watts – obviously selected as men who had reason to know the area well. This was done in connection with John Bastone's purchase of Middle Hill in that year. The wording of the document seems to imply that, in 1709, Bastone and Withycombe were in occupation, but this may not have been the case. The document was actually a 1791 copy of the 1709 original, so we cannot be sure whether the heading was copied accurately from the original or composed at the later date. After all, by 1791 both Bastones and Withycombes had been tenants of the two Hill farms for so long that their names had become synonymous with the properties. The details of the 'view' are not of great interest, but the fields belonging to Higher Hill were clearly mostly those listed in 1840: Clift Meadow, Middle Close, Broom Close, Wood Close, Oat Eddish (also called in the same sentence Oat Erish and in another Oat Irish!) and the orchard next to the house. There was a close called Bottom Close which was not listed in 1840 but which adjoined the Middle Hill field called 'Little Marrow', and a close next to the house was apparently called 'ye Ball'.

Perhaps John Withycombe arrived in 1717, because in that year the Manor Court of Withycombe Hadley instructed the homages (jurors) to view the estate of Mr Robinson. They reported: '... halfe a hundred of Reed will putt the thatching of the houses in good repair and... the Walls are in intolerable repair.' The 1722 lease clearly indicates that John Withycombe was already in place at that time, for he was described as a 'yeoman of Withycombe' and the property as 'late in the possession of David Robinson lately deceased, now in the possession of John Withycombe.' It was wrongly described as being within Withycombe Wyke,

probably through confusion with the intermingled Middle Hill Tenement. The rent was still the same, but 2s.6d. was now payable in lieu of the bushel of rye.

The name of John Withycombe continued to appear in the rent lists into the 1740s and he was a juror at the Manor Court of Michaelmas 1752; but he was buried in Carhampton in the following year and Grace Withycombe took over the property. In 1758 she was in trouble at the Manor Court over a familiar problem. Clearly the mill had been in a poor state for some time and the farmers upstream from it had been taking advantage of the situation. Thus she was presented for 'the Head-ware in Grace Withycombe's Court made to turn the Water away from the Grist-Mill... which ought to be broken down.' This is a puzzling accusation as surely her 'Court' was beside the house, well above the path of the brook.

Grace was named as paying the Higher Hill Church Rate in 1769 but by the following April she had joined her husband in the churchyard at Carhampton. She was described as 'of Hill', so it is clear that she was actually occupying the property up until her death. In the 1770s 'Hill or Robinson's Tenement' was in the hands of John Withycombe's executors. It included 41 acres, was valued at £40 and held on the life of William Withycombe, aged 60, son of John. The lease was finally determined in 1785, upon the death of William. The 1790 Church Rate shows that the estate was then in demesne, John Fownes Luttrell paying the usual amount for 'higher hill late Withycombe's'. Then in 1830 John Pearse (farmer of Higher Rodhuish and brother of William Pearse of Gupworthy Farm) was named as tenant when the farm was valued at £31.7s.5d.; and he was still the official occupier in 1840. However, probably since the death of Grace Withycombe the farmhouse had been let as a dwelling-house. The 1778 booklet of particulars noted beside the entry 'viz. a dw. house'; and in 1820 James and Grace Poling 'of Higher Hill' christened a daughter in the Parish Church. James Polling, a farm labourer, and wife Grace were still living there in 1841. This family (their name also written as 'Pullen') subsequently moved to Rodhuish.

William Hurford and his family followed the Pollings at Higher Hill, but in 1871 the house was listed as uninhabited, and probably remained that way until the building eventually fell down not many years afterwards.

Middle Hill Tenement was part of the manor of Withycombe Wyke and so we do not know as much about its early history as we do about the other two Hill farms. It was shown as No.210 on the Tithe Map, and its fields were listed as Eastern Land (No.156), Part of Baby's Pulpit (No.162), Borough (No.164), Barn Close (No.209), Home Orchard (No.213), Orchard (No.214), Beast Way (No.221), Little Marl (No.222), Chilly Close (No.253), Great Marl (No.254), Steepy Close (No.259), Wood Close (No.283) and Parry (or Penny) Meadow (No.285). However, there appears to be a mistake here: there is no field No.164 shown on the original map and Borough (a meadow) is in fact No.162.

The most comprehensive information concerning this property originates from the sale of the manor in 1709. The survey made at this time of course included 'Hill Tenement'. The leaseholders since at least 1697 were William Hill senr (born c.1654) and William Hill junr (1697). Was this why it was called Hill Tenement or was it named for its location? The two Hills paid a rent of 10s.0d. annually for the farm. However, they may not have been the occupants of the property, perhaps preferring Lower Dumbledeer, in which they also took an interest at that time. Arthur Edwards was probably the occupier.

Before 1697 it seems widow Anne Elsworthy held the property (and no doubt her husband preceded her). She was said to be deceased in 1709 but, as often happened, her name continued to represent the property on various, annually-copied lists. Most significantly a scrap of Withycombe Wyke rental of 1710 still has Ann Elsworthy paying 10s.10d. for a property. This surely harks back to her tenure of Hill Tenement, where 10s.0d. was the rent and 10d. the standard goose money payment.

At the sale of the manor Mr John Bastone bought 'Hills Tenement' for £500 plus two broad pieces. (A broad piece was an old coin worth 20s.) A document was accordingly drawn up to grant and release the property to Bastone. It described the farm as containing 40 acres in Withycombe Wyke and as being 'late in the tenancy or occupation of Anne Elsworthy widow deceased, now or late in the possession of Arthur Ewards and William Hill.' The fields were listed, having been accurately measured during the 'view' of Middle and Higher Hill's fields mentioned above. They were more or less identical to those named some 130 years later, although there were clearly more trees in the area surrounding Shiner's Wood (No.284 on the Tithe Map), as indicated by names such as 'Little Wood Close', etc.

So in 1709 the Bastone family became the owners of Middle Hill Tenement, having purchased it outright from John Codrington. In 1718 John Bastone paid the Church Rate of 1s.0d. for the property; and in 1727 Francis Bastone became due to take his turn as tithingman. However, the Bastones never lived at Middle Hill, or even in the village, so a substitute – Hugh Norman – was found to perform the duty. Francis Bastone was still being mentioned in connection with Middle Hill in 1739 but he was dead by 1752, when a document of transferral was drawn up. In it, Elizabeth Bastone, widow of Francis, a merchant, was said to be of Minehead.

The fields were again listed, much as previously, but with a few noteworthy differences. Chilley Mead was designated 'Chalway Mead', which is probably a more accurate version of its name. Burough had been divided into two closes 'called Burrows or Furze

closes' and there were two little orchards, expressly stated to be 'below the Burrows closes', i.e. against Combe Lane. And of the wood it was noted 'part of which has been lately converted to tillage'. Most interesting is the name of the occupant of Middle Hill at that time: John Withycombe, tenant of Higher Hill. Francis Bastone, the presumed son and heir of the previous tenant, continued to be named for Middle Hill throughout the second half of the eighteenth century, during which time one suspects that it remained in the hands of the Higher Hill Withycombes. This would explain why Higher Hill was repeatedly said to be 'part of Withycombe Wyke' at this period. Then in 1829 Francis, Cecilia and Hannah Bastone relinquished the family's hold on the farm, releasing it in fee to John Fownes Luttrell. Farmer Robert Burnell took over, paying the new Church Rate in the following year for Middle Hill Farm, which was valued at £40.3s.3d. He certainly lived at and worked the property, still being in residence at the time of the 1841 census, together with wife Mary and several grandchildren. Son James Burnell succeeded him, and was still there in 1866, according to trade directories, but by 1871 the family of farm labourer Robert Stanbury was in occupation, the building clearly having changed from farmhouse to simple dwelling. This was also the case in 1881, when either Thomas Chapman or widow Mary Gould, or both, were in residence.

We do not know who was there in 1891 but by 1901 the building had been converted into two cottages. Tom and Caroline Webber lived in one three-roomed dwelling, while shepherd John Baker and his family had four rooms. John Baker's wife was the unusually named Aylotte Davey. In the 1920 Register of Electors three people gave their address as 'Hill Cottage': Ernest Fry, Matilda Harvey and Sidney Wyburn. Ernie and Mabel Fry were still there in 1938, with Bill and Elizabeth Dyer next door. Middle Hill still survives as a house with outbuildings.

Mabel Fry, photographed outside Miss Edbrooke's 'Pear Tree Cottage'. Mabel, a daughter of Tom and Mary Wyburn, lived for a long time in one of the cottages at Middle Hill.

A view of Mill Street in the 1920s, with Jack Fifvel on horseback. The scene is little different today, except that the outbuilding up the street on the left – once part of Milton's Tenement – has gone. Both of the cottages on the right (separated by the cobbled way leading to the chapel) were created from buildings that once belonged to a single Withycombe Wyke tenement.

Albert Sully in Mill Street, c.1934.

Seven

Mill Street and Rattle Row

Between Hill Bridge and the old mill is an area where, until the twentieth century brought radical changes to our way of life, the flow of water dominated the environment. The village brook still flows alongside the road, but this natural bottleneck also used to channel two other watercourses. One ran down from Lower Hill Farm – via an outfall known as Tudball's Shute – through Buckhill Meadow to the east (beyond the row of modern bungalows), while above the level of the road to the west was the mill stream, which fed that most important of village buildings.

At the Manor Court of Withycombe Hadley in 1704 Andrew Newton of Combe Farm, not a tenant of that manor, was presented for diverting water running to the mill 'which we [the jurors] have heard & believe to be an ancient, tho' no Mannor Mill, out of its ancient, & usuall course...'. This statement, borne out by other records, accurately describes the situation regarding the mill, which stands fairly and squarely between the hill, village and Sandhill farms. There was no mill record-ed at Withycombe in the Domesday Book and its location, between the demesne farms rather than close by one of them, tends to bear out the opinion that it was not originally a manor mill, although its site was of course principally dependent upon the water-supply. In order to provide sufficient fall for the mill-wheel to function efficiently, the water was turned from the Withycombe Brook in Combe Lane and retained in a series of holding ponds above the mill. This elaborate construction meant that when-ever the mill needed rebuilding it made sense to do so on the same site.

It is likely that the first mill was operating when the manor of Withycombe was split into three parts

Parked across the road next to the mill (don't try this today!) are sisters Olive and Doris Leversha from Court Place.

during the reign of Henry III, around 1238. This is because the rent of the mill has always been shared equally between the three sub-manors, suggesting an arrangement made at the time of the division. Each third paid a high rent of 3s.4d., making a nice round total of 10s.0d. After the amalgamation, Withycombe Hadley paid 6s.8d. This remained remarkably con-stant for hundreds of years.

The earliest mention of the mill which has been found so far is in 1386, when James Durburgh, the owner of the larger manor, mortgaged his holdings, which included two thirds of the mill. In the reign of Henry VII (1485–1509), a series of rentals of Withycombe Hadley have survived which include the mill's tenants. These same tenants would also have been paying 3s.4d. to Withycombe Wyke; and it should be remembered that they were rarely if ever the actual miller, generally being local farmers or landowners who would themselves employ such a man. The 1502 rental names Robert Thorne as the holder of two parts of a corn-mill, paying 6s.8d. annually. He also held a ten-ement and a cottage and paid 8d. 'for water there flowing to the mill'. Then in 1506/7 John Thorne paid 7s.4d., clearly for the mill and its water.

Next, in the early-sixteenth-century survey of Withycombe Hadley, the two parts of the mill and its water-supply were stated to be in demesne. Mention was also made, among payments issuing from the manor, of 40d. due annually to 'the noble Lord Dawbney, knight' for a third of the mill. This was the 3s.4d. due to Withycombe Wyke. At this time, for some reason, the Hadleys seem to have found it convenient to rent that third of the mill themselves.

The mill, and its watercourse, were still in demesne in the 1570s but by the beginning of the seventeenth century it seems to have been rented by the family of Withey (alias Wheddon). At that time William 'Withie' owed 24s.1d. to Withycombe Hadley for certain property held 'in the right of his wife'. The evidence suggests that this payment included the rent of both the mill and what became known as Chester's Cottage, of which more below. We know from a 1655 survey that William Withey definitely held them both prior to 1640.

Several events occurred in the years just before the Civil War that must have led to the next change of tenancy. In 1637 Lucy, the wife of William Withey, was buried at Withycombe, and in the same year Richard Withey took on a moiety of a grist-mill in Watchet (yet still within the manor of Withycombe Hadley). Subsequently, in 1640 George Chester took on a cottage, two parts of a grist-mill and a close called Bere Wood. The association of these three, which probably had existed in earlier times, continued right through to the nineteenth century.

It is clear that no gentleman, such as invariably held the mill, would dream of living in the building; instead a substantial cottage was built nearby, probably either for the tenant of the mill or the miller himself. This was situated across the ford from the mill, near the bottom of Rattle Row, opposite the Rectory gates. Although it may have existed from an earlier period, it was henceforth known as Chester's Cottage and it survived until around 1800. The close known as Bere Wood consisted of just over an acre of woodland on Withycombe Hill, accessible via the path (Culver Lane) running behind the mill. It is likely that this close was reserved for the mill owner's use in order to provide the wood necessary for the maintenance of the mill machinery, including of course the great wheel.

In 1678 George Chester paid 12s.5d. to Withycombe Hadley, almost certainly comprising 6s.8d. for the mill plus 5s.9d. for Chester's Cottage. In September 1692 the Manor Court presented Robert Hosegood (crossed out) and George Chester, for 'suffering his Mill to be ruinous & in decay' and ordered him to make repairs or suffer a fine of £1.6s.8d., a considerable sum. Perhaps the erased name reveals the identity of the actual miller, as Hosegoods lived in the village at that time. George was clearly finding it difficult to maintain the mill and two years later he surrendered his copy in favour of John Maunder junr. John Maunder also acquired the copyhold of Withycombe Wyke's third of the mill around that time. The Maunders may have doubted the wisdom of taking on the mill, however, because it was obviously an old building in dire need of repair. John was presented to the Manor Court of Withycombe Hadley in 1700 'for not repairing & keeping in order the footway near his Mill' and was ordered to do so under penalty of four nobles. (A noble was a gold coin worth 6s.8d., so the fine – as in the earlier case – was severe.)

When John Codrington sold off the manor of Withycombe Wyke in 1709, John Maunder's third part of the mill remained unsold; so in 1714 it was released and conveyed from Codrington to Madam Luttrell, the owner of the manor of Withycombe Hadley.

John Maunder and his mill dominated business at the Easter Manor Court in 1715. First Samuel Kent of Bowden and Andrew Newton of Combe Farm were presented for diverting the water from Red Girts (the source of the Withycombe Brook), to the detriment of John Maunder and the tenant of the mill, who was named. Unfortunately the latter's name is unclear. Then Maunder himself was presented, again for his path being out of repair. The complaints made against him were repeated annually and in 1717 an admonishment 'for not laying planks or boards att the lower Mill Pond' was added. He paid the Church Rate of 3¹/₂d. due for the mill in 1718 but then died before the Easter Manor Court of the following year. The complaints were then directed briefly at his widow Catherine Maunder until she also died prior to 1723, whereupon Mary Escott was presented as the new tenant. At the same time Henry Escott took out a lease on 'all that water grist mill and dwelling-house called Withycombe Mills late in the possession of Catherine Maunders widow lately deceased.'

Henry Escott was another investor in village property, at one time holding four different properties. It was now his turn to take the blame for the mill's dilapidation. In 1726 he was presented for 'not repairing the foot path above the Mill & letting the Water over the same to the annoyance of the tenants of the manor.' He was given a fortnight to make repairs or face a fine of 13s.4d. However, the man who was in practical charge of the mill – presumably undertenant to Henry Escott – was Edward Jennings (alias Appledore), listed in that year as a cottage tenant for 'ye Mill'. The same complaint was directed at him in 1729 and then in subsequent years he was presented in the Manor Court for failing to appear to make his due homage. In 1734 his widow Sarah briefly replaced him, to be followed by yet another heavy investor in Withycombe property, William Oldman. He was presented to the Manor Court in 1740 for 'not keeping and cleaning his watercourse to the mill.' William Oldman formally leased the mill in 1753. It was described as:

... all that dwelling house and water grist mill thereunto belonging known as Withycombe Mills, formerly in possession of Katherine Maunders widow deceased, Since that and late of Henry Escott... now of William Oldman.

It was taken on the lives of his daughters Jane (42) and Mary (30). The rent was reduced to 5s.0d., perhaps a reflection of the poor state of the building.

The miller throughout the 1760s may have been Robert Trall, formerly a miller in Carhampton, because after his marriage to Withycombe's Jane Webber the couple clearly resided in the village.

A survey of 1777 names William Oldman and his daughter Jane for a dwelling-house and water grist-mill. He was buried in 1780 and in the following year Jane Oldman was sent a formal notice to repair 'ye Mills':

... to put all and every the dwelling house and outhouses, Mills, Bridge, Head Weare, Sluices, Mill ponds, mill banks, dams, wheeles, Mill Stones, Cogs, Rounds or Rings, and all other work belonging to the said Mills... in good & sufficient repair with all convenient speed.

However, it was surely expecting too much of a 70-year-old woman to put right something that had been allowed to slide for the best part of a century. Jane died in 1790, and it fell to the prosperous Withycombe family of Marshwood in Carhampton to do the radical work that was necessary. During the next decade, James Withycombe pulled down the old buildings and replaced them with the solid mill house that stands today. The large, overshot water-wheel was possibly an innovation of his.

His widow Mary Withycombe leased the new mill, together with Chester's Cottage and the close by Bere Wood in 1800, upon the lives of her children William, Sarah and Jane, for an annual rent of 12s.9d. Consideration was given for the deceased James having erected a new dwelling-house and set of water grist-mills on the ground where 'a set of decayed Water Grist Mills & house commonly called late Oldman's Mills' formerly stood.

We come at last to the period when the miller, rather than the manorial tenant, begins to be regularly recorded, and the first of these was John Ridler. He first appears in the parish registers as the miller in 1821. Then in 1830 he paid the new Church Rate for Withycombe Mills, which were valued at £7.14s.8d. On the Tithe Award of 1840 he is shown as holding, amongst others, the house, mill and garden (No.101 on the map), Mill Orchard – the site of Chester's Cottage, no longer standing (No.97), and Bere Close (No.233). The following year's census shows Withycombe Mills in the occupation of miller John Ridler, wife Hannah and children. Also there was a male servant, Thomas Davey, learning the miller's craft.

In 1851 John Ridler was the census enumerator for the village. He was still at the mill, describing himself as a miller and grocer, born at Timberscombe. Wife Hannah and children (including son John and daughter Lydia, who later married Robert Case of Withycombe Farm), and servant Benjamin Willis, a waggoner, were also there. Ten years later young John Ridler had taken over from his father as miller, but he obviously had greater aspirations, calling himself also a farmer of 38 acres, employing two men and a boy. By 1866 Thomas Davey had returned, after a

long spell working as the village baker, to take on the job of miller. His wife Jane had died by 1881, when Thomas and son Ephraim were both described as 'miller and baker'. Thomas, assisted by Ephraim, continued at the mill into old age: he was still described as a water miller at the time of *Kelly's Directory* of 1894. The 1897 *Directory*, however, has Ernest Beer in that role. He continued there until the Cockram brothers replaced him in the years leading up to the First World War. George Maidment recalled Beer in his letter to Fred Nicholas:

Ernie Beer the miller & Baker, we were glad to help him hitch the Chain on the Corn Sacks when he was hauling them aloft by the Water Wheel. Othertimes we were not as helpful, when we would empty one or other of the three millponds up Coombe Road, to stop it again so we could easier get the trout in that stretch of river.

Boys, as ever, will be boys!

The end of the conflict also marked the end of traditional milling, more or less, as the sudden surge in industrialisation made it sadly impractical. Gradually the building fell into decay, the working parts especially, but fortunately it has since been restored and, although the wheel has gone, it retains much of its original character and appearance.

The mill building, with its own small causey – an absolute necessity with all that water splashing about when it was working – was at one time divided into two parts, one section briefly seeing service as the village Post Office, and as the mill fell into disuse first the 'other' half and then eventually both came to be used as dwellings. Reg and Florrie Bindon and Frank and Nellie Griffiths lived there in the 1930s.

The importance to the village of the water flowing to the mill went beyond its use as that building's power source. In comparison to the waters that flowed across Rattle Row, there to be subject to pollution from traffic, etc., it was a relatively clean supply. In the eighteenth century, when the well in

This building was the old mill barn, pulled down in comparatively modern times to make way for a new dwelling, Millstream Cottage.

The Queen of the May (c.1934), photographed outside the mill. On the mill causey (left to right)*: Ruth Sully, Barbara Sully, Mildred Hall, Joan Hall, Pat Winter, ?, Mrs Bindon, Mrs Lewis, ?, Lizzie Burnett, Harry Cridge, ?, Thelma Young, June Nicholas; on the road:* John Davey, Cyril Bindon, ?, ?, Winnie Davey, ?, ? Nicholas (?), ?, Eileen Griffiths, Joyce Bindon, Phyllis Gould, Gordon Gould, ?, Valentine Lewis.*

the Vicarage orchard ran dry, as it often did in the summer, a servant was sent to the mill to request permission to take pot water from there. Perhaps this was how Jane Webber came to know Robert Trall, her future husband. No doubt other villagers did the same and so it was probably when James Withycombe built the new mill that an outlet was provided for village use. This pipe can still be seen between the mill and the house next door. During the nineteenth century excess water from this was allowed to simply run across the road and find its own way into the brook but later it was sensibly piped underground.

This system was subsequently extended to feed standpipes in other areas of the village. There was one in Lower Street, now opposite the Memorial Hall, and another in West Street, between the houses now called Simon's Steep and Tudor Cottage. A third was opposite the Causey, set against the churchyard hedge/bank, and a fourth in Rattle Row, near the Rectory gates. The brick housings for all four can still be seen, although two are largely hidden by overgrowth. The 1887 Ordnance Survey map indicates that there were once another four: one outside the smithy and another by Sully's Farmhouse, both in West Street, one opposite Myrtle Cottage and another next to Laurel Cottage in Lower Street.

To feed the village supply a reservoir was installed behind the mill. It was in place by 1887, shown as a water tank on the OS map. The system was replaced by mains water in the 1960s, we believe, as the author can recollect his grandmother complaining then that her cup of tea didn't taste half as good as it used to!

Adjoining the mill is a pair of dwellings, by their appearance originally intended to be one grander residence, known as Mill House (or variations on that name). It may have been built at the same time as the mill by James Withycombe to be just that, as Chester's Cottage had been before it. On the outside it bears a fire mark of the Royal Exchange Assurance company, which dates from the early 1800s at the latest and may be considerably earlier, possibly having been transferred from an earlier building such as the old mill. Internally there are clear signs that the building underwent several phases of major change. Initially the storage of grain, flour, etc. seems to have been catered for, with trapdoors opening into the loft, which still has traces of open lattice-work (for ventilation) at one gable-end. However, the situation quickly changed: the building was extended backwards and divided down the middle to create two habitable dwellings. Probably the mill owner had discovered that he had sufficient room in the mill itself for storage and looked to turn a profit from the house in another way.

The first tenant we know of was James Pearse. After living for most of his life at Bowden he brought his family down to be near his brother William the tailor when, in his fifties, his eyesight began to fail. He was named as tenant on the 1840 Tithe Apportionment and was also there in the following year's census. In the latter the adjacent entry shows two ladies of independent means both named Mary Bryant, probably mother and daughter: it is possible that they lived in the other half of the building. James and Betty Pearse continued there beyond 1861, their neighbours possibly being Thomas and Mary Bryant. This tends to be confirmed by the 1871 census, which indicates not only that Betty Pearse (then on her own, a widow of 84) was living next to the Bryant family, but also that they lived in the same building. Betty died and the Bryants moved on soon after, and there follows a period when it is very difficult to ascertain who was living on the premises. However, it does look as though Robert and Elizabeth Gould and their children were tenants in 1901.

In 1920 Bert Stevens, a carter at Sandhill Farm, lived in the house, as did George Webber (remembered as a tall man with a bit of a stutter). He also worked at Sandhill. In the 1930s and later the tenant was Harriet Davey, who had the nickname 'Harriet Sus', which she acquired because of her habit of

Mill Street, looking towards Top Cross, during the heavy snows of 1978.

repeatedly saying 'he (or she) sus (says)...' while reading aloud to those who had received letters (she worked at the Post Office) and whose eyesight or literacy skills were inadequate to read for themselves.

Another who lived there very briefly was Cyril Bindon, son of Reg who lived in the mill itself, who sadly died from polio just after moving in. Frank Griffiths also lived at Mill House later, probably moving from the mill itself when that building began to fall into disrepair.

When viewed on a map of the village, Mill House can be seen to be unusual, in that it does not conform to the standard house and garden plot that one usually finds: rather it seems squeezed into an area that was not originally intended to hold such a substantial property. If it was built by James Withycombe as a replacement for Chester's Cottage then this partly explains why this occurred, but it is thought that there may be another reason, one connected with the irregular origin of a previous house on the site. Without question, other houses stood there or thereabouts prior to Mill House's construction. In the early-sixteenth century we hear of a customary tenant of the manor by the name of William Stalewyqe (alias Hancok) holding a yard 'next to the lord's mill' with garden adjoining at a rent of 4s.0d. a year. An earlier rental (1502) includes a Richard Skalwike (another calls him Stallwyqe) paying 4s.0d. for a cottage called Stonyhouse. As 4s.0d. is far too much to be paying for a yard and garden it is probably fair to assume that between the times of the two references the cottage had fallen down. We do not know exactly where it stood, but there are few other options available apart from the Mill House site.

Of more interest is a later property, a house and garden referred to in 1655 as being on 'wast land adjoining the Mill Pond in Withycombe... lately bounded and inclosed by Hugh Moore.' The document refers back to a 1639 lease, and describes the house as being in the possession of John Slade, to whom it had been assigned by George Milton, who was himself the assignee of Hugh Moore. Moore's Cottage (in Withycombe Hadley, as distinct from the Lower Street property of the same name belonging to Withycombe Wyke) – like Clement's Cottage in Withycombe Lane – was clearly an example of the somewhat irregular practice of creating a new property on a bit of waste ground, without the prior agreement of the lord of the manor.

John Slade lived in the cottage, which comprised two 'low roomes' with two chambers over, for most of his life, paying the 1s.0d. rent due from it. The amount is indicative of its size and perhaps also of its condition, for as early as 1693 John Moore junr was presented to the Manor Court for his house being 'ruinous and in decay'. One year later John Slade was called upon to depose in open court that he had 'very well known a plot of ground adjacent to the mill pond wall in Withycombe to be held and enjoyed by the tenants of the Lord of the Manor,' etc. for more than 50 years previously. Clearly his age (he was said to be then over 60) and place of residence made him the ideal deponent. He lived on until 1710, but had been replaced as tenant of the cottage by John Moore himself a few years earlier. Moore died in 1743, and was entered in the burial register as John Noles, a variation on the family's common alias, and his 'house by the Mill' was assessed as being out of repair.

If Moore's Cottage was built on the site of the present Mill House, then this would explain the unusual shape of the site: but was it? References are to the Mill Pond, surely implying the main pond, which extended right behind the mill itself, and above we see it referred to as 'by the mill'. It also refers to waste ground, and we know that an earlier cottage had fallen down, leaving a yard and garden nearby; and finally its subsequent fate lends weight to the theory.

William Oldman was the next to take the property, in 1753, when it was described as 'all that toft or plot of ground whereon some time since stood a Cottage late in the possession of John Moore deceased', and significantly it was taken on the same lease as Milton's Tenement, the Top Cross property which abutted the site of the later Mill House. The only reason we can think of as to why this should have happened is that Moore's toft immediately adjoined Milton's, and therefore must have been on the Mill House site. William Oldman's purchase of this lease probably also explains how the site became intimately linked to the mill, as he also held that property at the same time.

We have arrived back at Top Cross in our virtual journey around Withycombe. Now we turn and begin the second loop by travelling up Rattle Row in the direction of Sandhill, examining the properties on the other side of Mill Street as we pass. What one sees nowadays between the top of the Causey and the ford at the foot of Rattle Row is a row of three adjoining cottages, separated from the fourth by an alleyway, so that one might expect their histories to reflect this split. In fact this is not the case. Anvil Cottage, as it is now called, is one property (with its neighbour Shell Cottage, more recently built, a sort of adjunct to it), while the two on either side of the alleyway together make up another. Chapel Cottage, tucked away behind and reached via this alleyway, is also part of Anvil's history. Although we will refer to it here by its current name (no older name has been found for it), it should be remembered that it was once a very different property from that which we see in 2003: it earlier comprised two or even three messuages, one of which was probably to the rear, perhaps behind the site of Shell Cottage, and for a long period part of it was also used as a shop.

It is likely that all of the houses on the east side of Mill Street belonged to the manor of Withycombe Wyke, as they abut the glebe lands, from which they may originally have been cut out. Certainly none of the buildings that directly adjoin the glebe have been found to be connected to the manor of Withycombe Hadley, and most were definitely part of the superior manor. That said, it has not been possible to positively identify Anvil Cottage among the properties sold off when that manor was dismembered in 1709. We do know that it consisted of three dwellings around that time, in the possession of William Games, William Moore and Joan Slocombe; and thus it is possible that it was one of the several properties belonging to the Moore family.

If this was the case, then the property remained unsold at this grand sale. The Moore family opted to purchase their farm at Carhampton Cross – a seriously expensive and ultimately doomed venture,

Left: *Mill Street bedecked with bunting for the silver jubilee of King George V in 1935. The old gentleman in the doorway is believed to be George Davey.*

as we have seen – and could not afford to splash out on their smaller properties. Eventually Withycombe tailor John Uppington, almost certainly a direct descendant of the village's Uppington vicars, purchased the property, with the aid of a loan from a Minehead gentleman named Robert Davis. The pair conveyed it in 1763 to Robert Birth, blacksmith of Timberscombe. The Birth family – often called Birth alias Tagbeard – leased at least one other cottage nearby, which they had also taken over from the Uppingtons.

Incidentally it may or may not be significant to the name Anvil Cottage that a blacksmith took it on at that time. The Birth family included blacksmiths who lived and worked in the village in the eighteenth century, but it is not known whether or not they plied their trade on these premises. We do know, however, that a blacksmith's workshop was constructed close by in the nineteenth century (see below).

The 1763 conveyance gives an unusually detailed description of the property at that time. It was clearly one building divided into three messuages, with a 'little court' in front and another behind. The 'Fore Court' was 28ft in length, 13ft in breadth, while the other 'on the backside' was 29ft by 20$\frac{1}{2}$ft. Given that Anvil Cottage extends right up to the highway, with no space for any sort of yard in front, this only makes sense if what we now see as the front of the building was originally the side. The house faced southwards, and would have been entered via the Fore Court (now the site of Shell Cottage) in Robert Birth's time. Part of the rear court is still visible as the yard that separates Anvil from the top house on the Causey.

Also included in the transaction was a garden, 92ft by 46ft, 'lying over the water East from the said house' adjacent to Robert Price's orchard (see below), and three closes of land, which were the little fields below Withycombe Hill known as Higher, Middle and Lower Perry.

We do not know for certain the names of the occupants of the house following Robert Birth's purchase, but it is likely that members of his family were among them. Beginning in 1769, we find mention of a property in the rate lists called 'The Seven Stars', in the hands of John Birth. This we can assume to have been a tavern or inn, the name signifying the constellation of The Plough, a well-known countryman's pub name. Land tax returns of 1795 indicate that John Birth was owner as well as tenant of the same, so it is likely that The Seven Stars and Anvil Cottage were one and the same.

Following his marriage to Mary Vickery in 1812, William Pearse the tailor made his home at Anvil. He was the brother of James at Bowden. Through William we have a clue that could be taken to support the view that Anvil included The Seven Stars, because the 1841 census calls him a tailor and licensed brewer.

Living nearby were the elderly brothers William and Thomas Birth, but they were probably at Chapel Cottage by then. A more likely fellow occupier of Anvil in 1841 was James Burnell who, with the aid of finance from John Lockyer Haddon, purchased the property at some time prior to 1850. Only a labourer in 1841, James was soon to inherit the tenancy of Middle Hill Farm from Robert Burnell; and in 1850 he agreed to pay 3d. annually to James Giles of Withycombe Farm, then the owner of the next-door property, for work done to the timber there which was to the benefit of Anvil Cottage. Burnell described 'his' house as being occupied by Mary Pearse, widow (William had died in 1842), and Thomas Court, and the following year's census shows these two to be neighbours. Clearly Anvil now consisted of two households rather than three, and part of it was being used as a shop, for widow Mary was described as a pauper/shopkeeper.

In 1858 the ownership of the house returned to the Uppington family when Burnell and Haddon conveyed it to Charles Uppington of Rodhuish. It was described as 'all those two messuages or dwelling-houses adjoining each other then in the respective occupations of John Sully and William Pearse.' William Pearse was a tailor like his father before him, and also – now that he had a shop – a grocer. A few years previously he had married Elizabeth Burnell, a relative of his landlord. John Sully was a shoemaker, newly arrived in the village from Old Cleeve. His move can be linked to his marriage, for he is believed to have wed William Pearse's sister Charlotte.

William continued there as a tailor and grocer until the end of the nineteenth century. We can guess that he was a keen churchman from the names he gave his children – Levi, Mahala, Josiah, Matthew and Mark – to name but a few. Several of his boys worked as millers, daughter Mahala having married William Denbury, the miller at Old Cleeve. William Pearse made the short, final journey across to the churchyard in 1902.

John Sully also plied his shoemaking trade at Anvil for a good many years, later moving to the West Street cottage that had been Hannah Gay's dame-school. It is possible that John's son Charles had replaced him at Anvil in 1881, while another son, William, also enjoyed a period there. William, principally a shoemaker like his father, was a well-known figure in the village at the turn of the century. George Maidment again:

Bill Sully the Snob & Rabbiter Auctioners men, etc., who on Sundays kept order among the boys in the Gallery (now gone) in the Parish Church. I well remember him hammering wet leather on a large smooth Peeble Stone held on his knees.

Most tradesmen in a small village could also turn their hands to farm work, and William Sully was no exception. His speciality was sheep-shearing and photographs show him working at West Street *(see*

Above: *Taken on the lawn at Halswell/Foxwarren, upon the occasion of Barbara Sully's wedding. Albert Sully is on the right of the picture, with best man Dick Pearse on the left.*

Right: *Gertrude Sully with Miss Winfield and girls of Croydon Hall School, preparing to walk the local footpaths. Croydon Hall lies just beyond the parish boundary, close to Rodhuish.*

Below: *Preparing to set off to the school centenary celebrations in 1966 are Lilian Woodcock, Gertrude Sully and Mary Cridge.*

Above: *Mill Street during the 1935 silver jubilee celebrations. Three of Bob Gould's daughters feature: Kit (Griffiths) and Blanche are on the left, while Olive (Spracklan) is holding the flowers. Alfie Gratton is standing in the doorway of Anvil Cottage. It is believed that the man in the centre is Arthur James, and the old man on the right George Davey.*

Right: *The school centenary celebrations in 1966. Left to right: Ann Fielding, Norma Stevens, Mrs Slater, Gertrude Sully, Mary Cridge, Miss Huntley (or Lilian Woodcock?), Mabel Fry, Audrey Case and Ann Palfrey.*

page 42) and Combe Farms with a set of hand-cranked mechanical clippers, which he may well have owned.

It is likely that the Sullys moved out of their part of Anvil as an indirect result of the marriage of William Pearse's daughter Jemima to mason Ephraim Hobbs. The new family needed a home and what was more convenient than the dwelling next door? The move was not immediate, but no doubt made as soon as the other part of the house became available. Ephraim and Jemima were certainly installed by 1891. Old Frederick Willis, who had lived nearby all his married life, had been taken in as a lodger. In 1901 Jemima was a widow, her husband having died in 1894. She still had her lodger. Her ailing father William Pearse had moved out of the village, leaving his part of the property in the hands of Thomas Burge, who had moved down from Rodhuish with three of his sons. The Pearses' connection with Anvil Cottage ended with Jemima's death in 1912: Fred Willis lived on for another two years.

It was probably around the time of the First World War that Anvil became a single dwelling, perhaps coinciding with the arrival of new tenants Jack and Alice Gratton. Jack worked on Withycombe Farm for Edgar Case while his wife continued to run the little shop. At this time customers would tap on the window beside the road for service. This was still operating in 1923, for it was included in the description of the property when it was advertised for sale in that year. After the Grattons left it might not be a coincidence that Albert Sully, the son of William the shoemaker, was the next occupant. Albert was also a cobbler and he had been fitted with a wooden leg following an accident. Apparently, this artificial limb had been known to 'go missing': Harry Cridge recalls being sent to retrieve it from a hedge at Dumbledeer on one occasion! Albert's wife Gertrude was very active in village life throughout the twentieth century, living to a good age, and Anvil Cottage remains in the family to this day.

Adjoining Anvil is Shell Cottage, which stands on what was the Fore Court, once the front entrance of its older neighbour. Maps of 1840 and earlier clearly show that no building stood on the site at that time. The first indications of a building there can be found in a document referring to Charles Uppington's purchase of Anvil Cottage in 1858, which mentions 'that court or yard then called the Forecourt together with the Blacksmith's shop then lately erected thereon and then in the occupation of James Elliott.' The evidence is not altogether clear, but it is likely that this included a residential part fronting the highway. This is reinforced by the census taken three years later, when James and his family can be seen living in the general area. James was a haulier (probably working for Sandhill Farm) rather than a blacksmith himself, who later moved to the house close by Bilbrook that is now called Bournstream.

It has proved difficult to establish who followed the Elliotts at Shell, but leading candidates are Robert and Martha Stanbury. They lived briefly at Middle Hill before moving to Mill Street after 1871, when they were clearly close neighbours of the occupants of Anvil Cottage. Perhaps the connection to the Burnells (who had farmed at Middle Hill and owned Anvil, together with its associated properties, for a time) led them there. Thomas and Anna Date were there in 1901 but may not have stayed for long.

Throughout the first half of the twentieth century, the family of Alfred James – so christened but always known as Arthur – was at the forefront at Shell Cottage. He was named as the tenant at the disposal of Charles Uppington's estate, when his stone-built and slated cottage, containing two sitting-rooms (one with range), pantry, wash-house and two 'fair-sized' bedrooms was sold. Arthur worked as a groom for Mrs Hennessey at nearby Halswell. He was still living with his second wife Emily (Davey) at Shell in 1938, and his children Ronnie and Edna grew up there. One of their toys was a very large rocking horse that is still fondly remembered by at least one of their playmates of that era.

Next we come to the two cottages separated by the short passageway leading to the chapel. Adjoining Shell is Forde Cottage, while the other – next to the ford – is unnamed, although it was long thought of as Lizzie Burnett's house. However, what we see now is the result of the conversion of an old Withycombe Wyke property known in the nineteenth century as Jabez Helliar's (or Hellier's) House.

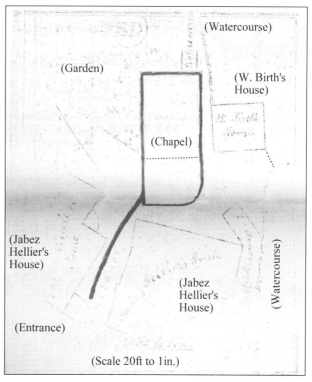

Enhanced copy of a map reproduced for the conveyance of the Ebenezer Chapel in 1974. The original clearly dates from its construction 130 years earlier.

John Slocombe was the tenant at the time of the 1709 sale of that manor and he decided to try to purchase the family home. He paid £50 plus a guinea for it, which also included some land – the three Perry fields that Robert Birth was later to acquire with his purchase of Anvil Cottage. William Giles, tailor of Dunster, also took a share in the property, possibly because of a family connection, as the sale document describes the copyhold cottage as 'formerly in the possession of Elizabeth Giles or Elizabeth Wilcox'. The Wilcox family lived in Withycombe around 1670 and can be assumed to have preceded the Slocombes as tenants.

However, like quite a few of those tenants who aspired to ownership of their own estates, the Slocombes overstretched their resources. To fund the purchase they demised the property to William Blackford for the sum of £60, which they should have paid back in 1724. They failed to do so and consequently forfeited their estate to him. Blacksmith Robert Price stepped in to purchase the house, etc. from Blackford for the sum of £22, promptly assigning it to the churchwardens (at that time John Question and John Withycombe), to be held in trust for his heirs. When Price bought it, there was a single dwelling-house, described as being 30ft by 15ft, with 9ft of ground 'from the north side backward' and 'part of the Court as it was agreed to be divided'. This evidently refers to the 'Fore Court', as the residents of Anvil Cottage thought of it. There was also a garden and orchard across the stream, adjoining the gardens belonging to Anvil's tenants.

Robert Price had arrived in Withycombe around 1711, and might well have been living in the house prior to his purchase of it. However, his son and heir John Price, who later took on the tenancy of Hoare's Tenement in Lower Street, probably let his father's property to undertenants. Ownership passed to John's sons William (who died without issue) and Robert, and then to Robert's only surviving child, Jane. She had married Jabez Helliar at Bedminster in 1805, who thus became the owner after the death of William Price in 1816.

The complexity surrounding the ownership of the title to the property prompted a subsequent legal inquiry, which has added to our knowledge of the house's history. In 1850 a carpenter living in Gloucestershire, one Thomas Burnell Horn, made a declaration concerning the title. He was the son of William Horn and Elizabeth Burnell of Minehead, where he was born in 1803. He stated that he had known Withycombe and the Helliars, and we can speculate that this was because of a connection between his mother and the Withycombe Burnells. Thomas said that he had known the Helliars for 25 years, when they had 'enjoyed the property', which had formerly consisted of one dwelling-house and stabling. He recalled that they had converted the stabling into two other cottages, and 'particularly

remembered' that in 1838 or thereabouts one William Hobbs 'who was the tenant of one of the cottages in my presence gave up the possession thereof to the said Jane Helliar by delivering to her the key thereof.' Thus we have a picture of the two cottages today as originally a house plus a stable, the latter being converted into two dwellings during the 1820s; but which was the original house and which the stable? The 1887 map clearly depicts Burnett's Cottage as two adjoining structures, aligned at right angles to the building's current orientation, so that would seem to point to it being the converted stables. However, by that time it looks as if the house itself might also have been converted to two dwellings, so that evidence is not conclusive, and, if anything, the 1724 description of the old house possibly best fits Burnett's Cottage. Probably conclusive, however, is a photograph of the property taken just after 1900, which seems to show that Burnett's Cottage had no windows upstairs at that time, making it the prime candidate for the stable conversion.

William Hobbs became the tenant of the house in 1817, coincident with Jabez Helliar's acquisition of it, replacing George Milton. As we have seen, he remained there until at least 1838 and was still named as the tenant of No.92, a house and garden belonging to 'Jabez Hylliar', on the Tithe Apportionment of 1840, for which the information was compiled in advance. In 1841 it is likely that the occupants of the now three dwellings were John Hobbs, Hugh Griffiths and Benjamin Lettey. Both John Hobbs and Benjamin Lettey were related to William Hobbs (Lettey by marriage to Jane Hobbs), while Hugh and his wife Fanny had both lived close by prior to their marriage.

Jabez Helliar died in Bristol in 1848 and his heirs sold it to James Giles of Withycombe Farm for the sum of £103. It was then in the occupation of tenant John Griffiths; while the two others 'mostly adjoining' were occupied by Hugh Griffiths and Nancy Blake. John can be seen to have been there in 1851, but his neighbours in the converted stables are not apparent, and in 1861 only George Davey and Frederick Willis can confidently be placed in two of the dwellings belonging to Helliar's House.

The tenants are revealed again in 1871 when, following the death of James Giles, his executor sold the property to the Luttrells. By this time there were four cottages, occupied by Aaron Ellis, William Case, George Davey and William Gould. The census which was taken a month before the sale shows these four in logical sequence. Davey and Gould appear to have been in Forde Cottage, while Ellis and Case occupied Burnett's. William Case was the blacksmith, father of Beadon Case who later worked the West Street smithy (not blind William Case). Was he working from the cottage, perhaps in the blacksmith's workshop built nearby by James Elliott? Lizzie Burnett told a journalist some 75 years later that her cottage had once been a smithy.

By 1881 only William Gould remained, perhaps sharing Forde Cottage with elderly farm worker Job Orchard, a Wootton Courtenay man. William Case had moved to the West Street smithy, leaving the other house to mason Ephraim Hobbs and William Cridland (a young farm-hand, not the older man of the same name who lived in West Street). Ten years on, William Gould was still in place: interestingly his house was stated to have only three rooms, evidence that Forde Cottage had indeed been divided to make the fourth messuage? The same was said of Walter Case's and Robert Gould's houses, entered next on the census, probably the two halves of Burnett's Cottage. If so, then Walter Case had returned to his childhood home after commencing married life at Old Cleeve, for he was the son of blacksmith William.

This seemingly excessive division of property looks to have been reversed by 1901. William Gould was still there, although now with four rooms and no sign of another family crammed in close by. John and Lizzie Burnett moved into the other house around this time.

In 1906 William Gould sent a postcard to Clara Gould, which showed the two dwellings comprising Helliar's House, with occupants and neighbours posed outside. This presumably means that William was still living in his part of the house. Certainly Lavinia Gould, wife of William's son George, is in the picture. Also there is Tom Webber's wife Caroline, who may have been living in part of the same house, but more likely was in Chapel Cottage, Lizzie Burnett, who had clearly moved into the cottage beside the ford, and Lizzie's unmarried brother Mark Osman, later known as 'Marky Blew', who lived with the Burnetts.

Marky Blew, something of a local character, worked at Briddicott Farm in Carhampton and eventually returned to that parish to live with his mother Betsey Blew. She was burned to death in her cottage one day after an accident with a candle, and Marky ended up living in what was little more than a shed behind The Butcher's Arms.

Tom Webber too met with an untimely end following an accident. He worked at Court Place and

Right: *Bert Webber operating a piece of equipment known as a tumble-sweep, which was used to collect hay from the ground.*

Below: *Some of the residents of Mill Street c.1905. This was a postcard sent by William Gould to Miss C. Gould 'c/o Miss North' the following year. It is thought that he lived in the house on the left. Lizzie Burnett* (dark dress, centre) *lived in the cottage on the right, as did her brother Marky Blew, who is standing next to her, holding a hoe. On the other side of Lizzie is Lavinia Gould, then Caroline Webber, who may have been living then at Chapel Cottage, reached via the passageway between the two cottages.*

while returning home from there one dark night in 1917 he was knocked over by a speeding bicycle outside of the Pearses' cottage in Lower Street. He was carried inside but died from his injuries shortly afterwards. The cyclist, a local lad, was not prosecuted, the police regarding the incident as an unfortunate accident. Tom Webber's son Bert was promptly sent for to take over his job and his cottage in Mill Street. Ever mindful of the sad fate of his father, Bert made sure that he always carried a torch with him when out and about at night. The Webbers are remembered by several people as definitely living in Forde Cottage, although documents name them as tenants of nearby Chapel Cottage.

Bert Webber and his family continued to reside at Forde Cottage between the wars and were followed by Sid Pateman, the one-legged tailor, who had married Bert's daughter Ivy. Lizzie Burnett was a fixture next door throughout that period and well beyond. The alleyway between the two parts of Helliar's property leads down to Chapel Cottage, which seems to have been built on part of the garden 'over the water' belonging to Anvil Cottage, following Robert Birth's purchase of that property in 1763. It was in the possession of three men – grandfather, father and son – all named William Birth, from then until the mid-nineteenth century.

One of these Williams was named as owner and occupier in 1840, and the census taken in the following year shows him and his brother Thomas (both men in their sixties) in residence. By 1851 Thomas was there on his own, in 'Halloway Cottage', this name no doubt reflecting the construction of the adjoining chapel in the intervening period.

When the cottage was sold as part of James Burnell's Anvil Cottage property in 1858, its tenant was named as Richard Taylor, the farm worker who had previously lived at Lower Hill. He was gone by 1871, and it is not known who replaced him. Tom Webber's widow, Caroline, was named as the tenant in 1923, when it was sold as part of Charles Uppington's estate. The sale document described it as 'a well-built stone and slated cottage' which contained living-room with range, larder, two bedrooms and a boxroom. Outside were the usual washhouse, with furnace to heat the water, and WC.

In 1938 Tom and Caroline's son Bert Webber was named on the electoral roll for Chapel Cottage. However, as already noted, he is remembered as living in Forde Cottage at that time: the occupants of Chapel

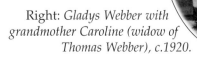

Right: *Gladys Webber with grandmother Caroline (widow of Thomas Webber), c.1920.*

Cottage in 1938 were Chris and Maud Carter. This was the gypsy couple who were previously at Dumbledeer. Later Chapel Cottage was home to a pair of ladies known as Big Florrie and Little Florrie!

Chapel Cottage was named after the Bible Christian Ebenezer Chapel built next to it in 1844. It stands now as part of the cottage but served as a place of worship for Nonconformists for 130 years. Although there is little evidence to suggest that many people in Withycombe were lured away from the orthodox Church by John Wesley's sermons, a Bible Christian society was set up there in 1843. William Birth must have been one of the prime movers in this venture for within a year the chapel was being constructed next to his house. Space was at a premium, so it was built above the Withycombe Brook, on a specially constructed platform that spanned the watercourse! William seems to have relied on the access-way to his cottage for the building site.

In 1845 a group of trustees was nominated to administer the new building and in this list we surely see the nucleus of the village's Bible Christian society. William Birth (the elder) is first on the list, followed by farmer Samuel Hobbs and cordwainer Thomas Poole, all from Withycombe. Next come their younger family members: mason James Hobbs and labourer William Birth (the younger), again of Withycombe, and finally two men from Timberscombe, William Hole (the younger) and John Poole. Shoemaker Tom Poole, originally a Luxborough man, had a paralysis of one arm and it is said that he later lost his wits upon hearing a sermon on 'the man with a withered arm'.

Only three Withycombe families were involved then, and this is possibly reflected in the support that the chapel received because, from the start, the congregation was small, although larger than its official membership. By 1852, when the membership was just one or two, the building debt of £92 had increased through unpaid interest and the situation was becoming desperate. A special Anniversary Tea Meeting was arranged in an attempt to attract support. Fortunately James Giles and his wife had arrived in the village to take over at Withycombe Farm and were showing an interest in this part of the village, as their purchase of Helliar's property a year or two earlier reveals. They were active practical Christians, previously members of Minehead's Baptist Church, and the Tea Meeting won them over to the cause. They continued to support the chapel until James' death in 1866. Despite this though, the crippling building debt meant that there was little money to spare for the chapel's upkeep and consequently it fell into disrepair and was temporarily closed, to be reopened in 1878 by the celebrated Methodist minister, the Revd Vanstone.

The chapel's perennial problem was its lack of a membership large enough to pay for its continued existence. It was not uncommon for the minister to

Top left: *Features of the chapel exterior, as the work of conversion progresses.*

Left: *In 1974 permission was given for the Methodist Chapel to be closed down and converted to residential use. Work is in progress here involving the adjoining residence, the old Chapel Cottage.*

Above: *Chapel interior.*

Right: *A three-shilling bank token from the era of George III lost and found in the Vicarage orchard.*

preach to just a single worshipper on his Sunday visit. The chapel generally had one or two loyal members: Worthington Sutton, the well-known ruddy-faced lime-burner who lived at Bilbrook was one such, until he became a Salvationist, and Betsy Dent, the little old widow from Lower Street, another. For years she cared for the building, cleaning and preparing it for services, and afterwards inviting the minister back to her cottage for tea.

In the twentieth century the Chapel Sunday School enjoyed a period of popularity among the village children, in part because of the annual outings to Weston or Burnham, which it organised. Two ladies came on the bus from Alcombe to take the Sunday school, Mrs Chidgey and Miss Whittington. The former would occasionally perform the service, while the latter played the organ. New trustees were authorised in 1920, nearly all of them Methodists from beyond Withycombe. The only local man was grocer William Eames, from the West Street shop. Things later improved in this respect, so that by 1971 the trustees had come to include Arthur Bryant and Lilian Tibbles of Lower Street, Alan Sanderson (again from the West Street grocer's shop) and Edith Spencer of Pinns Cottage, Rodhuish. However, the poor condition of the chapel by that time meant that a decision had to be taken to sell the building. Consequently, in 1974 it was purchased by the owners of the adjoining Chapel Cottage, with the proviso that the premises were not to be used for anything involving drink, gambling or as a public dance hall! It was subsequently converted to become an extension to William Birth's little cottage.

Crossing the brook by the ford outside Burnett's Cottage we come to Rattle Row, the steep, narrow way going up and over Buckhill, connecting the village to Sandhill. Apart from the Rectory, and a few modern houses constructed towards the foot of the hill, these days it is just a quiet, leafy lane. However, this was not always the case. Dwellings once adjoined the highway on the opposite side to the Rectory all along its length, and the building plots are still readily discernible.

All of the land on the left-hand side of the road (as one goes up the hill) belonged to the glebe, with the Rectory and its gardens situated on the flatter ground near the hill's foot. Above the Rectory was an orchard and, on the steepest section, the four-acre field called Oakey. Throughout the twentieth century the fields were rented to the Pearses of Christopher's Farm, although Dick recalls a time when the Revd Govan used to keep his two ponies, David and Jonathon, in the orchard.

There must have been a Rectory on the site since the church of Withycombe was endowed, when an area of the village was allocated for the use of the institution and its priest, and this area – the glebe – is

Left: *Children gathered in the doorway of the Ebenezer Chapel, c.1936. Left to right, back: Joy Griffiths, Ruth Sully, Barbara Sully, Joan Hall, George Nicholas (in porch), Freda Pearse, June Nicholas (looking sideways), ?; in the middle: Eileen Griffiths, Nancy Windsor, Betty Davey, Donald Young, ?, Thelma Young (in front of Freda Pearse), Wilfred Nicholas, Clarence Winter; in front: Violet Nicholas, Hazel Nicholas, ?, several Windsors, Charlie Cridge, Ainsley Scudamore.*

Right: *This sketch is an enhanced version of the oldest detailed map of Withycombe's streets. The original (scrawled on the back of a lease by or for the Luttrells' solicitor) was drawn to clarify the situation regarding the flow of water from Tudball's Shute to the Rectory ponds, blocked in 1790 by the Luttrells' bailiff. Note that Mill Street has been drawn at a wildly incorrect angle.* (REPRODUCED COURTESY OF THE SOMERSET ARCHIVE AND RECORD SERVICE.)

in many respects similar to that allocated to a manor's demesne farm, with house, outbuildings, some agricultural land, orchards, fish-ponds, a supply of drinking water, etc. These are all contained within a clearly bounded area, with the church itself separated from the rest only by the highway.

The Rectory would have been home for many of Withycombe's incumbents, although it is wrong to assume that all would have lived there. Some were presented to more than one living, and would have employed the services of a curate to fulfil their duty in the least-favoured parish. George Inman was one of these distant clerics, being referred to as 'of Burrington' throughout his 24-year incumbency in the late-eighteenth century. To leave one's property personally unsupervised for such a long period as this was risky: in 1791 he was forced to take legal action against Mr Gale, the Luttrells' bailiff, for diverting the watercourse which ran from Tudball's Shute, through Buckhill Meadow and across Rattle Row into the Rectory grounds (where it was used to fill the fish-ponds) 'and by that Means depriving my Tenant of the Parsonage House of Withycombe the Benefit of having the Water run thro' my Court Yard and garden.' The court's judgement was apparently that a lead pipe should be installed to convey water 'to a depth of seven inches' to supply the ponds.

Most of Withycombe's vicars wished to be on hand, not only to administer to their flock but also to monitor their rightful dues or tithes. The details of these were laid out in the Glebe Terrier of 1639, the year that saw the death of Laurence Uppington after 51 years of service in the village and the succession to the living of his son John. All fields and closes of land in the village were supposed to pay a tenth part of their crop to the vicar, with the exception of certain fields, namely Meatlands, Clehills and Harpmeads, all of which lay close by Bilbrook (in the adjoining parish of Old Cleeve). It is likely that in much earlier times those fields had been granted to the Fernacre estate in that area, which belonged to the brothers of Cleeve Abbey, and consequently the tithes from them went to the Rectory at Old Cleeve.

The vicar was also supposed to receive one in ten lambs, geese, pigs, apples, pears and hops, and a small sum of money for each larger animal, such as cattle. From sheep he was due 'all the tythe of woole in kinde the fleece the loaks the Neckinge Woole', and similarly with copse woodland he required a tenth part of the wood produced, with one exception. This was 'the farme wood wherin the tyth acer is knowen and lyeth out by it close in the side next adioyninge to the Glebe Close.' This is a part of Great

Wood Close, once the area of coppice woodland adjoining Withycombe Wood, which lay beyond the top of Oakey. Two ancient stone gateposts can still be seen in the hedge in this area, marking the parson's route to his private source of coppice wood.

Not many years after the composition of the Glebe Terrier, its beneficiary, vicar John Uppington, was forced to give up the living as a result of Parliament's war with the Royalists, when Puritanism gained a brief ascendancy over the established Church; this despite the fact that John's patron Francis Wyndham, a staunch Royalist, was living just over the hill at Sandhill at the time. John Moore was the layman who replaced him at the Rectory. In the difficult years that followed John Uppington probably relied heavily on his patron for support: it is known that he preached at St Peter's Church at Williton, close by Orchard Wyndham, the Wyndham's family seat, despite grumblings from the Puritans who were supposedly in charge there. He returned to the Rectory following his reinstatement after the restoration of the monarchy in 1660, and continued there until his death ten years later.

The house must have been in a poor state by then, possibly in part as a result of neglect during its period of lay occupation, because the next incumbent, Thomas Collard, had it rebuilt. This was done in 1688, at a cost of £336, according to an inscription above the door in the Rectory porch. Thomas came from a relatively wealthy family, one of his patrons being John Collard of Spaxton, and it is probable that he or his family desired a building that was more in keeping with their status. However, he did not long survive to enjoy the property as he was buried in 1690, just a few months after his wife Elizabeth and their infant daughter Margaret.

His successor, John Jenkins, was very much a resident, christening a large number of his own children in the village between 1692 and 1712, and being described as 'minister', 'clerk' or 'rector' in the registers, despite the fact that officially Andrew Verryard supposedly served until his death in or around 1715!

The next man to feature so conspicuously in the village records that it is highly improbable that he lived anywhere else but the Rectory was Samuel Rogers, who served the community for 42 years, before finally being laid to rest in the village in 1767. In stark contrast he was succeeded by the distant George Inman, and for a quarter of a century at least the building would have been home to a succession of curates, in all probability, or perhaps not even that. For the five years before Revd Arthur Verelst's arrival in 1819, most of the services at Withycombe seem to have been performed by the rector at Old Cleeve, William Newton. The Verelsts lived in the village, although they went away occasionally for short periods, when a curate would move in temporarily. These young curates were a source of great interest to the more genteel young ladies of the neighbourhood,

being regarded as potentially eligible husband material, in true Jane Austen style. Sophia Pearse of Binham Farm, Old Cleeve, a sister of the previously mentioned William Newton, wrote a series of letters (1824–30, now in the County Record Office) to her daughter Anne who was at school in Taunton. In 1830 she informed her daughter that Mr and Mrs Verelst were leaving Withycombe and that the new curate was a Mr Weymouth. Furthermore, she reported that Anne's cousin Mary Pearse (of Gupworthy Farm) had heard him preach, and been 'delighted with the sermon'! Alas, Charles Weymouth stayed only for a short period, the Verelsts returning after all too brief an absence.

Charles Cooke followed the Verelsts at the Rectory in 1844, with just one or two gaps in his tenure. He was notable for making significant changes at the Rectory. The driving force for these lay in the desperate need for a village school, for which he gave over part of his own gardens. The alterations gave the Revd Cooke the opportunity to create a new driveway to the Rectory from the Lower Street direction, which largely replaced the old Rattle Row approach around this time.

The Church's sponsorship of the new school meant that it was now vital for Withycombe's rectors to be on hand to supervise its running, so no more was seen of absentee incumbents while the school remained open. Robert Birtwhistle, George Govan, Albert Ford and Ernest Williams successively followed Charles Cooke, between them spanning the years from 1873 until the end of the Second World War.

Opposite the Rectory gates in Rattle Row is an attractive garden plot, cultivated by two of Mill Street's residents. This was once the site of the important property known as Chester's Cottage, one of the buildings associated with the nearby mill. Its history prior to 1687 has been documented in the account of the mill (because until that time it was always included with that property), but in that year the lease was split and the story of the cottage took a separate path.

After the death of George Chester of Slowley (Luxborough), who had held the mill for many years, Henry Chester was granted the cottage and the part of Bere Wood, at a rent of 5s.9d., on the lives of himself, his wife Elianor and Joane, the wife of Thomas Gimlett of Watchet. Henry died in 1698 and, after payment of a heriot for the property 'that formerly was part of ye Mill', his widow was taken tenant. Elianor then married Giles Daubenny – one of the many members of that family who took that christian name presumably in honour of the Lord Giles Daubenny who had held the manor of Withycombe Wyke in the early 1500s. Giles was an interesting character, almost certainly a descendant of the noble family (his will bore their coat of arms). He also subsequently lived at Slowley. Elianor died in 1730, Giles in 1731/32, and both were buried inside

Left: *The Rectory, 1906. The Revd Hickman, rector from 1968, is thought to have been the last to use the Rectory as such: it is now in private hands.*

Below: *Withycombe ladies in the Rectory gardens, 1930s. Left to right, back row: ?, Kit Griffiths, ?, Mabel Burnett (?), Violet Cook, Dorothy Copp, Clara (Gould) Nicholas, Mary Cridge, ?; middle: Florrie Cridland, Mrs Hall, ?, Kitty Liversedge, ?, Vera Gould, Ada Irish, Eliza Gould, Annie Thomas, Lizzie Burnett, Lydia Gould; front, seated: Maud Pearse, ?, Rose Gould, Rhoda Wyburn, Bessie Case, Elsie Gould, Mrs Bright (?), Maria Davey, Lavinia Gould, Mrs Couzens, Alice Webber; on ground: ?, ?, Caroline Chilcott, Annie Gould.*

Above: *Village girls in the Rectory garden, c.1930. Left to right, back row: Joan Griffiths, Linda Cridge, Winnie Nicholas, Gladys Fry, Winnie Davey, Dorothy Cridland; middle: Joan Hall, Bet Griffiths, Barbara Sully, Phyllis Gould, Freda Pearse; front: Mildred Hall, Ruth Sully, Beatrice Gould.*

Right: *When Albert Ford was at the Rectory in the early 1930s, many entertainers (friends of his wife) used to visit. This lady and her troupe of girls were among such visitors. The lads are Withycombe's choirboys of that time and they are (left to right): Dennis Young, Fred Nicholas, Reg Young, Arthur Irish, Dick Pearse, George Hall, Harold Sully and Charlie Cridge.*

Withycombe Church. Two years later William Brewer leased the property. His period of occupation was an eventful one, and it is clear that he was something of an 'awkward customer', and possibly not one with whom to argue. To begin with, he was reprimanded by the Manor Court for not coming to be taken tenant. This was not unusual, especially when a tenant lived out of the parish. However, this was not the case with Brewer: he simply refused to be taken tenant, and for this was eventually fined a noble.

Nevertheless, he began to make the office of tithingman his own, one suspects because it was considered politic to have such a potential troublemaker on the side of the law. To perform the office, which in many respects was not dissimilar to the later village 'bobby', the candidate had to be one of the tougher characters in the parish – so Brewer's appointment must have seemed a good idea. However, as a tithingman, he was apparently somewhat less than effective. In 1741 he was presented to the court for not repairing the village stocks (part of his tithingman's duties) and for letting his house fall into disrepair. Then in the following year he was fined 1s.0d. for appearing at the court in a drunken state and consequently being unable to discharge his duty (which was to act as a sort of sergeant-at-arms during the proceedings). Therein probably lay the root cause of William Brewer's problems. The court was typically held at ten or eleven o'clock in the morning, so a man who was incapable through drink at that time of day had to have been a very serious drinker indeed.

He died in 1753, causing his widow Joan (previously Oatway) to take a new lease on the property. It was noted that the cottage was held in reversion of Joane Wheddon, widow, who was either the Joane Gimlett mentioned earlier, or possibly a descendant of the Wheddon family who held the entire mill package prior to George Chester, or even both of these; and when the death of a Margaret Wheddon was recorded four years later, Joan Brewer's new husband Henry Mitchell was asked to pay a heriot with respect to Chester's Cottage.

Joan survived until 1805, with the cottage remaining in her name and that of her son John Brewer (who died in 1785) until at least 1777. A document of 1778 calls it 'Chester's Cottage... Brewer's House'. However, even before this time it came to be linked with Thomas Gough, who paid the 2d. Church Rate due on it in 1769. Thomas was a respected member of the village community, becoming a churchwarden in 1781 and remaining as such until his death nine years later.

John Uppington was named as being responsible for the land tax due on 'late Goffs' in 1795, possibly in his capacity as Gough's successor as churchwarden, and it is likely that the cottage was abandoned around this time. It received a final mention in 1800, when Mrs Withycombe (whose husband had just built the new mill) took out a lease which reunited

the three parts of the old property. It referred to 'late Chesters Cottage and orchard', of three-quarters of an acre, previously in the possession of Thomas Goff, deceased, now Christopher Harding. The cottage certainly disappeared shortly afterwards, the site being described in 1840 as simply the mill orchard, in the occupation of miller John Ridler.

Continuing up the narrow lane, we come rapidly to its steepest part, beside which – quite improbably, it now seems – once stood as many as four dwellings! The evidence suggests that they were all once part of a single original property, further structures being built upon its garden and orchard as the years rolled by. The individual dwellings were referred to by many different names over the centuries, but the group as a whole was known as William Watts' cottages. The property is first heard of during the Tudor period when, in 1587, 'all that one cottage and garden and one Orchard hereunto belonging contayning by estimation halfe an aker of ground… lyinge and beinge by Buckwell' was granted by Richard and Margaret Hill to John Way. The name Buckwell is not remembered today, but logic suggests that it was to be found upon Buckhill and later evidence supports this. The site of this house – which represents the earliest stage of the property's development – was probably close to the piece of ground whereon a little stable, etc. now stands. Here an old hearthstone was discovered some years ago, and the 1840 Tithe Map shows a substantial house on the site at that time.

A further grant on the property was made by the Hills in 1596, when it was assigned to John Dyer the younger of Nettlecombe, his tenure to begin after the termination of Way's lease. However, not long after this William Watts came on the scene. In 1602 John Way assigned his interest in the property to him, and in 1606 John Dyer did likewise. Thus in Withycombe Hadley rentals from 1604 onwards we see William Watts listed as paying 6d. at Michaelmas for his cottage.

William took out a new lease on his 'tenement near Buckwell' in 1628, upon the lives of his children, George and Elizabeth Watts. It seems that his family actually lived there around this time, as George, Gregory and William Watts all put their names to the Protestation Rolls of 1641, William and Gregory both christened children in the village, and Gregory was buried there in the 1660s. Furthermore we have confirmation of the situation in the Withycombe Hadley survey of 1655, wherein the development of the property is apparent. In this document George Watts and his wife Elizabeth are listed as being responsible for a cottage, garden and orchard of half an acre, as well as other dwellings in the tenure of Peter Hallicar, Peter Sully and William Elsworthy. To make things even clearer, the writer goes on to explain that there were four dwelling-houses: 'one George Watts hath, one Peter Sulley Als Farmer hath, one Elsworthy hath, and one Allis Hellicar widow hath.' This gives us an unusually clear picture of the Rattle Row residents in 1655, rather than merely the official tenants. Also it is apparent that the original cottage had by then become four dwellings. The additions were probably fairly basic structures: all three of George Watts' undertenants were certified as exempt from paying Hearth Tax in the 1670s, so they must have been among the poorer villagers at that time.

By 1684 George Watts had moved to Devon, assigning his interest in the cottages to George Norris; but little changed until 1694 when, after the death of Watts, new leases were taken on each of them. Immediately John Uppington and George Pearse were taken tenants of the manor of Withycombe Hadley for part of George Watts' estate. It is noticeable that the Uppingtons took a keen interest in the little cottages, which is understandable when one considers that most of them grew up in the Rectory just across the road. John Uppington, tailor, almost certainly a son of the vicar of the same name and born around 1642, took the lease of one of them, described as a 'little house with little garden adjoining, over against the Parsonage.' Mary Hellicar 'lately dwelt' there. Clearly this was Peter and Alice Hellicar's cottage mentioned above. The rent was 1s.0d. It is likely that Mary continued to live there as John's undertenant until her death in 1704, whereupon blacksmith John Birth took out a new lease on it, for the lives of his children John and Joan. John the blacksmith died in 1723, leaving his wife in possession of the cottage. She was accordingly taken tenant by the Manor Court, being called Joan or Joanna Tagbeard, the common alias of the Birth family. Daughter Joan married John Webber in 1730 and so when the mother died in 1741 it was he who was taken as the new tenant. Then when Joan Webber died in 1759 a new lease was drawn up in favour of the Webbers' daughter Jane.

From the age of nine Jane lived and worked as a servant in the Rectory, initially for Samuel Rogers, then for whomever George Inman had installed as his tenant. She married the miller Robert Trall in 1761. By 1772 though, both husband and father were deceased, leaving Jane in possession of the little cottage, which she continued to occupy until her own death in 1792. Her cottage was probably the lowest of the group, adjoining the plot containing Chester's Cottage and just yards from the Rectory gates, which seems fitting when one considers her early life.

The final chapter of its history is not at all clear, but after the death of Jane the tenancy was apparently taken up by one of the Gay families. William Gay was listed as the occupier of No.98 on the Tithe Map in 1840, and the next year's census reveals Sarah Gay, in her seventies, living with the family of John Gage. It is likely that Sarah was the widow of James Gay and that William was her son: the Gages, despite the similarity of surname, were probably not related, as they were not born locally.

Although on its last legs by this time the house may have finally been home to another Ephraim Hobbs and his wife Mary. This Ephraim died in 1853 at the age of 30, but his widow was still there in 1871. She was the daughter of Richard and Mary Griffiths whose home was another of the Rattle Row cottages. George Pearse, husbandman, had been granted a lease for another of the cottages, again described as a 'little house and little garden lying over agst ye Parsonage House' in 1687, to commence after the death of Watts. The occupier then was said to be Thomas Uppington, husbandman, and the rent was 6d. As George had married Ann Elsworthy it may be that this property was previously William Elsworthy's (he had died in 1676), but this is by no means certain. The lease notes that the cottage had 'lately' been made one dwelling-house, possibly implying that it may have been a pair of dwellings, now knocked into one. This Pearse family came from Carhampton, having held property there at 'Gill Chapple' and near the seashore at Blue Anchor.

After George's death in 1715 his son Thomas took charge, remaining there for the next 40 years, only troubling the Manor Court in 1740 when he was admonished for attempting to make a little orchard in the waste by Buckhill. Richard Williams, husbandman of Carhampton, took over from Thomas in 1753, three years before the latter's death. A note on the back of the lease identified it as 'Uppington's over at the parsonage'. Richard later married Joan Hoare and had several children, but when he died in 1774 his brother-in-law John Hoare stepped in to help out, naming nephew John and niece Grace Williams as lives on his new lease. A Withycombe Hadley manorial survey made three years later named John Hoare for the late Richard Williams' cottage and garden 'opposite the Vicarage', with a note added later that John died in 1792.

Grace Williams married William Griffiths in 1790, and so in due course the cottage became their family's home. William was listed as occupier of this house and garden, valued at 15s.0d., in the rate list of 1830. Both husband and wife died in the 1830s, but not before William was again listed as occupier of No.100 on the Tithe Map, a house and garden near the top of Rattle Row.

Elderly couple William and Elizabeth Case, together with their blind son, also called William, were the next occupiers. The elder William and his Irish wife died in the 1850s, but blind William continued to live in the village for the rest of his life. Despite his blindness he managed to cope well in the community, working sometimes as a farm labourer, at other times weaving baskets from the withies that gave the village its name. He married Mary Cridland from Old Cleeve. This cottage fell out of use at some time in the second half of the nineteenth century.

Left: *Mary Ann (Chidgey), eldest child of blind William Case and his wife Mary who lived in a cottage at the top of Rattle Row until the old place became uninhabitable c.1850.*

Left: *This is thought to be Mary Ann Chidgey as a young woman.*

The third of Watts' cottages (the one used by George Watts himself, perhaps?) was also secured via a new lease in 1687, scheduled to commence after the death of Watts. Husbandman Thomas Bowing, also called a-Boyne or Boyne, took the cottage and two gardens for his own life and that of Elizabeth Williams of Old Cleeve, at the rent of 1s.0d. It is likely that Thomas Bowing subsequently married Elizabeth Williams, because after the death of Watts, Thomas and his wife Elizabeth were presented to the Manor Court as leasehold tenants. She died in 1706, Thomas in 1729, to be replaced as tenant by one John Jones. There was at least one resident of Withycombe at the time with this name, but this was probably another man, sometimes referred to as John Jones 'of Milverton'. He failed to attend the Manor Court to be officially accepted as tenant during the next five years, which also suggests that he was not a local man.

The cottage was gone by 1764, when it was included in the lease of the fourth of Watts' cottages, and listed as:

... all that plott of garden ground whereon formerly stood a cottage called Bowings Cottage, likewise in Rattle Row lying on the right hand side of the highway leading to Sandhill Farm and late in the possession of John Jones his assigns, undertenants, etc.

The fourth cottage was probably the one inhabited in 1655 by Peter Sully. He died in 1688, and it is likely that Hester Sully, widow, who was buried in Withycombe in 1696, had been his wife. By custom she would have been allowed to continue there in her widowhood. In 1698 John Uppington the younger, tailor, was granted the cottage previously in the occupation of Hester Sully, for the lives of himself, wife Joan and brother William. This John Uppington, born in 1675, was the son of Thomas, who had previously held one of the other three, and, as was so often the case, his acquisition of the property coincided with his marriage, to Joan Williams.

John Uppington remained as the tenant until his death in 1743, followed by his widow for another six years, and then their son Lawrence, until the year

1764, which saw a radical change in tenancy, when carpenter Jonathon Griffiths moved in with his young family. The lease was for 'all that dwelling-house or cottage and garden in Rattle Row, late in the possession of Lawrence Uppington, deceased' and also included what was left of Bowing's property, as mentioned above.

Jonathon set about converting the property into two dwellings, which he had achieved by 1778, when it was stated to also comprise two gardens, an orchard behind (of half an acre) and a field above the orchard. He may well have erected a second house on the ready-made site of Bowing's toft, perhaps, rather than dividing the existing one.

Jonathon was a son of Richard and Hannah Griffiths, who came to Withycombe from Carhampton in the first quarter of the eighteenth century. Richard was Parish Clerk in the 1750s, and was the ancestor of just about all the Griffiths who have lived in the village ever since. They were a prolific family, with many households producing predominantly sons, and the need to find buildings to house them was always in the mind of the family patriarchs. Fortunately many of the Griffiths men were carpenters, ably equipped to go about the business of improving existing houses or building new ones. Jonathon began the trend in Rattle Row, with the work on his own property. After Jonathon's death in 1797, his son Richard replaced him. He was also a carpenter, as was his son Jonathon, who replaced him in 1824. This second Jonathon was the man named as tenant of the 'house etc.' in Rattle Row, valued at £1, in the rate list of 1830. It should be remembered, however, that the 'house etc.' was two dwellings, and this was made apparent in the Tithe Apportionment, where No.99, a house and garden noted as two dwellings, was said to be occupied jointly by Jonathon and Richard Griffiths. Richard was Jonathon's younger brother, shown in the 1841 census as living next door to his sibling, with their elderly mother Betty (who lived to be 90) in his household.

Richard and his wife Mary were still there in 1851, but son Thomas and his wife Eliza (Webber) had set up home in the other house. The children of the latter included many long-lived Griffiths who are still remembered by some of Withycombe's older residents today, such as Samuel, Uriah and Harry. All of them were born in the forgotten cottage at Buckwell. The family remained there for much of the next 50 years.

In 1861 Grace Griffiths, widow of Jonathon, lived in the other house with her son – yet another Jonathon; Grace died in 1867, but the son and his family were still there in 1871. It was unoccupied in 1881 and no more is heard of it. Thomas and Eliza continued in the other dwelling beyond 1891, both of them dying a year or two later. With their passing went the last of William Watts' cottages.

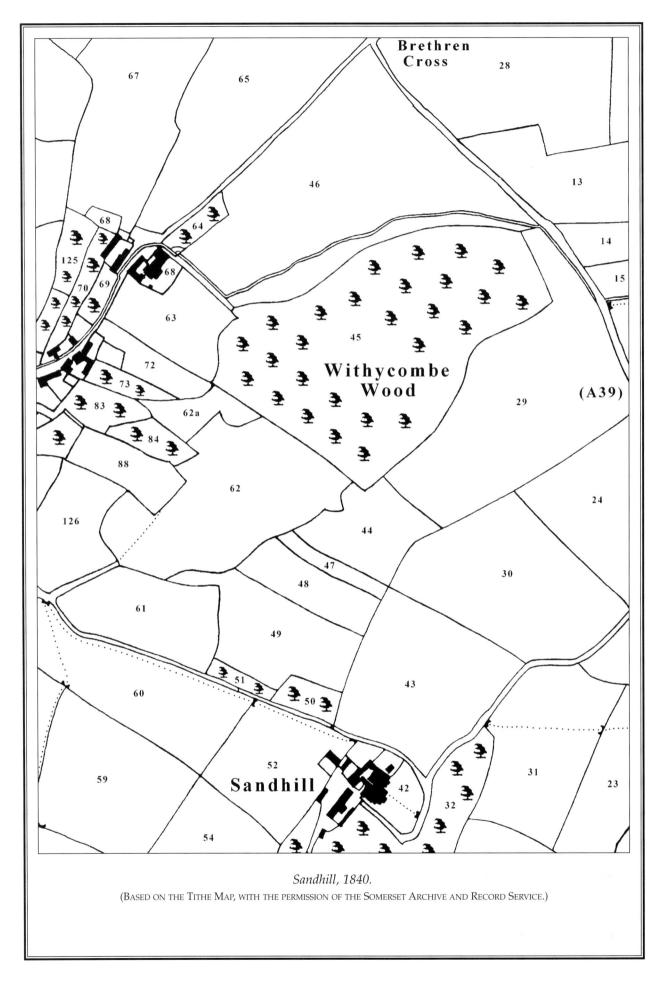

Sandhill, 1840.
(BASED ON THE TITHE MAP, WITH THE PERMISSION OF THE SOMERSET ARCHIVE AND RECORD SERVICE.)

Eight

Sandhill

Rattle Row terminates at a crossing of ways near the top of the ridge that effectively divides the village from the manor of Sandhill. Here one road turns southwards, connecting to Lower Rodhuish, an old rutted track runs north to Withycombe Wood, while Sandhill Lane falls away eastwards to the house built for Joan Carne, the alleged witch of Withycombe. Before heading off down the hill towards it though, the track to the wood merits some consideration.

At the end of this short lane is Great Wood Close (now known simply as Wood Close), a pasture field mirroring its neighbour, Withycombe Wood, in shape and size. A glance at a map makes it quite apparent that it was indeed originally part of a larger area of woodland, intentionally divided into two halves, the surviving timber wood to the north being reserved for the lord of the fee as a vital national resource (for ship-building, etc.), while the southern section consisted of coppice woodland. Quite a few of its trees survived into the twentieth century, until in the 1920s the Chapman family of West Street was given the job of clearing the last of them. Great Wood Close was also one of the areas used by the village boys as a football pitch in the early 1900s. However, its major disadvantage was that any ball propelled too robustly out of play was liable to disappear rapidly downhill towards either the village or Sandhill, necessitating an arduous recovery operation!

Looking to the east one has a panoramic view of the fields around Sandhill. However, the fields that belonged to that manor did not stretch quite as far as the crest of the ridge. Although today it is no longer visually apparent, an open field, divided into individual strips, used to run along the top part of the east-facing slope below Great Wood Close. This system of communal cultivation had been abandoned long before the end of the Middle Ages, but the group of fertile little fields (which were only gradually melded together to form larger closes of land) remained, belonging to the manor of Withycombe rather than Sandhill, but on the 'wrong' side of the ridge. It is probably because of this that a farmstead was built nearby, named Little Sandhill Tenement. The house was gone by the time the earliest reliable maps were drawn up, but it must have been in the general area of the field known in 1840 as Neddy's Close, No.49 on the Tithe Map.

Little Sandhill's tenants paid 12s.0d. rent plus 8d. goose money annually to the manor of Withycombe Hadley. Confusingly, it was sometimes referred to simply as 'Sandhill', but it should not be confused with the large farm and house of that name. Sandhill proper was exempt from many types of payment to either of the Withycombe manors, its owners being regarded as 'free suitors' of the Withycombe Hadley court.

Thomas Willway was Little Sandhill's first known tenant during the 1570s, followed in 1604 by widow Joan. Thomas Flower was paying its rent by 1617. The 1655 survey of Withycombe Hadley names John Hiles the elder (aged 68) as the holder of (Little) Sandhill since 1621. It was described as being late in the tenure of Thomas Flower, and consisted of 12 acres of land, which included some woodland. An added note states '(247 trees in Hilles his wood)'. This wood was surely part of Great Wood Close, indicating that this too was then part of Little Sandhill's ground. John Hiles granted the property to his brother Hugh Hiles for his life.

John Hiles and brother Hugh were dead by 1670, and the next we learn is that in a rental of 1678 'Sandhill Tenement' was in the hands of George Thorne. George held other property in the village, including Pyle's Hill Tenement, so it is not certain that he occupied the farm himself. However, it is known that his widow occupied it later, so it is possible that he did. There are gaps in our knowledge of George's story and it could be that there was more than one individual with that name, but it was probably one man who married three times. His first wife Agnes died in 1689, his second, Frances, in 1703, and he himself in 1704, leaving a third wife, Eleanor, as his widow. From then on Eleanor took over the responsibility for Little Sandhill. This was formalised in a lease of 1713, wherein Eleanor 'widow and relict of George Thorne' officially took on 'all that tenement... called Little Sandhill consisting of a dwelling-house, outhouses, orchard and garden and 9 acres in Withycombe Week... wherein she now lives.' The mention of Withycombe Week (Wyke), unless it refers specifically to some of the land associated with the property, is likely to be a mistake: Little Sandhill belonged to Withycombe Hadley. Quite soon after the lease was taken out, Eleanor married one William Edwards, who became responsible for the property in right of his wife. He paid the 3^1/$_2$d. Church Rate for Little Sandhill in 1718 and was still there in 1732.

In 1736 William Clarke, yeoman of Over Stowey, took on the lease of the property for the lives of his wife Susanna and son John Clarke, in reversion of Eleanor Edwards. Both Eleanor and her husband were getting on in years and were probably finding it hard to make ends meet. She was buried a couple of months later and he followed within two years. The 1736 lease described the property as 'Little Sandhill or Thorne's Tenement... consisting of dwelling-house, outhouses, a court, garden and two orchards (1 acre)' together with ten acres of land. The Clarke family put in an under-tenant after the death of both of the Edwards: this was Edward Thorne, who was perhaps a relative of the earlier George Thorne. Together with his wife Mary, he ran the farm until its break-up in the 1770s.

No definitive list of Little Sandhill's fields has been found, but all of the evidence indicates that they lay in the general area of Neddy's Close. The two orchards mentioned in the 1736 lease were surely Lower and Higher Neddy's Orchards (Nos 50 and 51 on the 1840 map). Did the name Neddy refer to Edward Thorne? There is evidence to suggest that Little Sandhill Field was part of No.48, Little Wood Close, and further along the ridge is Edwards Close, perhaps named after William Edwards.

There is some further evidence relating to Little Sandhill's location in two complaints made by George Thorne's widow, Eleanor, to the Manor Court in 1708 and 1710. In the first she asserted her right to a 'halfe-path' which led northwards across the little fields to the eastern edge of Withycombe Wood. She named the fields beyond Neddy's Close and Little Sandhill Field, together with their owners. The field known as Edwards Close in 1840 was referred to as 'Joanna Thorne's Wood Close' – part of William Thorne's Lower Street holding – which perhaps lends weight to the theory that it was acquired by Little Sandhill after Eleanor's later second marriage.

In her second complaint she claimed the right to use a path 'leading from her house athwart [across] the Highway into a close called Chilkey... '. This field lay directly across Sandhill Lane from Neddy's Orchards, placing Little Sandhill firmly in this area.

As already stated, Little Sandhill met its end in the 1770s. A survey of 1777 still lists it under the tenancy of Edward Thorne, held for the life of John Clarke of Over Stowey, consisting of nine acres and valued at £10.10s.0d. The rent was recorded as 12s.8d. (inclusive of goose money). John Clarke died in 1779, terminating the lease, and in 1780 the tenement was described as 'in demesne' and as 'an old ruinous dwelling-house'. Edward Thorne was old and ailing, and so probably had no desire or ability to continue there. He died the following year. Subsequently Little Sandhill's land was absorbed into the estate of Sandhill Farm, then in the hands of Thomas Escott.

We pass on down Sandhill Lane to the property, now a racing stables, that has existed for something like 1,000 years, Sandhill Farm. Originally the demesne farm of the manor of Sandhill, which was created during the Norman period in part out of the manor of Withycombe. We are fortunate in being able to name quite a few of its early occupants. We can do this because the family who held the manor in fee of the lords of Dunster Castle (via the intermediate manor of Withycombe – at first, at any rate) took the surname 'de Sandhulle' from their place of residence. They would hardly have done that if they lived elsewhere, nor would they have lived anywhere in Sandhill but on their own demesne farm.

While Sandhill was not mentioned in the Domesday Book, being created at a slightly later date, it has been deduced that it was part of the five and a half fees held of the lords of Dunster by William fitz Durand in 1166 and his son Ralph fitz William in 1196, both of whom also held Withycombe. Probably from its creation it was in the occupation of the family who styled themselves 'of Sandhill', as William of Sandhill was a witness to two deeds executed by Ralph fitz William.

Certain things were regarded as essential adjuncts to a manor-house: these included a dovecote, fish-ponds, and – if there was no church nearby – a private chapel. Several of Sandhill's fields were granted to Cleeve Abbey but the de Sandhulles also had dealings with other religious houses. In 1243 Ralph de Sandhulle came to an agreement with the Prior of Dunster, his 'tenant', quitclaiming his rights concerning land in Doverhay (Porlock) and an acre of land and an acre of meadow in 'Wyldalre' to the latter for a payment of ten marcs. Wyldalre is likely to have been Willaller or Willalders, an area of meadowland near Sandhill. This may have been purely business, but there was surely also an element of gaining favour with the Church involved here.

Roger of Sandhill held the manor in fee of the lords of the superior manor of Withycombe during the period 1280–1303, and three people with that surname appeared in the Subsidy Rolls of 1327. Alice of Sandhill paid the most (12d.) and so was probably the widowed lady of the manor. William and Ellen of Sandhill paid smaller amounts. Three years later a certain John Dygon held the property, and it is likely that he had married a Sandhill widow, for when the manor was granted to him and wife Elizabeth in 1329 it was to them both and the heirs of Elizabeth.

By 1346 John of Sandhill held the manor, and a man of the same name was still there in 1410. By 1417 Peter of Sandhill had taken over, being a suitor to the

Hundred Court of Carhampton in that year. He may have been the last of the de Sandhills to hold the manor (and by this time there is no guarantee that the family still lived there), for around 1427 William Newton took over at Sandhill, holding the manor from Thomas Beaumont, the owner of Withycombe Wyke at that time. This is the last one hears specifically of Sandhill being held through mesne lordship: henceforth it was regarded as being held directly of the lords of Dunster Castle.

The Newton family proceeded to hold the manor of Sandhill for the next 150 years or so, possibly occupying the farm themselves. They owned estates elsewhere, but that at Sandhill may have been of sufficiently high status to have been preferred by some of the family. Certainly in slightly later times other wealthy gentry were happy to live there, although admittedly in a new manor-house.

William Newton died in 1453 and was replaced by son and heir Alexander, who was then 18 years old. John Newton succeeded him, followed by his son, another Alexander. We know that in 1494 this Alexander had a wife named Maud, and five years later they effected a settlement upon their son Thomas and his wife Alice. Later though, Alexander took a second wife, Agnes, from the Clavelshaye family of Curry Rivel. He died in 1523. He had also possessed an estate at Swell, near Taunton, which had been his preferred residence, and son Thomas inherited this, not Sandhill, which fell to a younger son, John, who was probably the child of Alexander and Agnes. In 1524 Agnes was granted wardship of the boy (thus effectively gaining Sandhill for herself) from Alexander Luttrell. She subsequently married Giles Wadham, and it was 'Mistress Wadham' who

was still being named as the holder of Sandhill as late as 1558.

John Newton died without issue in 1584, leaving all of his lands to John Popham, the King's Attorney. John Newton's widow Joan – said to be originally from Dunster – was a famous character in the history of Withycombe, later to be known as the witch Joan Carne. She swiftly remarried after her first husband's death, her new husband Charles Wyndham receiving a conveyance in fee of the Sandhill estate from Popham. The Wyndhams were the wealthy lords of nearby Williton, their home the grand house known as Orchard Wyndham.

However, Charles did not last long, his will of 1585 leaving Sandhill to his godson Francis Wyndham, after the death of his wife. Joan then made a third advantageous marriage, this time to Thomas Carne of Ewenny, Glamorgan. She outlived him as well, finally dying herself in 1612. It was then that the rumours started: Joan had murdered at least two of her husbands; she could turn into a hare at will; her ghost haunted Sandhill; and upon returning to the house after her funeral she was found in the kitchen, frying eggs and bacon!

At this distance in time, it is difficult to know what to make of the murder accusations, probably made long after the events. The marriage to Charles Wyndham was clearly a pragmatic affair, made in order to secure the Sandhill estate for herself and, it should be remembered, her spouse's family. This was simply how things were done. Perhaps the third marriage was also made for personal financial benefit. But where was the gain in murdering any of her husbands? She had no offspring, and the custom was that, as a widow, she would continue to enjoy the

The big house at Sandhill, built by Charles Wyndham in 1588.

SANDHILL WITHYCOMBE (VOWLES)

property for the term of her life anyway. These fortunate marriages and deaths were surely just grist to the village rumour-mill, at a time when witch-hunts were very real and at the forefront of the public mind. There is a brass plaque in the chancel of the church commemorating thrice-married Joan Carne 'of Sandel': would that have been placed there if there had been any substance to the rumours? What Joan should be remembered for is the erection of the present house at Sandhill, completed in 1588, thanks to her advantageous marriages. Instead, her name has become attached to several rural myths, all of which can be found in just about any part of the country: she was seen wearing a bandage the day after a huntsman wounded a white hare; and each year since her death her ghost takes a cock's stride towards the house, the attainment of that goal presaging doom for anyone living there at that time!

However, in the village the belief in the stories concerning the 'witch' Joan Carne was very much a reality. One later occupant of Sandhill Farm was said to have kept a room above the porch in the house empty and furnished, ready for the spirit's return; and such was the fear generated around Sandhill by the myth, that an exorcism was attempted in the early 1800s. The intention had been to lay the ghost in one of Sandhill's manorial ponds, but the affair degenerated into farce when the large party of clergymen and spectators managed to spook themselves and ended up racing in full flight back to the village. So much for myth and legend then, but the reality at Sandhill after Joan's death was equally dramatic. Her estate had been worth the astronomical sum of £6,000, and it had been placed in the hands of administrators William Pound of Timberscombe, clothier, and Richard Keene of Broadways Downe, gentleman, while the matter of inheritance was settled. The heir, as already mentioned, was Colonel Francis Wyndham, but this had to be proved of course, and until this was done the estate appears to have been eyed with avarice by another member of the Wyndham clan. According to proceedings of the Star Chamber (written down by Revd Camplin-Coggan in a booklet compiled for the Festival of Britain):

Francis Robertes, a poor Runagate person, was hired by Zachary Windham, out of Wales, to commit some desperate and outrageous action. He took a great pot from the clothier [Pound], *and 7 persons on horseback with long piked staves, Welsh hooks, guns, swords and daggers came to my ground at Crodon* [Croydon?] *in the night time to drive off the cattle of the late Joane Carne, and drove off 17 udder cattle and 184 sheep, and then repaired to the house of John Vicarie at Old Knoll, where four kine remained in a close court, tore down part of the covering of the walls of this court and broke open the door thereof, and assaulted Richard Keene in the highway.*

Sandhill itself was also raided. Francis Wyndham (aware perhaps of what was in the wind) had hired Thomas Burge, who had worked as a ploughman for Joan Carne, to take care of eight oxen in their stall, to which end he locked himself in with them overnight. He reported that he was awakened around midnight by ten or a dozen persons attempting to gain access. He attempted to resist 'according to his small power' and heard one of the attackers say 'thou art a crook-legged rogue, a trissell-legged rogue, and it were no matter if we did kill thee' whereupon he made such an outcry that the gang ran off! One of the defendants in the case attempted to put a different gloss on the whole affair, stating that he had driven off cattle belonging to Zachary Windham in a peaceable manner by order of the Sheriff of Somerset, although this seems an unlikely explanation, in light of the evidence.

Francis Wyndham did take over at Sandhill, occupying the house and clearly playing a dominant role in village life. The Civil War was rapidly approaching and Francis was very much a King's man. He was active in his support of the King's cause throughout the conflict and it was a letter from him which persuaded the Luttrells at Dunster Castle to switch their support to the Royalists, an act which ultimately led to the siege and partial destruction of their home.

In 1645 a force of Roundheads descended upon Sandhill, intending to surprise Colonel Wyndham. According to Revd Camplin-Coggan, the soldiers pillaged the house 'not even respecting the women, whose clothes they tore off their backs.' Sir Hugh Wyndham escaped by the back door and made his way to Francis at Dunster Castle, where he had been appointed governor. He mustered what troops he could at short notice (some 30 horse) and set off in pursuit of the Parliamentarians, catching up with them at Nettlecombe. He claimed a victory in the ensuing battle against 250 horse, and returned with five prisoners and 14 horses, but perhaps the Roundheads were more concerned with getting their booty back to their base at Wiveliscombe than fighting.

A weather-vane on the gable of the house at Sandhill bears the initials of Francis Wyndham. His daughter Elizabeth had married Thomas Morgan of Tredegar and Machen in Glamorgan at some time around 1633 and, as she was her father's heir, Sandhill passed into the hands of the Morgan family. They definitely did not live at Sandhill, and it is possible that the undertenants from this time onwards were members of the Escott family. Thomas Morgan was paying the rent for the manor to the lords of Withycombe Hadley in 1655, the payment being 10s.11$\frac{1}{2}$d., due at Michaelmas. An archaic tradition decreed that the bailiff had to deliver 15 horseshoe nails to the mansion house at Sandhill before receiving the rent! This later became 24 nails, or 2d. The origin of this custom is obscure, but it was possibly intended as compensation for carriage of the rent from Sandhill.

Thomas Morgan died in May 1664, and his wife two years later. Thus Sandhill passed to their younger son John, a turkey merchant who lived in London. John died in 1716, unmarried, and left Sandhill to his nephew, John Morgan of Tredegar. When he died three years later, leaving the estate to his second son Thomas Morgan, Hugh Escott was said to be in occupation of the farm. Hugh was still there when, in 1736, Thomas Morgan sold his interest in Sandhill to the Smyth family of St Audries, near Williton, via intermediary Edward Dyke. The Manor Court of Withycombe Hadley moved swiftly to present that it was the custom of the manor 'that any free tenant that owes free suit and service... dies or aliens, a releife [sic] of double the chief rent is payable', and to demand this payment from Thomas Morgan for the sale of 'Sandle Farm' to Dyke.

Within a short time Thomas Escott took over from his father at Sandhill as undertenant to the Smyths; and then in 1761 he was able to purchase the freehold from them for the princely sum of £5,250. He died four years later, his son of the same name taking over from him and promptly marrying Joan Withycombe, a member of the equally prosperous Carhampton family. At the same time Thomas leased his lands for one year to William Withycombe (see below). The success of this venture from the point of view of a tactical alliance is open to question, as it may have led indirectly to a dispute in Chancery in 1772 between the two families. Nevertheless, the ownership of Sandhill Farm brought considerable prestige to the Escott family. The farm paid the highest Church Rate and the most land tax in the parish at this time, and Thomas was churchwarden – regarded as a position of honour – throughout his time in charge of the farm.

Thomas was buried at Carhampton in 1789 and was succeeded at Sandhill by three of his sons. The first was yet another Thomas, who died in 1808, then John, who only survived for a further year, and finally Hugh. Both Thomas junr and Hugh were also churchwardens.

Hugh was the last of his family to hold Sandhill. In 1813 he sold the estate to John Fownes Luttrell of Dunster Castle, but remained as tenant until 1821, when all of his stock and household goods were sold off at a grand sale. The stock consisted of:

163 ewes in lamb of the Nott kind, 107 lambs, 6 capital rams, 14 wether rams, 7 milch cows, 1 guernsey in calf, 5 fat oxen, 2 fat heifers, 12 plough oxen, 5 two year old steers, 5 two year old heifers, 5 steer yearlings, 6 heifer yearlings, 7 calves, 1 hackney horse, 1 hackney mare and colt, 3 cart horses, 6 Exmore and other Ponies, 48 store pigs, 30 hogsheads of excellent Cider in Cask, large quantity of empty pipes, puncheons and hogsheads in good condition, Sulls, Drags and Harrows, Yokes, Bows and Chains, Waggons, Carts, Putts and wheels, Cart and other Harness, etc.

Household goods included:

Four-post, Field and other Bedsteads, with Cotton and other Furniture; prime Goose Feather Beds, Bolsters and Pillows; Marseilles Counterpanes, Quilts and Blankets; bed and table linen; Mahogany Dining, Card and other tables; Mahogany and other chairs; Mahogany Bureau; Mahogany and other chests of drawers; 2 8-day clocks; 1 30-hour clock; Chimney, Pier and Swing Glasses in burnished Gilt Frames; etc.

James Copp was the Luttrells' next tenant at Sandhill, in residence from the time of Hugh Escott's departure until around 1832, when Richard Oatway replaced him. Both of these also took their turn as churchwarden, in what was becoming almost a mandatory appointment. Oatway was the tenant of Sandhill when the Tithe Map was drawn up, and it reveals that at that time practically the entire eastern end of the parish was associated with the farm. Indeed, those fields probably correspond almost exactly with the area originally assigned to the manor of Sandhill. However, they include fields which had been let out at an early date in the manor's history, then later recovered. These reclaimed areas historically belonged to such smallholdings as Little Sandhill, Baker's and Poole's Tenements, and to Cleeve Abbey, and they lay mostly close by Sandhill Farm. Most of the fields that were actually farmed by the tenant of Sandhill throughout the majority of its history seem to lie in a block to the south of the farm, on the higher ground.

These fields were listed in the short-term lease made in 1766 by Thomas Escott to William Withycombe, as Sand Croft, Lower Chilkey, Higher Chilkey, Slade, three hills called Turner's Hills, Bottom Close, Great Hensty, Higher, Middle and Lower Bradley, Mardle Close, Higher Hensty, Broad Meadow, Broom Close, Bush Close, Long Close and Long Meadow, altogether comprising 85 acres. By the mid-nineteenth century, however, the farm had expanded to take in roughly 250 acres.

By 1841 Richard Oatway had died, leaving his widow Sarah in charge. She ran the farm herself until well into the 1860s, when son John took over, remaining at the helm for most of the remainder of the century. His arrival saw the return of the Sandhill/churchwarden connection, which had been held in abeyance while his mother was in control.

During the first half of the twentieth century Sandhill was the home of George Reed, who lived there before the First World War, and then the King family, who occupied the farm continuously between the wars. Later Anthony Hobbs was the tenant at Sandhill and at the time of writing his son Philip runs his highly successful racing stables from there.

Mention has already been made of Sandhill land that was granted to Cleeve Abbey in early times: generally speaking, the monks would have let these

The Girls' Friendly Society was popular in the village during the 1930s, meetings being held at Sandhill.
This picture of the diamond jubilee celebrations at Wells in 1935 must contain at least one Withycombe member, possibly a Cridge.

fields to local farmers, receiving the rents and tithes due from them. Whether tenements were established on these grounds or they were simply fields to be worked from nearby farms is not always apparent and the situation probably varied. However, two that were likely to have been independent holdings, situated close to Sandhill Farm itself, were Baker's and Poole's. Baker's lands lay to the south-east of the manor farm and must have included the fields named Baker's Orchard (No.33) and Baker's Close (No.34); and it is likely that the adjacent field named Metland (No.35) was also included, that being mentioned in the Glebe Terrier of 1639 as part of the old Cleeve Abbey estate. Baker's Barn – situated in one corner of Metland, next to Baker's Orchard – is still marked on Ordnance Survey maps.

Baker's Tenement was referred to in a case brought before the Court of Chancery after the Dissolution of the Monasteries. John Baker (alias Ferrer) and his wife Alys had taken on the tenement before the Dissolution, after the death of John Chapman and his wife Margaret, as tenants of William Dovell, the Abbot of Cleeve. Now, because the Abbey's lands had been seized by the Crown, Sir John Sydenham (presumably as lord of the manor of Old Cleeve) decided that Baker's tenement was his for the taking and made off with their corn, as well as causing general 'vexation' to the tenants. John Baker argued that because he had been granted the copyhold lawfully, this was a gross injustice. Other tenants of the dissolved Abbey suffered similar abuses at this time.

'Baker's lands' are recorded as part of the Sandhill estate from the seventeenth century onwards, so the tenement may have ceased to exist as an independent farmstead not long after the court case. Poole's was similarly brought back into the Sandhill fold, but survived on its own for a little longer. When Thomas Escott bought the freehold of Sandhill Farm in 1761,

the property included 'all that tenement (where was formerly a messuage) late Poole's & now parcell of Sandhill Farm.' It is likely to have been situated immediately to the west of the manor farm, its fields including Lower (and probably also Higher) Chilkey or Chalkey.

Beyond the manor farmhouse Sandhill Lane turns northwards to meet the A39 road. It enters the parish a short distance to the east, where a house stands perilously close to the roadside. This house is named Bournstream. Like several fields nearby, within the hamlet of Bilbrook, it used to be part of Withycombe parish, and was referred to in the nineteenth century as Sandhill Plot. The first indication of a house on the site is to be found in the 1851 census, where the family of Thomas and Elizabeth White were listed as living at Sandhill Plot. Thomas had been born at Luxborough in the 1790s, had married a Withycombe girl and subsequently lived at Oak. The family was still there in 1861, the address being given then as Bilbrook.

In 1871 James Elliott, the man who had erected the blacksmith's workshop in Mill Street, had gone there to live. This time the address was noted as Keynham – a name for the Withycombe end of Bilbrook. He was still there ten years later, a farmer (at 'Kinarn'), but was dead by 1891, leaving his widow Eliza as the farmer, helped by three of their grown-up daughters. One of these daughters, Charlotte, was named as farmer in 1901, with another, Sarah Date, employed there as a cook. In 1891 and 1901 the house was referred to once again as Sandhill Plot.

Subsequently Sandhill Plot saw a variety of tenants, Irishman James Pearce being there in 1920 and a Colonel Durand in 1927. The latter kept kennels there, where he bred Irish wolfhounds and Pekinese. A Mrs Beynon also lived at Bournstream then, and she was followed in the 1930s by a Mrs Delzell.

The house's location being at the parish's eastern boundary, we now take the highway back, past Sandhill Lane and Withycombe Wood, to Court Place Lane. No other houses abut the busy highway as it skirts the parish nowadays, although in quieter times this was not the case. Its path has only been slightly changed with the passing of the centuries, the major 'improvement' taking place around 1960, when part of it was widened and straightened. In early times the road was in notoriously bad condition, necessitating its reconstruction as a turnpike road with tolls payable to use it. There is a village legend that the road did not exist before the establishment of the turnpike trust and that all vehicles had previously been obliged to use the route between Withycombe Lane and Sandhill Lane to travel between Carhampton and Bilbrook. This is incorrect; the main highway had existed for many centuries before the turnpike road's introduction.

Beyond the Sandhill Lane turning, on rising ground on the other side of the road, is a field (once more than one) known as Clayhills or 'Cliles'. It was one of those pieces granted to Cleeve Abbey. Its tenants are known from the time of Henry VII, when John and Thomas Heyward held it, until the early 1900s, when it was one of Henry Pearse's fields. For much of its history it was rented to whomever was at Sandhill Farm. However, what is unusual is that it was described as 'floated ground' and every fourth year the Withycombe Brook was diverted from its usual course in order to water it.

Normally (as today) the brook flowed alongside Court Place Lane to Brethren Cross. To water Clayhills, the stream was turned from its course at Court Place and redirected across Cherry Field to Withycombe Wood, skirting it before crossing the highway. We may suspect that this diversion was only effected for a short period in each fourth year, when water was plentiful: but it is notable that this was the course of the brook recorded on the 1840 Tithe Map, rather than its proper course.

Next to Clayhills is an area of valuable meadowland known as Willaller or Willalders. Part of this, as we have noted, was granted to the Prior of Dunster by Ralph of Sandhill in 1243: this led to the creation of two distinct properties there, one of which was retained by the clergy, more or less. The tenants of one part tended to be farmers from Old Cleeve, such as the Whitlocks, while those of the other were the occupants of Sandhill. All of these meadows were treated as overland properties (fields detached from the farmer's home estate), far too valuable to set a tenement upon. However, in the period immediately after the Civil War a house was set up by the roadside at Willaller.

Pound's House was authorised to be erected in 1660, by a lease granted to blacksmith William Pound by Francis Luttrell. It was taken on the lives of himself, wife Joane and son James, at a rent of 1s.0d. The house was to be built on a parcel of waste ground on the other side of 'a stony foote path' which divided Willaller from Clayhills. This William Pound is unlikely to have been the same man as the clothier of Timberscombe who was one of the administrators of Joan Carne's estate, but he may well have been a relative.

The Pounds do not seem to have prospered in their new home, for most of them were laid to rest in the churchyard within a dozen years of its building. William himself was listed among those too poor to have to pay Hearth Tax in 1670, two years before his own death. Widow Elianor Milton acquired the house subsequently, being presented to the Manor Court in 1685 for not repairing the highway before 'her house att Willaller wch was formerly Pounde's'. Her son Christopher replaced her as tenant after she died in 1696, followed by his widow Ann ten years later. She continued to be named as a cottage tenant until 1713 but in the following year 'Ann Melton's cottage' was said to be in the lord's hands. The last we hear of it is in 1718, when it was named as one of John Hiles' properties.

Across the road from Pound's House is Withycombe Wood, an imposing landmark that signals the village's proximity to the passing traveller. Once known as Court Wood, it has dominated the scene for hundreds and perhaps thousands of years – but not continuously. In 1830 the Revd Savage wrote:

> In this parish there is a wood of twenty acres on the left of the turnpike road going westward; it covers the sides and top of the northern part of a ridge that passes down to the eastward of the village, and was a very fine object from any part of the neighbourhood before it was cut down, about ten years since; but it has again been replanted by J.F. Luttrell esq. and is now becoming a prominent and conspicuous feature in the face of the country.

The levelling of the wood was no doubt prompted by the war at sea which Nelson had been waging with the French throughout the early years of the nineteenth century. The trees – 931 oak and 115 ash – were advertised as 'Prime Navy Timber' when they were put up for sale in 1816. The wood was replanted five years later. A Mr Veitch was paid for planting 8,500 larch, 8,500 oak and 500 ash trees on 26 November 1821; and almost as many larch and oak on the following day. Clearly these had developed well by the time Savage passed by a few years later. The road from here to the Court Place Lane turning is wide and straight now. Though never so wide, its route is not much different from that of the turnpike road and the old highway that existed before it, although one feature of the old road that has long since vanished is the stretch of causey that once edged it as far as Willaller. We tend to think of these raised pavements as features of town and village

Above: *Perhaps Carhampton's 1922 football team, rather than Withycombe's, although the players are drawn from both parishes. Left to right, back row: Revd Dawson, Bob Willis, Reg Young, Phil Back, Cliff Rawle, ? Fenwick; middle: Harry Sutton, Archie Chilcott, Reg Chilcott; front: Bussy Watts, George Chilcott, Frank Case, Harry Simmonds, Joe Williams.*

Below: *Withycombe's football team c.1938 before a match against Carhampton. The pitch was in the field called Higher Nothams, between the main road and Black Monkey Lane. Left to right, back row: Professor Bright (referee, lived at Merton House), Percy Lewis, Joe Strong, Archie Chidgey, Bill Nicholas; middle: Ted Gould, Jack Routley, Alan 'Shiner' Burnell; front: Jack Lewis, Harry Martin, Bill Copp, Fred Hawkins, Harry Lewis.*

Right: *Withycombe's football team in the early 1930s. Left to right, standing: Percy Lewis, Joe Strong, Jack Lewis; kneeling: Ted Gould, Bill Nicholas, Alfie Gratton; seated: Jack Gould, Harry Lewis, Bill Willis, Fred 'Tussy' Hawkins, Reg Chilcott.*

streets, but clearly the road was walked frequently enough to justify the trouble of maintaining such a structure here. At least this was the case in the Middle Ages: by the early 1700s this causey, like the one in Withycombe Lane, was in constant need of repair; and there is no evidence that either received the necessary attention then or later.

The junction which takes us back to the village of Withycombe is more than just a turning. It is an ancient crossroads, although the opposing fourth arm – Black Monkey Lane – is rarely used these days, being heavily overgrown, and no drivers would dream of taking that direction. The crossroads tends to be referred to today as Withycombe Cross, but some still remember it as Brenton or Brendon Cross, names noted in early-nineteenth-century documents. However, these are but variations on Brethren Cross, its true name. There may well have been an actual preaching cross here at one time, but whether or not this was the case it was certainly travelling monks who gave it its name, for the name 'Black Monkey Lane' derives from a misinterpretation of the word monkyes (a common spelling of monks in the late Middle Ages). Black monks were the Benedictines, the order favoured by the de Mohuns of Dunster Castle.

Just beyond the junction between the road to Carhampton and Black Monkey Lane is a field where Withycombe's football team used to play. The team benefited from the support of club president Rupert Leversha, who provided much of the necessary equipment and allowed the use of the field, called Higher Nothams. Resplendent in their colours of scarlet and emerald, they enjoyed some success from the 1920s to the 1950s. The local derby against Carhampton's team was always the most keenly anticipated and fought, like all such games. Someone, possibly Gertrude Sully, made up a song about Withycombe's footballing heroes, the first verse of which was:

The captain's Freddy Hawkins,
The goalie's Joey Strong,
Young Teddy Gould is on the wing,
Reggie Chilcott's running along!

Withycombe's 1949–50 football team. Left to right, back row: *Walter Gould, Jeff Dyer, Alec Windsor, John Nicholas, Ray Tarr, Ernie Potter, Gordon Fry, Harry Martin, Fred Jones;* middle: *Rupert Leversha, Timmy Burnett, Roger Scudamore, Tom Stephenson, Charlie Cridge, Walter Ashe, Revd Camplin-Coggan, Bill Griffiths;* front: *John Prout, Gertrude Sully, Ray Fry, Bill Shopland, Phil Pope, Jack Dyer, Albert Sully;* kneeling: *Benny Griffiths.*

Left: *Doris Leversha in her wartime nurse's uniform.*

Below: *A good morning's haymaking work done, the Leversha family heads back to Court Place presumably for a well-earned lunch.*

Left: *Rabbiting was always popular in the village, among the farming community in particular, principally in order to limit the numbers of these animals. Pictured here at the rear of Court Place is Olive Leversha, a crack shot, with her 'bag', no doubt destined for the cooking pot.*

Below: *Many of these workers outside Court Place, c.1921, were not employees of the farm; were they helping to deal with a serious rick fire that occurred there around that time? On the wall on the left are Harry Nicholas, Bill Nicholas and Bill Gould (seated left to right); in the centre is George Gould (holding a pitchfork), with Walter Gould and Tom Burnett (behind); Bill Griffiths is holding baby daughter Joan, with Bowler Nicholas (in front), and Bert Webber (one from the end).*

The 'Mansion House' of Court Place, photographed on a slightly misty morning in 1906.

Nine

Lower Street (Court Place to Christopher's)

At the top of a short but steep rise in level, Court Place Lane gives way to Lower Street and we are once again in the village proper. The first property we encounter is Court Place Farm, the manor farm of Withycombe Hadley and – as its name suggests – the location of the Manor Court.

Court Place Farm, at some periods confusingly called Withycombe Farm, must have been in existence since at least 1238, when the old manor of Withycombe was divided into three parts. At that time it became necessary to establish two new manor-houses in order to provide fitting accommodation for their new overlords, and Court Place must have been chosen for the third granted to Ilaria and her husband Richard of Combe, which quickly passed into the hands of the Fitzurse family.

It is not known whether there was a farm already on the site but certainly the structure of the property as seen in 2003 (more or less) must have been established when it became a manor farm. A substantial area of ground around the farmhouse would have been allocated for its demesne, and other elements deemed necessary for the life of a manorial lord would have been put in place, such as fish-ponds, a dovecote, etc. The demesne enclosed an area around and mostly to the north of the farm, extending eastwards as far as Wood Field on the far side of Withycombe Wood. Over the centuries Court Place's lands have varied as some fields were let out while others were acquired, but in general the heart has remained intact: Bean Meadow, Cherry Field, Wood Field, the two Barn Fields, Brethren Cross Field.

We know who its owners have been since the thirteenth century (although few of those owners would have lived there) because it was the demesne farm of one of the sub-manors. For most of its history Court Place Farm would have been let to local farming families, drawn from among the wealthier members of that class, such as the Chesters, Escotts, etc., as befitted the status of the property. On the odd occasion the house may have been the home of the lord of the manor, or a member of his family: Christopher Hadley, for example, heir to the manor before his early death in 1540, declared his wish to be buried in the chancel of Withycombe's church, perhaps indicating that he had more than a remote connection to the parish; and Court Place was referred to as 'Hadley's House' by George Luttrell around that time. Generally speaking, however, the lord preferred grander residences elsewhere.

The survey of the manor of Withycombe Hadley made in the early years of the sixteenth century describes the 'capital messuage' and the demesne lands associated with it. It is not named but the description makes it absolutely clear that Court Place was the property concerned.

The house, etc. consisted of: capital messuage with garden adjoining; bakehouse with court and woodhouse; court with garden and orchard adjoining; an orchard with fish-pond below the wood; barn, dovecote, stable and barton. The fish-pond below the wood can be seen marked on the 1887 OS map, sited in the south-east corner of Cherry Field, next to Withycombe Wood. It is believed to have been supplied by a streamlet outflowing from the Rectory ponds, which were themselves fed from a source located at the Hill farms on the Higher Rodhuish Road, already discussed. This stream was slight and prone to dry up during the summer months, but water from the main Withycombe Brook could be turned into the Court Place pond via the route specified in the previous chapter, which supplied the Clayhill fields every fourth year.

Nearby demesne lands named included: Beneclose [Bean Meadow], valued at 10s.0d.; one close on the east side of the wood, estimated at 15 acres (Wood Field), 15s.0d.; one close below the wood (probably Cherry Field), 25s.0d.; one close on the northern side of the barn (probably Hither Barn Field), 15s.0d.; one meadow in the same place called Chalcroftmede, 23s.4d.; one meadow called Longmede (Ways Meadow, next to Higher Nothams); one close near Brotherscross and opposite to the close below the wood (Lower and Higher Brenton Cross Fields, which used to be one field), 54s.0d.; one meadow called Wodwalmede in the same place (Wallin Meadow), 10s.0d.; a meadow called Fostersmede estimated at one acre (probably part of Old Meadow), 20d.; a pasture by the road which leads all the way from the capital messuage to Brotherscross; a pasture by the road which leads from Bilbrook towards Carhampton; and a close near

Below: *Haymaking at Court Place Farm around 1930, with the large elevator making it possible to create massive ricks. At ground level, left to right: Percy Griffiths, boss Rupert Leversha, Walter Gould and his father George Gould, another Leversha (?), Bill Griffiths, Jack Hawkins, Bert Webber and Fred Hawkins. Now, who's got the cider jar...*

Above: *Doris and Olive Leversha are among those playing croquet on the lawn in front of the house at Court Place in 1911.*

Left: *Alec Windsor, following in the tradition of lifelong workers at Court Place Farm, receives a retirement present from Stephen Crossman.*

Below: *The Goulds taking Hay Tea in Cherry Field in 1917 after helping the Leversha family bring in the harvest. From the left: Walter Gould (Leonard's younger brother), ? (possibly another Gould), Lavinia Gould, George Gould, Leonard Gould and his wife Annie (Burnett).*

The haymaking at Court Place Farm complete, a Hay Tea is held in Cherry Field, 1908. Doris and Olive Leversha are on the ground with their dogs, close by their parents. Rupert and Geoff are on the haystack with the two North boys, sons of the artist, John William North. Among the workers George Gould can just be seen, third from the left of the group of six standing at the back.

the farmyard called Monkeshey, 16d. Not every field can be identified with certainty but it is clear that they are all close by Court Place. Monkeshey, or 'Monkshay' (see below), later associated with the Tuttle family, was on the south side of the farmyard.

There were other fields described as demesne lands in the sixteenth-century document, notably several around Gildencote, but these were probably not originally linked with Court Place. The document names several tenants paying rent for various parcels of dominical land, but hardly any for the fields directly associated with Court Place (Thomas Darch, for Fostersmede, being the exception).

The manor of Withycombe Hadley subsequently passed via Margaret Hadley's marriage to Thomas Luttrell into the hands of that family at Dunster Castle. Thomas and Margaret definitely did not live at the capital house (no surprise there really), the house and demesne lands being described in 1571 as in the joint, or several, occupations of George Escott and Robert Darch, clerk.

In 1622 a 'true valuation' was made of the lands belonging to Withycombe Farm (meaning Court Place). The demesne fields listed include: Brethren Cross Field (24 acres), the Barn Field (20 acres), Cherry Field (18 acres) and Wood Field (12 acres). The total valuation conveniently came to £80, plus £25 for the lands at Gildencote, making a grand total of £105.

During the seventeenth century Francis Luttrell and Roger Hill granted 'all that capital messuage and farme called Withecombe Farme or Court Place' to various people, culminating in a transfer in 1704 to John Mordant, knight of London. The document that records the details notes that in 1655 the property was 'then or late in the tenure of Henry Chester'. It is not until the eighteenth century that we start to find consistent evidence for the occupants of the farm. In 1715 Mr John Withycombe leased Court Place Farm for two years at £115 rent. Madam Luttrell paid the Church Rates (5s.4d.) in 1718, which seems to have been the general practice. John Withycombe remained in possession until his death, which probably occurred in 1729, his burial taking place in Carhampton. A 1739 lease granted to Mr (James) Newton 'all that Mansion house Capital Farm and Tenement commonly called and known by the name of Withycombe Farm (or Court place)', plus all of its lands. These included a messuage and tenement called formerly Vellacott's or Hill's Tenement, part of which was Chalcroft Meadow, two and a half acres upon which a house and garden had been erected (the rest remained as meadow). Chalcroft Meadow had long been associated with Court Place, but its exact location remains a mystery. The farm was described as 'late in possession of John Withycombe, now deceased.'

In 1759 another lease for Court Place Farm was granted to James Newton by Henry Fownes Luttrell,

for 14 years at a rent of £150. This time Fern Acre, of 18 acres, 'in Carhampton', was included; and specifically excluded was Carmoore (Kermoor) in Carhampton, said to have formerly been enjoyed with Court Place Farm.

In 1765 Mrs Newton 'of Court Place' was buried at Carhampton. Then in 1773 Mr James Newton followed his wife, bringing about an auction for the tenancy of the farm. This took place on 4 December. The bidders (together with their high bids) were as follows: William Withycombe (£170), Thomas Escott (£171), John Newton (£172), John North (£176), John Bindon (£177), James Taylor (£181), James Pearse (£182), William Oatway (£186), John Thresher (£190) and Joshua Veysey (£191). Joshua Veysey's high bid failed to meet the reserve, which was apparently 200 guineas. The asking price was reduced in stages to £200 but when this was refused it looked like there would be no sale. However, 13 days later an agreement was made: Veysey would pay £200 a year if his landlord would pay all rates, etc. and make certain repairs. The arrangements were confirmed the following year when Veysey took out a 21-year lease on the property at a rent of £200 per annum. In the lease he was described as 'late of Exford, now of Withycombe' and the property as 'Court Place Farm with late Chapman's and the Gilcotts and other grounds... '.

In 1778 Court Place was stated to consist of farmhouse, two barns, stable, pound-house, bakehouse, three linneys, two courts (altogether half an acre), garden and orchard. Remember that bakehouse from the description some 250 years earlier?

It looks as if Veysey was determined to hold the Luttrells to their promise to make repairs to Court Place, for John Fownes Luttrell paid a succession of bills to workmen on his behalf during Veysey's period of tenure. In 1784, for example, he allowed Jonathon Griffiths' bill for:

Carpinters Work don For the Honbl John Founds Luttrel Esq Work don at Curtplas farm by Jonthan Griffith for lasting of the linmey and plancing of the chamber in the side hous.

The following year saw mason John Jones' bill for Court Place, for repairing:

... the hols in the Barns walls…the tops of the Bakes, and Kichen Chimilys… the Back of the Kichen Chimily… the hols in the walls of the Corn Chambers… the walls ag'st the Court… the Pan-tile over the Dary, and Lenny, & pigs-stys and other Jobbs.

And again in the next year there were bills allowed for payments to: Richard Greenslade for lime; John Hucklebridge the glazier; Thomas Weetch the blacksmith; Jonathon Griffiths the carpenter and mason; John Jones again; two locks for new doors; John Case the thatcher; etc. Such was the extent of the work done that perhaps the appearance of the current house owes more than a little to this period of its history.

Joshua Veysey was clearly a relatively prosperous man, for he not only took on the demesne farm of Withycombe Hadley, but also one of the major farms of Withycombe Wyke, namely Gupworthy. As befitted his position he swiftly became churchwarden. He had married Elizabeth Lyddon of Winsford at Withycombe in 1774, at which time he was called a gentleman. However, it looks as if he had overstretched his resources somewhat because in 1789 he received notice to quit Court Place Farm, together with Gilcotts, Fern Acre, etc. at the following Michaelmas. Joshua Veysey continued as churchwarden until 1799 and he is probably the man of that name buried at Exford in 1801, who 'died suddenly in bed'.

Veysey's successor at Court Place seems to have been another member of the Withycombe family, for in 1820 James Withycombe, aged 34, 'of Court Place', was buried at Carhampton. However, in 1829 it was taken on by farmer William Boucher for seven years. He paid the Church Rate in the following year, when Court Place was valued at £124.1s.5d., second only to Sandhill Farm, and he also paid for Hiles Farm nearby, which had been amalgamated with Court Place a few years earlier. Part of Hiles Barton later became the pound and still exists as such in 2003.

It looks like William Boucher did not extend his tenancy beyond the agreed seven years, because by 1840 James Leversha had taken over. One of a family said to be descended from Flemish plaster-workers brought to England to work for the Luttrells at Dunster Castle and at East Quantoxhead, where many of the Luttrells chose to live, James was the first of his family to occupy Court Place, which they continued to do for a century or so thereafter. The Tithe Apportionment of 1840 shows that James Leversha held not only Court Place and the amalgamated Hiles Farm, but also Lower Hill Farm, which was let to an undertenant. At that time James – a man of over 60 – lived at Court Place with wife Izott, their children and servants.

By 1851 James was dead and his son William was in charge. His widowed mother Izott was also there with three more of her offspring, all employed either in the house or on the farm. Also resident were two farm labourers and a general servant. The farm was stated to consist of 182 acres, providing employment for eight men, three women and a boy. In 1861 William's brother John was in charge. He was also the census enumerator for the village. He had a wife, Elizabeth, and seven children.

John and his family remained in charge at Court Place into the 1890s. His son Thomas Leversha was in partnership with his father by 1889, although until John's death he farmed himself at Higher Rodhuish. In 1891 Thomas was living at Rodhuish with his wife Florence and several children, including three-

Right: Doris Leversha celebrating her 93rd birthday. She survived to become a centenarian and must have been one of the few people to have lived in three centuries.

month-old son Rupert. Ten years later they could be found at Court Place. Daughters Olive and Doris, familiar Withycombe figures throughout the century to come, were there as well. In the electoral returns of 1920, Thomas, Florence and Rupert can be found listed at Court Place Farm. Rupert subsequently took over from his father, featuring in the electoral returns for 1938, together with wife Beatrice. Rupert Leversha was a dapper figure in the village throughout the first half of the twentieth century.

The Levershas maintained a benevolent attitude towards the villagers. We have already seen how Rupert gave his support to the football team. He also allowed the use of Bean Meadow for village fêtes, etc., and the mangel barn next to it was frequently used for events that required some protection from the elements. This consideration was due in part to the family's generosity of spirit, but can also be seen as a continuation of the traditions associated with a manor-house. As one of the major employers within the village it always made sense to support the community in any way possible. A fine example of this was the Hay Tea, a major event at Court Place under the Levershas. This was effectively a huge picnic, held in Cherry Field after haymaking was complete, as a 'thank you' to everyone who had helped with the work. Haymaking used to be a massively labour-intensive task, frequently undertaken in intense heat and under pressure from the threat of rain, so that sometimes the workers continued to labour until it became too dark to see. Whole families would be called upon to help. The 1908 photo of the Hay Tea seems to include half of the village!

After Rupert's retirement, Court Place was farmed briefly by a certain Mr R. Tatchell-Poole, before the family of George Crossman took over – they are still farming there in 2003.

Many Withycombe men worked all their lives at Court Place Farm: men such as Jim Gay, George Gould, Tom Webber and, more recently, Bill Griffiths; and often their sons would follow in their footsteps, so that their association with the farm became almost viewed as a hereditary right. Bill Griffiths started working at Court Place for Thomas Leversha in about 1902, aged 14, for a shilling a day, and continued under Rupert Tatchell-Poole and the Crossmans, carrying on into his seventies. In common with many farm labourers who began their lives before the coming of the tractor, his preference and talent was for working with horses.

Above Court Place, Lower Street provides the boundary between land which belonged to Withycombe Wyke on the west side and Withycombe Hadley on the east, the former comprising the demesne land of the ancient Withycombe manor, which became the demesne of Withycombe Wyke after the 1238 split. However, there is an exception to this in the land immediately to the south of Court Place's barton on the west of the road, whereon some houses built by the Crown Estates in the twentieth century and an old thatched dwelling now called Lower Cottage stand. During the sixteenth century this was a meadow (the brook still runs close beside it) known as Monkshay, and as already noted above, it belonged to the manor of Withycombe Hadley. From its name we can assume that it was associated with one of the monastic orders, probably the Benedictines at Dunster Priory. Certainly the owners of Withycombe Hadley made a payment of $3^1/_2$d. to Dunster Castle every Michaelmas in respect of Monkshay.

In 1653 this piece of land was granted by George Luttrell to Thomas Tuttle of Withycombe, weaver, his wife Margaret Tuttle and Henry Chester, the son of Henry Chester of Rodhuish. It was described as being 'neer unto the Sowther pte of the Barne wch belongeth unto the Farme called the Court place of Withicombe Hadley now or late… held by Henry Chester the father.' The intention here was for Thomas Tuttle to establish a messuage, and this had been done by 1655, because a survey made in that year mentions a dwelling-house on the site. Thomas and Margaret were named as freehold tenants, paying rent to Henry Chester (the son). This house is the present Lower Cottage, and below it a garden was created with, beyond that (where the Crown houses now stand), an orchard. Henry Chester, who lived himself at Slowley in Luxborough, was the principal tenant and was responsible for the manor rent of 2s.0d. and its 1d. rate, but it was the Tuttle (or Tuthill) family who inhabited the property. A friend of Henry Chester was Giles Daubenny, whom we have met in connection with Chester's Cottage in Rattle Row. In the 1680s Henry added Daubenny's name to the lease of the cottage, which was gradually becoming known as Tuttle's. Consequently he inherited the tenancy after Henry's death in 1698.

Meanwhile members of the Tuttle family continued to occupy the cottage. Thomas the weaver died in 1677, his widow Margaret in 1688, and after them either John or Thomas Tuttle, or both, who were probably their children, may have succeeded them. John was a shoemaker who was certainly there in 1720, when he took over the Daubennys' lease on the property, in his own name and those of his son John and daughter-in-law Mary Tuttle. However, after his death in 1731 it was a Joseph Tuttle who was taken as the new tenant 'for the house wherein he now lives'. He may have been the son born to John and wife Dorothy in 1699 but

this is not certain. It may have been no coincidence that in 1732 at Carhampton it was deemed necessary to establish the legal place of settlement for a Joseph Tuttle, son of Thomas (who was receiving parish relief there): this was declared to be Withycombe. Joseph Tuttle was the last of that family to hold the tenancy, which he did until his death in 1781.

The year 1790 saw the property's acquisition by Robert Webber, described then as a labourer of Withycombe, aged 59. No christening has been found for him at Withycombe, but he married Joan Davis in the village in 1756 and raised a family during the years that followed. His son John (born 1762) and granddaughter Joan Webber (daughter of eldest son Thomas) were also named on Robert's lease. We know a little about the early life of Thomas, the elder son, because in 1781 he was also examined in Carhampton as to his place of legal settlement. At that time living in Carhampton as a cordwainer, he declared that he had been born in Withycombe and apprenticed to Richard Ballifant of Old Cleeve for six years from the age of 17. He worked in that capacity for two years before moving with his master to Carhampton, where he continued as before for another 18 months, before returning to reside in Withycombe with his father for a short period, at the same time travelling daily to Carhampton to work for his master. He then cancelled his indenture by agreement but continued to work for Ballifant 'by the piece', and was married within a month. He wed Mary Webber (a cousin perhaps) in January 1781, and daughter Joan was born shortly afterwards – explaining the need for the abandonment of his apprenticeship, no doubt!

Robert Webber's lease of Tuttle's makes it clear that the orchard was detached from the property at that time and returned to the demesne, where it can be seen on the 1840 Tithe Map as 'Tithole's Orchard', in the possession of the tenants of Court Place. Robert died in 1801, to be replaced as tenant by his son John, and from around this point we begin to find the cottage being described as two dwellings. In 1833 the heriot of 10s.0d. that was traditionally due on this property when a new tenant was admitted was paid in two halves – 5s.0d. from William Webber (son of John) and the same from a John Bryant – indicating dual occupancy; and the Tithe Apportionment composed shortly afterwards names John Webber as the tenant of a cottage and garden, 'two dwellings', No.71 on the map. It is quite likely, given the size of the original cottage, that it had always been used in this way, with perhaps extended family living in different parts of it.

The families of William Webber (father John died in 1846) and John Bryant occupied the adjoining dwellings for a considerable part of the nineteenth century. When William's daughter Ann (who had already given birth to Tom Webber) married thatcher James Edbrooke, that family moved in, so that by

Above: *Although around 90 years old, Miss Edbrooke managed to attend the celebrations of the village school's centenary in 1966. Here she is ably supported by the vicar's wife Pat Watson and young Stephen Crossman.*

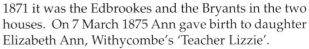

Left: *A photograph of Leonard Gould sent by him to Caroline Webber and her grand-daughters Violet and Gladys around 1920.*

1871 it was the Edbrookes and the Bryants in the two houses. On 7 March 1875 Ann gave birth to daughter Elizabeth Ann, Withycombe's 'Teacher Lizzie'.

By 1891 Elizabeth Edbrooke, aged 16, was already being described as a 'pupil-teacher' – the phenomenon whereby a senior girl who had proved herself bright enough was chosen to be what today we might call a classroom assistant. She was living at home with her widowed mother and several of her siblings. The elderly John Bryant and his wife in the adjoining cottage had moved to Bristol some years before and had been replaced by John and Harriet Perkins. They were still there at the turn of the century but next door Elizabeth Edbrooke was by that time on her own, and a qualified assistant teacher. She is principally remembered as a teacher at Carhampton School but it is thought that she may have taught briefly at Withycombe in her early career (as she definitely did as a pupil-teacher). She remained in the cottage where she was born throughout her long life, never marrying, and lived to experience the centenary and then the closure of Withycombe's school in 1966.

John Perkins died before the First World War but his widow continued to live beside Teacher Lizzie into the 1920s. Bill and Kit Griffiths were the next tenants but later they swapped houses with Fred and Cath Hawkins, who lived just a few yards up and on the other side of the road. Their part of Tuttle's Cottage was that furthest from the road and Miss Edbrooke lived in the roadside half, which she called Pear Tree Cottage. Today the two halves of the building have been reunited and the house is one of a handful in the

A group posing in front of Bradbeer's van at a fête in Bean Meadow. The men are, left to right: Harry Martin, Jack Routley, Bill Nicholas, Edward Chapman (behind), Revd Ernest Williams, Walter Gould, Fred Jones (behind), Bill Copp, Timmy Burnett, Reg Sully (behind), Alan Burnell, Monty Cook, Fred Nicholas and Sid Wyburn. The ladies are, left to right: Olive Spracklan, Annie Gould, Rhoda Wyburn, Polly Cridge, Lavinia Gould, Clara Nicholas (?) and Mabel Fry.

village that still sports a handsome head of thatch.

Above Court Place on the other side of Lower Street is a group of eight 1920s dwellings, originally built as council-houses but now known as Meadow Cottages. They were built upon part of Bean Meadow. The bean has always been a significant crop in Withycombe and the name of the field has remained unchanged since at least the Tudor period.

The introduction of social housing to the village was a source of some excitement at the time, especially among those used to the primitive conditions of the older, more dilapidated cottages – and the eight new houses would have been keenly snapped up. *Lenthall's Directory* of 1927 lists some of the earliest occupants of 'Council Cottages'. These included: William George Nicholas, tanyard worker, at No.4; Reginald William Young at No.5; John Montague Cook, mechanic, and Sid Wyburn at No.6; William Henry Cridland, a painter from Old Cleeve, at No.7; and Ernest Gould and chauffeur Ernest Hunt at No.8. Arthur Gould and Edgar Hawkins were also there but no house number was listed. A decade later we find Goulds in Nos 1, 2 and 3 (including Arthur in No.2) so it is quite likely that George Gould, whose address was simply listed as 'Lower Street', also had one of them in 1927. As a lifelong worker for Court Place Farm it seems probable that he would have been one of the first in the queue for one of these smart new houses, so conveniently sited for his workplace!

Beyond Meadow Cottages we come to Laurel Cottage, which nestles close by the roadside opposite Tuttle's Cottage. In 1948 a journalist, Lewis Brown, writing an article about the village for *The Somerset Countryman*, singled out this building. He wrote:

In the lane which winds up the main road to the village is a quaint white-walled and thatched cottage, with bread ovens bulging into the road at the base of its substantial chimney.

Now considerably modernised and having lost its thatch, it is not quite so eye-catching as then, but it is clearly a dwelling of some antiquity. However, its early history is uncertain. The first positive mention of it is in the Tithe Apportionment of 1840, where it is shown as No.76, a cottage and garden in the occupation of William Case junr. The owner was John Fownes Luttrell, as one would expect, seeing as all of the land on this side of Lower Street as far as the Rectory grounds belonged to the manor of Withycombe Hadley. This must be the same cottage and garden mentioned ten years earlier as being occupied by Thomas Case.

This Thomas Case was the eldest son of William Case (a descendant of Simon Case the thatcher) and his Irish wife Elizabeth. Thomas had married Ann Webber, known as Nancy, who seems to have been a

daughter of Thomas and Mary Webber, whom we have just met in connection with Tuttle's Cottage just across the road. The William Case junr mentioned must have been blind William Case, the younger brother of Thomas, who may have lived there as a young man. However, it was Thomas and his children who inherited the cottage.

Perhaps it was through Ann Webber that the cottage came to this family, for at the same time that Robert Webber was leasing Tuttle's Cottage he also acquired a property known as John Norman's Cottage, naming Ann's father Thomas Webber as one of the lives on the lease. This has a history dating from Robert Blundell's tenancy in the 1570s but no conclusive evidence of its location has been established. Was Laurel Cottage the former John Norman's? We can only say that it is a possibility.

We are on firm ground though with Thomas Case. Initially just a labourer, by 1851 he was describing himself as a laver manufacturer. This involved the production of various edible products from seaweed (see also *The Book of Barnstaple, Volume I*). This may have been collected at Blue Anchor, close to Pill Bridge, which spanned the Withycombe Brook close to its outflow into the Bristol Channel. The fields on either side of the bridge were a detached portion of Withycombe parish, called Pill or Peel Meadows, intended to give Withycombe residents some access to the sea's bounty. At the same time a Carhampton lady, Elizabeth Webber, was listed as having the same occupation. Surely she must have been a relation of Thomas' wife Nancy (by then deceased) – her mother, it is thought – and the two were working together, perhaps with him doing the gathering and her the preparation of the food. Hilary Binding wrote of Elizabeth Webber's business in her column in the *West Somerset Free Press*, mentioning that she may have been the lady of Carhampton who was recorded by the Revd William Thornton as being a regular supplier of laver to Fortnum & Mason!

Thomas died in 1858, having also taught at Sunday school in his latter years. After the death of wife Nancy he had remarried, taking as his partner Mary Cridland of Old Cleeve. Coincidentally blind William, his brother, had also married a Mary Cridland of Old Cleeve, but from a different family. Thomas and Mary had one son, Edwin, who continued to live with his mother at Laurel Cottage after his father's death until adulthood. Mary Case then lived there alone until her own passing in 1899.

It is believed that the family of Jim Gay and wife Elizabeth (Baker) took over the cottage at this time, moving down the road from their previous home nearby. Jim worked as a stockman for the Levershas at Court Place. The couple were still there in 1920, but Daniel Gould and his wife replaced them in the years following. Old Dan was remembered fondly by Henry Pearse, for if he heard the sound of Henry's wagon returning home at night, he would come out unbidden and see to it and the horse, allowing Henry to go on home to rest. Sadly Dan died after a few years in Lower Street, and when he was perceived to be failing Henry was sent for to have a few last words with the old chap. He found Dan sitting up in bed smoking a last pipe of tobacco. When he returned home Henry was less than happy: although not averse to anyone having a drop of cider, he was firmly opposed to smoking.

By 1938 Fred and Mary Jones were the occupants of Laurel Cottage, and Fred was still the tenant when the house was sold as part of the Luttrell estate in 1951. It was described as a little detached cottage, built of stone and cob, rendered over, and it still had its thatched roof.

Next to Laurel Cottage, and extending from the modern Reid House to the older building that stands close against the road opposite to the Memorial Hall, we have the site of Pritchard's or Hiles Farm, one of the more substantial of the village's ancient tenements. This can be gauged from the large manor rent of 26s.0d., which it paid annually to Withycombe Hadley, plus goose money at the highest rate of 8d. A considerable part of its structure survives, in the form of the abovementioned older building and the outbuildings behind it. Old maps indicate that there was originally a similar arrangement on the site of Reid House, so that the whole consisted of a range of buildings around a courtyard, with an entrance between the two buildings abutting the road.

The first tenant that we know of was Davye Thorne, who held the property in the years around 1580. It is possible that he was the same David Thorne, billman, who was named as one of the eight 'ablemen' of Withycombe in the 1569 muster. Peter Poole held it between 1604 and 1617, and after him it came to George Pritchard, who was described as a clerk. He held it 'in right of his wife Grace'. There is no evidence to suggest that the Pritchards ever lived in Withycombe.

Butcher John Hiles, called 'the Younger' of Withycombe, took on the property in 1657 on his own life and that of his wife Joane, when it was said to include 19 acres of land. However, the question of who the occupants were at that time is far from clear, as in the 1670s we find Alexander Prole named as the tenant and after him briefly Joane Prole. Then in 1680 Mary Hiles took a new lease on the tenement 'wherein Alexander Prole now dwelleth, now in the tenure of Joane Prole', on the lives of her mother Joane Hiles and her brother John.

Although Hiles Farm was in many ways a typical smallholding in that it contained house and

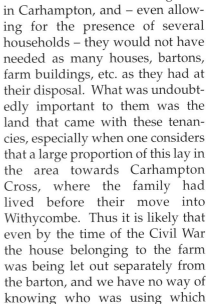

A young Rupert Leversha and Jim Gay, one of his farm-hands, in the road outside the farmyard at Court Place.

outbuildings around a courtyard, with gardens and orchard adjoining, one cannot avoid the impression that by the time the Hiles family became associated with it the farm was no longer being operated as a single, coherent whole. Members of the Hiles family were tenants of several small farms in the village and in Carhampton, and – even allowing for the presence of several households – they would not have needed as many houses, bartons, farm buildings, etc. as they had at their disposal. What was undoubtedly important to them was the land that came with these tenancies, especially when one considers that a large proportion of this lay in the area towards Carhampton Cross, where the family had lived before their move into Withycombe. Thus it is likely that even by the time of the Civil War the house belonging to the farm was being let out separately from the barton, and we have no way of knowing who was using which part at any one time.

We have an indication that this sort of usage was still occurring in 1753 when, following the death of John Hiles, almost his whole Withycombe estate was transferred to James Newton, described as a yeoman of the village. The lease includes, among a group of fields that were associated with the Lower Street farm, a barn and court 'all now in the occupation of William Oldman'. Yet the dwelling-house, garden and orchard were listed separately, being in the hands of Robert Oldman, who had died just a couple of months previously.

James Newton, yeoman, was followed by his son the Revd James Newton. He remained as the official tenant until 1790 at least. Then in 1795 there was a change, with Charles Hurford listed as paying land tax for 'Hilles'. By this time Hiles Farm was definitely no longer functioning as a tenement and so in 1820 it was amalgamated with Court Place Farm, the barton belonging to the former being close enough to be of practical use to the latter; but of course it was the associated land that was of most value to Court Place. A map was carefully drawn up to accompany the transaction, listing all of Court Place's and Hiles' fields. The latter included all of those closes that once belonged to that family's various properties, such as the Buckhill fields, Furze Close and a parcel of strip fields adjoining Withycombe Lane that were once a parcel of Withycombe Wyke, as well as those that must have belonged to the Lower Street tenement. Of the 41 acres of land mentioned it is not easy to find the 19 that were originally said to belong. Unusually, apart from Hiles Orchard immediately behind, none of the fields are in the vicinity of the farm itself.

As mentioned above it was around this time that part of the Hiles Farm Barton began to be used as the Withycombe Hadley pound, the secure enclosure for the detention of stray animals that all rural parishes had. The house on the site continued to be sublet as before but it is very difficult to name the tenants from the nineteenth century with any certainty. The census returns suggest that there was more than one family living on the site, with two sometimes sharing a dwelling, and perhaps another using a converted outbuilding in the early period. There would certainly have been room for more than one dwelling on the site, as indeed is the situation at the time of writing. From 1841 the main occupants seem to have been Thomas and Hannah Thorne. Thomas was from Brompton Regis, Hannah a Withycombe girl, and both lived to a good age, Hannah surviving until 1900. Following her death the house fell empty for a time, being listed as uninhabited in the census of the following year. However, somewhere nearby was another dwelling which housed another Case family throughout much of this same period. The patriarch of this branch was a John Case (born around 1785) who had married Fanny Pugsley of Cutcombe in 1811. His origins are unknown (he is believed not to

Among those digging a trench in Lower Street in the early 1930s are Clifford Burge, Jack Fifoel and Lionel Thresher. The house in the foreground belonged formerly to Hiles Farm, while Laurel Cottage with its tall chimney is further down the road.

have been the brother of Robert of Withycombe Farm, although of the same name and age) but the fact that he lived next door to the Cases of Laurel Cottage suggests that he may have belonged to that family. John was described as a gardener in 1841 and he was also Parish Clerk.

John Case's son of the same name married Mary Pullen in 1846 and they took over the house after father John's death two years later. They continued there until at least 1881 but thereafter there is no further sign of the dwelling.

During the twentieth century Fred and Cath Hawkins inhabited the Thornes' old house between the wars before moving to make way for Bill and Kit Griffiths. It is probably no coincidence that both Fred and Bill were Court Place workers, remembering that Hiles Farm now belonged to Court Place. We may surmise that Thomas Thorne, himself a farm labourer, had also obtained his tenancy via that route.

Next along Lower Street we come to a range of farm buildings, all of which present their backs to the highway. They are what remain of another ancient, comparatively valuable small farm, known as William Thorne's Tenement. Only the house associated with it is missing but this must originally have stood close by. This paid the highest manor rent of all of the Withycombe Hadley properties, £1.8s.4d. annually, plus 8d. goose money. Someone named William Thorne held it around 1580, in 1617 and again in 1655, although clearly this was more than one individual. The holding comprised 12 acres of land, including one and a half acres of meadow and a close called White's Orchard, and also two other fields (not part of the original farm) called Seven Acres and Footland. There was a field called Seven Acres, No.13 on the Tithe Map, to the north of the A39, which is probably the same one.

The last William Thorne died in 1681 and was succeeded by his widow, Jane. After her death in 1702 another widow, Joanna Thorne, became the new tenant. She had been Joanna Bedon before her Carhampton marriage to Robert Thorne in 1686.

Robert Thorne, the son of Robert and Joanna, formally leased the property in 1732, when it was similarly described as before, except that the overland field previously called Footland was now called Two Acres. However, neither Robert nor his mother worked the farm that they had inherited. Joanna was amerced at the Manor Court of 1737 for failing to pay her rent and for letting out the property without permission. A roster of those eligible to do the duty of tithingman drawn up two years later included the comment next to Robert Thorne's name: 'late Bartlett's in Water Street' (that being the older name of Lower Street). Whoever this Bartlett fellow was he left little trace of his brief time in Withycombe, except for lending his name to William Thorne's Tenement and to a field belonging to it, later known as Wood Close, next to Little Sandhill.

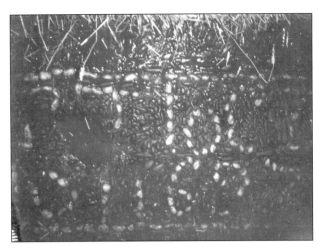

Some enigmatic writing – created by embedding white pebbles between darker stones – that was once to be seen on the floor of one of the farm buildings belonging to William Thorne's Tenement, which still stands opposite the entrance to Christopher's. Damage has obscured the message but what may be the date '1697' is apparent.

Another man with an interest in the property was yeoman John Farthing, of Nettlecombe. He had apparently surrendered a lease in 1732 in favour of Robert Thorne, and this he reclaimed in reversion ten years later following Robert's death. He held the tenancy for the next 30 years or so, the property being listed in 1778 as 'Thorn's late Farthing's'. It included a dwelling-house near a barn, stable, linhay, court and adjoining small garden. There was also an orchard and a close named 'Croft', which were the fields immediately behind the buildings, shown on the Tithe Map as No.84 Tithole's Orchard and No.83 Tithole's Croft. The map also shows that vehicles could gain access to the latter by turning off Lower Street and taking a track that led to what became Chilcott's wheelwright business and later Stevens' garage/workshop, then turning left to pass through the barton of Hoare's Tenement. This is a fairly good indication that the house originally associated with the farm was in that area, as the name 'croft' might suggest; and an estate map of 1820 shows a building in just such a position. Other fields listed were: 'a large garden and mead next to Court Place' (No.72, Tithole's Meadow, and No.74, a garden inset); 'ye 5 acre field under Beer Wood'; 'Down Close by ye hill Gate'; and the already mentioned Wood Close. It is strange that all of the fields near and belonging to William Thorne's Tenement had the name Tithole appended to them by 1840, as this was not the case in earlier times. The old house by the pound, belonging to Hiles Farm, also became linked with this name. It is a form of Tuttle/Tuthill and we have seen that that family had their original property on the other side of the road. However, they must have had some connection to the fields and the adjoining house in the

early years of the nineteenth century, by which time the Webbers had replaced them at their old family home. There is no official record of this though; by 1778 most of the property had been let to John Sully of the West Street farm that came to bear his name. The exception was the overland, which had been taken on by Thomas Escott of Sandhill.

From this point on the holding effectively ceased to exist as a unit, instead taking a similar path to Hiles Farm next door, with the fields becoming part of the Sullys' West Street business. No more is heard of the dwelling-house. The tiny farmyard in Lower Street has survived though, against the odds, proving useful not so many years ago as accommodation for several generations of pigs.

On the other side of Lower Street, beyond Tuttle's Cottage, we find ourselves within the manor of Withycombe Wyke, on what is likely to have been part of its demesne land. Here, on the site occupied by the Memorial Hall, was a house and garden known as Moore's, yet another property named after the family of Moore (alias Knowles). The house stood just across the brook, while a long narrow garden ran behind the ground occupied by Tuttle's, extending as far as Court Place. The lower part of this has since been taken into Lower Maunder's Orchard.

As with all Withycombe Wyke properties we know very little about it before 1700. We cannot even identify it for certain in the 1709 sale of that manor, but it may have been John Moore's cottage that was unsold on the day. Not long afterwards we find John Question of Gupworthy Farm paying rates, etc. for it, but this could possibly have been in his role of churchwarden, rather than in his own right. Certainly after John's death in 1734 Thomas Escott took over responsibility for the house, and a Thomas Escott also followed him as churchwarden, but we do not know if the two were the same, their being several Escott families in Withycombe – some wealthy, some artisans – at that time. As will be seen, both rich and (relatively) poor Escotts were connected with the property in the years that followed.

Despite the fact that Moore's was unsold and possibly not in great condition in 1709 it had obviously once been a substantial property as it was one of the 20 selected in the eighteenth century as eligible to provide a tithingman. Thomas Tuttle served in 1725 as a substitute for 'John Question for Moors'. By 1769 the property had been split into two parts, with the Church Rate of 3d. being paid as $1^1/_4$d. by George Escott and $1^3/_4$d. by Thomas Dyke Acland. George Escott was a son of Henry Escott of the family who lived in West Street and it is likely that he occupied the house. Had the house been divided into two parts? Although there appears to be little evidence to suggest that it included two dwellings in the years that followed the split, the building in its final years was remembered as 'two old cottages'.

LOWER STREET (COURT PLACE TO CHRISTOPHER'S)

George died the following year and his son Thomas, born in 1744, eventually came to inherit his father's part of the property. In 1790 it was Thomas Escott, labourer, who paid for his 'pt of Moors', while Mr Thomas Escott (of Sandhill Farm, the 'Mr' implying the status of gentleman) paid the remainder. Five years later the same two men were assessed for land tax on the property belonging to Sir Thomas Dyke Acland, in the same proportion as the Church Rate.

Thomas Escott the labourer married Sarah Smith in Carhampton in 1772 and raised his family in the Withycombe house, including another Thomas, who was to take over after his father's death in 1825. Young Thomas had married Jane Morish in the early years of the century, but the couple only seem to have had one son – John – and it was his family who filled the house with the sounds of small children in the 1830s and '40s. He had married Susanna Baker, beginning a connection to that family that was to continue at the old house throughout the rest of the century; for in 1846 James Baker of Watchet married Mary Escott and came to live at Moore's. Mary lived there for the rest of her life, continuing into widowhood in the company of son-in-law Jim Gay and his family. She died in 1894 and it was probably at this time that the Gays moved to the smaller Laurel Cottage nearby. The old house was approaching the end of its useful life and it appears to have been unoccupied in 1901. It was eventually demolished in the early 1920s, to be replaced by Withycombe's own Memorial Hall.

The First World War had taken its toll on the young men of the village. Most shocking was the loss of three of Sam Griffiths' sons, all killed while fighting on the Western Front, as were Edwin, a son of Bill Sully, and Edward, the son of John 'Noble' Davey. Frederick Howe was another casualty, dying in India after the war's end. Major Douglas Govan of the Fifth Gurkha Rifles, the vicar's son, also met his end during the fierce fighting of the summer of 1915.

The village felt the need to create something positive out of this terrible loss and the idea of erecting a community building in commemoration of the dead men was seized upon eagerly. At the time the only rooms available for general meetings, etc. were those belonging to the little village school, which were not really suitable or intended for such a purpose, so the need for a proper Village Hall was there; and so was the support from officialdom, as the government was encouraging projects of this type in order to provide work for returning servicemen. The third piece of the jigsaw was the generosity of Alexander Fownes Luttrell in presenting the property to the village free of charge. Nevertheless, £500 still had to be raised in order to fund the project and the familiar array of money-raising activities was organised to that end. The total was amassed within two to three years and village carpenter Jack Chilcott and his sons were given the task of erecting the new building.

The Memorial Hall was opened with a grand ceremony in September 1924, when practically the whole village attended to hear Alexander Luttrell himself formally open the building, with prayers and a few words from the Revd Govan. The vicar had played a large part in seeing the project through, no doubt partly because of his own personal loss; and it was decided that a replica of the War Memorial tablet in the church should be set up in the hall. Mr Luttrell exhorted the village to make sure that the hall was available for all – not just the men. Perhaps he had spotted the splendid billiards table that had been acquired for £50 from Chargot Lodge, Luxborough!

Following the opening ceremony a small fair was held in the building in order to raise further funds. In the evening there was a whist drive and dance, with Edward White's Dance Orchestra, to finish up the day's proceedings.

The hall was initially lit by two powerful oil lamps and it was not until October 1944, when the Minehead Electric Company ran a supply into the village via a pole situated next to the Memorial Hall, that electric lighting was installed. The hall has proved to be an invaluable resource to the village, no more so than during the Second World War. In true 'Dad's Army' style, Bob Gould used it to conduct Home Guard exercises, while it was the scene of regular morale-boosting dances, whist drives, etc., with the necessary precaution of blackout curtains, provided in 1943 by Mrs Burnett, Mrs Hall and Mrs Pearse. Close attention has always been paid to its upkeep and only recently it has undergone a major refit to ensure that it continues to benefit Withycombe for many years to come. It has certainly proved a fitting memorial to those brave young men who made the ultimate sacrifice in the early 1900s.

Above: *Short-mat bowls in the hall, 1999. Left to right: Maurice Pope (just visible), Mike Rutty, Anthony Shopland, Don Staight, Mike Jackson, Donald Parsons, Mike Burnett, June Harris, Myra Burnett.*

Above: *Erecting a wishing-well in 1993 are Donald Parsons, Derrick Fowler and (bending down) John Williams.*

Withycombe WI performing 'The Singing Maid' in 1964. Left to right: Mrs N. Stevens, Mrs Cridge, Miss Camplin-Coggan, Mrs B. Sherrin, Miss Chatwin, Miss Huntley, Mrs Caulfield, Mrs Watts, Mrs Davies, Mrs V. Scudamore, Mrs Tubes, Mrs Crossman, Mrs T. Davey.

Above: *Dinner at the Memorial Hall for the members of Withycombe Football Club, c.1950. Club president Rupert Leversha sits at the head of the table next to the Revd Camplin-Coggan.*

Right: *Withycombe WI performing 'Sanctuary', 1967. Left to right: Ivy Davies, Evelyn Camplin-Coggan, Marjorie Chatwin, Margaret Bird, Violet Scudamore, Bridget Roberts, Kathleen Ferris.*

In the Memorial Hall, 1933, for the Christmas party. Left to right, standing at back: Jack Maisey, Leonard Gould (Santa), Admiral Hope-Robertson, a young Scudamore (?), Ethel Scudamore, Rita Fry, Reg Young senr, Alan 'Shiner' Burnell; seventh row, seated at back: Effie Gould, ?, Polly Cridge, Gert Sully, Olive Spracklan, Mrs Hall, Vera Maisey, ?; sixth row: Lily Jones (or Annie Gould?), Mrs Coles, Mrs Eames, Mrs Lewis, Mrs Young; fifth row: Harold Sully, Kathleen Eames, ?, ?, Mrs Bindon holding Cyril, ? (holding Valentine Lewis), Alice Webber; fourth row: Bob Gould, George Hall, Joyce Griffiths, ?, Gordon Gould, ?, Clarence Winter (?), Arthur Davey, ?; third row: Patty Winter, ?, Barbara Sully, Betty Griffiths, Joan Hall, Charlie Cridge, ?, Beatrice Gould, Thelma Young, Joy Griffiths, Jack Gould, Dick Davey, ?; second row: Betty Davey, Hazel Coles, Violet Nicholas, Vivian Coles, Ruth Sully, Mildred Hall; front: June Nicholas, ?, ?, Margaret Lewis, Eileen Griffiths, Nancy Windsor, Lilian Cridge, Donald Young, Jack Eames, Roy Fry, Bob Willis; on ground: Gordon Fry, Clifford Case, Tony Young, Dennis Young, Dick Pearse, Reg Young junr.

The Memorial Hall adjoins a cluster of houses that were created in recent years in the barton belonging to Christopher's Farm, another small Withycombe Wyke property. The oldest records, dating from the seventeenth century, refer to it as Hedford's Tenement, linking it to the family of that name who had already lived in Withycombe for a century or so. Their main base had been at Lower Hill Farm, belonging to Withycombe Hadley, but they may have moved to the smaller property towards the end of their time in the parish.

During this period the farm consisted of house and farmyard with barn, outbuildings, etc., below which were two long orchards sandwiched between Withycombe Farm's Culver Close and Moore's long garden. In 1840 they were known as Higher and Lower Maunder's Orchards. All of the other fields associated with it were little strips, dotted all around the parish. This may be an indication that the farm had remained in a 'fossilised' state since medieval times; that while other farms gradually rearranged their holdings into a more convenient structure after the demise of the open-field system, Hedford's retained its allocation of field strips. If this was the case, it is a most unusual phenomenon, unique in Withycombe.

The Hedfords left the village after the Civil War, apparently moving to Rodhuish as a result of a marriage into the Uppington family who lived there, and in 1689 John Maunder leased the Lower Street Farm. The Manor Court of Withycombe Hadley immediately drew his attention to the state of disrepair of 'the pales adjoining Court Place Barton'. This was the fence at the bottom of the lower orchard.

Eight years later John Maunder leased Durland Head, formerly a tenement in Withycombe Lane (see Chapter Four), but by then probably just a field. This was later added to the farm.

John Maunder's family aspired to the class of gentleman farmer, more investors in property than hands-on farmers, with John eventually moving to Stogumber and his son John junr to Bicknoller, but there seems little doubt that the elder John did originally live and work on his farm, for a while at least. He christened a son, Roger, in Withycombe in 1675, and it may have been the same boy who was buried here four years later. He was also called to give evidence at the Manor Court of 1706, when aged 65, in the case concerning the water rights of the owners of Sandhill Farm; this would only have happened if Maunder had direct experience of the situation through having lived in the village.

John Maunder purchased the farm at the 1709 sale of Withycombe Wyke for £48 plus 1 guinea. This included Hedford's and Durland Head. He died in 1719 and was replaced as owner by his son of the same name. The heir definitely did not live in the village and would have let the farm to a tenant.

Hedford's Tenement was one of the properties obliged to provide a tithingman every 20 years or so

and it was listed in 1739 as 'John Manders for his estate in Water Street'. Not being a resident, Maunder was obliged to employ a substitute. The troublesome William Brewer did the job for him in 1740, while John Gold (Gould) was nominated for the year 1759.

In the 1770s John Maunder, who had by then moved to the family's home in Stogumber, sold off his Withycombe interests. One of his little strip fields – called Headford's Rap in 1708 and Maunder's or Lower Rap later – was situated close to Little Sandhill, an area of land that Thomas Escott of Sandhill was in the process of acquiring. He moved quickly to purchase the field and fortunately the document of release reveals the name of Maunder's undertenant at the time. He was Christopher Webber, who had probably had the farm at the time of his marriage to Joan Withycombe in 1769, when he was described as a husbandman. It is likely that he held the entire farm, the fact that he was named as tithingman in 1777 (clearly for the farm's turn) being further evidence of this. Christopher Webber's origins are unknown at the time of writing, but there were several Webber families in the village prior to his appearance, notably a Samuel Webber who was a regular juror at the Manor Court. Christopher and Joan subsequently raised a large family in the village, and probably kept the farm until 1817, the year of Christopher's death. He was surely the man who gave his name to 'Christopher's Farm' as it came to be called.

This period was probably the last in which the farm was used in its ancient state, that is to say, with house, barton and the original fields all together. When it was next transferred, it followed the tendency of other small farms in that the house was let out as a cottage and the fields absorbed into a larger property. The barton was transferred with the fields, but would one day revert to independent usage.

John Maunder had sold the farm to Andrew Gill, whose name appeared 'for late Maunders' on a list of ratepayers in 1790, but inserted after the entry were the names 'J & S Hobbs', the new tenants. A tithing office list of the 1780s also has 'Sam Hobs for Manders Estate'. John and Samuel Hobbs had arrived in the village and taken on the tenancy of Price's Farm just across the road from Maunder's, and had added the latter's lands to their own.

The location of the dwelling associated with Hedford's Tenement is revealed by the 1840 Tithe Map, where Robert Gill was listed as the owner of two properties: the farm itself, in the tenancy of John and Samuel Hobbs; and a house and garden adjoining the barton to the south, with tenant John Dent. Throughout the twentieth century the latter was simply a garden belonging to Christopher's Farm but at the lower end of it, close to the main entrance to Withycombe Farm, Hedford's farmhouse once stood. The Dent family may have taken the tenancy of the old house immediately after Christopher Webber's departure. Widow Mary Dent was certainly living there in 1830, her husband John having died many years earlier. Her son John, a stonemason, and his wife Elizabeth (Stephens) followed, and they lived there for the rest of their lives. After John's death in 1875 Betsy lived there alone, with occasional help from the parish. She was a stalwart of the little Bible Christian chapel in Mill Street and as such the visiting preacher would decamp to her little cottage for tea after the service. We have been left a legacy in the form of an account of Betsy Dent and her little cottage in *The Romance of a Country Circuit* by Lewis Court (1921), who was one of these preachers. He tells the story of Betsy and her devotion, and recounts how her only son Michael – who had been an apprentice to shoemaker Tom Poole – ran off to America as a lad and after 30 years away was contacted by a friend, and subsequently renewed contact with his aged mother to brighten her final years; but of even more interest is his description of the now vanished cottage. It was of the typical Somerset type, with cob walls, latticed windows and thatched roof – all in bad repair – with gardens at front and back. Roses, ivy and other plants festooned its walls.

Inside could be found old oak beams and crumbling plaster. Downstairs there was a large living-room with whitewashed walls and a kitchen, reached by a long passage leading from the front door, while up some rickety stairs was a big bedroom containing an ancient bed.

Betsy died in 1894 and was buried in the churchyard 'by the shadow of the old grey tower' and the 'poor, thatched tenement' followed her by quickly crumbling into the earth, leaving no trace of its existence behind.

However, the farm was not quite finished yet. Samuel Hobbs (the second of that name to hold the property) continued to work his farm, including that part of it which had been Hedford's, into the 1860s, still being listed as a farmer in *Kelly's Directory* of 1866. At this time, John Pearse was establishing himself as the village's road contractor, and it is thought that he initially took on the farmyard principally as a convenient base for this operation. Stabling for the necessary horses and a shed for the wagon would have been a minimum requirement. John, together with son Henry, continued to do this job into the 1880s at least, with Henry continuing to do it part-time long afterwards. Henry's son Dick Pearse

Right: *Posing on the new seat are Mrs Cridge, Mrs Carter (of Carhampton) and Mrs Pearse.*

Below: *In 1965 the WI presented the village with a new seat to replace another given nine years earlier. President Margaret Bird is making the presentation to Arthur Case, Chairman of the Parish Council. Those standing behind the wall are in the garden belonging to Christopher's Farm, where the Dents' cottage once stood.*

remembers that a 'stone depot' was located by the side of the road exactly opposite the entrance to Christopher's Farm. These were places where loads of stone would be delivered to be cracked into small enough pieces to be used when needed on the roads, and another was sited at the northern end of Withycombe Wood, by the main road. Dick remembers an old, slightly crippled chap known as 'Chumpy' Wedlake, who used to sit all day at the stone depot opposite Christopher's entrance, breaking rocks. Earlier Jimmy Moore had been a regular stone-cracker. However, with the farmyard came the adjoining Maunder's Orchards at least, and the opportunity for John to expand into the business of farming was too good to pass up. He began to lease land, including Cox's Close, Keynham Meadow (in the detached part of the parish in Bilbrook) and Clayhills. In early 1882, after injuring a leg by overturning a cartload of straw on the bridge leading from the farm on to Lower Street, John (forced to rest and so given the job of writing to his daughters away in London) penned these lines:

... it has been the Best year last we have had since we had the ground we had the Best lot of hay we ever had in one year we sold 7 tuns From Coxesclose at £5.5s. per tun...

John had also sold a quantity of apples and walnuts, the latter selling 'on that tree up by the old stable' for 4d. a hundred. Judging by the profit made on them he must have sold some 12,600 nuts! He also produced a dozen hogsheads of cider in that year. Potatoes were plentiful, but consequently their price was low.

At some time three fields near Withycombe Lane were added (Broom Close, Causeway Close and Little Buss) which had been leased together as a parcel of fields belonging to Withycombe Wyke since at least 1670, when they were held by Joan Hiles; as were the glebe fields – Oakey and the orchard below; and a piece of land comprising orchard, garden and fowl house at Top Cross – what remained of ancient Milton's Tenement. Thus the farm was reborn and was to enjoy a final century of existence under the Pearses. Son Henry succeeded John, and towards the end of his time (when he feared his sons would be too young to manage the farm after his death) the fields at Bilbrook and in Withycombe Lane were sold off. Yet the nucleus of the farm remained; and after the disappearance of Betsy Dent's ancient cottage that piece of ground also regained its association with the farm, as a garden with a couple of pigsties near the old barn.

The barn had clearly stood for a great many centuries. The barn door had a massive iron key, which was put down the neck of any child (the author included) who was suffering from a nosebleed, allegedly an infallible cure! As a child, the author was puzzled by the presence of another,

equally large door at the back of the barn, which opened only on to a hedge or fence, the other side of which was Culver Close, belonging to Withycombe Farm. In the central portion of the barn, between the two doors, was a raised wooden floor, with the gaps between the boards plugged by iron strips. This was once a threshing floor, and when this operation was being performed both doors were opened wide so that a through draught would blow the chaff away. There was also a stable of ancient vintage. When it was finally demolished to make way for the houses now standing on the site the builders removed no less than three floors, laid one on top of the other. A stone floor lay beneath the modern concrete one, and a brick floor below that.

Henry Pearse died in the 1930s, the farm being left in the hands of his widow Maud and their several sons. The others being called away to the Armed Forces at the commencement of the Second World War, the youngest son, Dick, was left to take care of the farm. This he ably did right up until his retirement in the mid-1980s and beyond, for even though Christopher's Farm has since been turned into a close containing several houses, he still keeps Maunder's Orchards and the glebe fields: at the start of the new millennium he single-handedly made a new hedge all around Oakey. He recalls a previous occasion when it was done. It was the 1920s and he was the small boy sent to deliver flagons of cider to the man hired to do the job – Walter Gulliver, a chap with a memorably large gold ring through his ear.

At some time during the nineteenth century the Gill family must have sold the farm to the Luttrells, because at the 1951 sale of much of their Dunster estate, the farm (called 'a valuable small holding') was one of the sale items. It was said to consist of a range of stone, brick and timber buildings with slated or iron roofs, including: barn, three-stall stable, garage, cow house (7), implement shed, stone shed and yard with water trough. Mrs Pearse (Henry's widow, who lived on into the 1960s) was named as the tenant and she was successful in purchasing the freehold.

Gathering in the hay on Oakey, c.1911. Henry Pearse is on the cart, his second wife Maud is on the right.

Above: *Farmer Dick Pearse, displaying a prize-winning cart-horse in full show array.*

Left: *Freda Pearse, with niece Janice and friend, feeding the fowls in Maunder's Orchard in 1941.*

Below left: *Pictured just before Christopher's Farm was converted to residential use, this picture shows the cow shed, trap-house, stables, cart linhay and fowl-houses.*

Below right: *The old barn belonging to Christopher's Farm, the sliding door a modern replacement for the traditional type. This was a home for many generations of farm cats, whose job it was to keep rats and mice at bay.*

Ten

Lower Street (Withycombe Farm to Top Cross)

Once past William Thorne's and Hedford's Tenements the narrow street opens out to create a space that is (in the absence of the traditional village green) the heart of the village. This luxury of space is the result of the proximity of the main entrance to Withycombe Farm, the predominant manorial property in the village for at least 1,000 years, during which time a generous access-way would have been carefully maintained. Originally a grand manor-house would have stood on or near the site of the current farmhouse, with an equally grand entrance to match. The manor-house was replaced by a succession of more practical dwelling-houses as tenant farmers came to replace the lords and ladies of Withycombe – a process that was probably well underway by the fourteenth century. If the stone effigies in the village church are indeed of Lucy de Meriet and her husband Thomas of Timworth, then these are likely to have been the last of the manorial proprietors to have had even a possible connection with the house. By the time Savage penned his 1830 history of the area there was no memory of Withycombe Farm ever having been a manorial site.

A procession of sheep wends its way from Withycombe Hill to the haven of Withycombe Farm via Lower Street, after the unusually heavy snowfalls of March 1978.

Sadly our knowledge of the history of this important farm is somewhat thin as it became the manor-house of Withycombe Wyke after the 1238 division, the early records of which have apparently not survived.

We know the history of the owners of the manor, but that tells us little or nothing about the history of the farm. Who were those first tenant farmers? As with tenants of other manorial demesne farms, only the more prosperous or those of respectable lineage would have been considered. Quite possibly they came from England's old Saxon stock, from the generations that had farmed in the area before the coming of the Normans, for they had the expertise.

We cannot know for certain who they were but it is possible to hazard a guess.

There is a family that lived in the general area of Withycombe in later centuries who were successful and relatively wealthy gentleman farmers for the most part. They could often be found farming important properties such as Eastbury and Marshwood in Carhampton, some of which had originally been small manor-houses. They bore the name that linked them to a certain English place: Withycombe.

It is thought that a family would not have acquired that surname simply by living in the parish, as this would fail to distinguish them from every other resident. Instead, perhaps, it signified – especially to the feudal overlords of Dunster Castle, who were the people making the early written records referring to their tenants – the occupiers of the demesne farm of Withycombe. While other tenants were distinguished according to their location within the village, such as William Boghdone (Bowden) and Thomas Uppehulle (up hill), the name of the manor alone would suffice for the most important of them all.

The Withycombes would certainly have been the class of family to be given the tenancy of the farm during and after the medieval period, but we lack the concrete facts to be certain. We can only say, as with Court Place Farm, that the tenants would have come from the wealthier families, such as the Withycombes, Chesters, Escotts, etc.

Even when we investigate the records of the sale of the manor in 1709 there is little information to be found concerning its largest asset, Withycombe Farm. It seems that its details were so well known that it was not necessary to say much about it! (This was also the case with Withycombe Hadley, where Court Place was often omitted from its records.) In the sale documents Withycombe Farm was referred

125

A splendid picture of Withycombe Farm's threshing machine at work. 'Bowler' Nicholas operates the traction engine. Expensive equipment like this was not only used on the farm itself, but was taken around the district for use elsewhere, under contract.

The children of Edgar Case looking very smart, early 1920s.
They are (left to right) *Tom, Pat, Mary, Arthur, Herbert, John and Margaret.*

The village with Withycombe Farmhouse on the right. One car is stopped at the foot of the church path, waiting to take on fuel at the petrol pumps.

to simply as 'the farme' and it was purchased, together with Question's Tenement (Gupworthy Farm), by Madam Whitlocke for a total of £1,850. This was a considerable sum, especially when one considers that the next highest amount was £520, paid for Combe Farm and Bowden together.

The Whitlocks were gentleman farmers from Old Cleeve and investors in property. There is no evidence to suggest that they ever lived in Withycombe. Were they backing John Question perhaps, as with the Gupworthy purchase? They still owned the farm in 1718, paying the Church Rate of 4s.3d. for it, but it had been sold by 1769 when this payment was made by Sir Thomas Dyke Acland and the property was named as Withycombe Farm. Unfortunately we have no clues as to the occupant of the farm at this time.

Then in 1795, when an assessment was made for land tax, the same owner was named for what was simply called 'Farm', but this time the occupier was named – as one Mr Escott. This just adds another layer to the problem, however: he was in fact the occupant of Sandhill Farm and could hardly have lived in two places at once so we must assume that he had an undertenant or perhaps a bailiff at Withycombe Farm. Richard Locke, in his supplement to Collinson's 1791 history, wrote that Withycombe 'came to the Escott family' – although, like many others, he may have mistakenly assumed that Sandhill was the seat of the manor of Withycombe.

The farm remained in the hands of the Escotts until the last of them, Hugh, departed the parish in the early 1820s. From 1823 it was in the hands of William Giles, and he was named as the occupant again in 1830 when the rateable value of the property was set at £123.14s.7d., just a few shillings less

than Court Place Farm. When Savage published his history in that year William Giles did not subscribe, but Mr James Giles of Vellow Farm, Stogumber, did. This may be significant when we consider that a James Giles replaced William at Withycombe Farm shortly after this.

James was the occupant in 1840, with Thomas Dyke Acland the owner. The layout of its fields then does not show a great amount of coherence, indicating that many changes had taken place over the centuries. This is apparent in various recognisable acquisitions, such as William Thorne's old Seven Acres field and the Sully family's Woodwall – now called Wallin – Meadow. Some fields close to the farm, such as Culver Close, were clearly originally demesne fields; and there is a significant group based around and including Great Wood Close, the half of Withycombe Wood that seems to have been used for coppicing in ancient times. Just as the surviving half was associated with the demesne farm of Withycombe Hadley, was this originally for the use of the superior manor of Withycombe Wyke?

James Giles and his wife Sarah definitely lived on the farm, as the first census returns show. James was born at Selworthy and Sarah at Stogumber, a daughter of the Allen family there. No children are apparent during their time in the village but they seem to have had a niece named Fanny Giles living with them for much of the time. The farm was said to comprise some 110 acres, requiring the services of six to eight farm workers. As noted previously, James was a staunch supporter of the Bible Christian chapel in Mill Street and he died in 1866.

His widow Sarah remained at the property in 1871, described as a retired farmer, with niece Fanny

Arthur Case and stockman Jack Badcock, at the Christmas Fatstock Show.

Top left: Robert Case (standing, left) features in this formal group portrait, probably taken in the 1870s. The other man is Mr Strong of Carhampton, whose daughter married Robert's son Herbert Case, while Laura Case (later Watts) stands between them. One of the three seated ladies is surely Robert's wife Lydia (née Ridler).

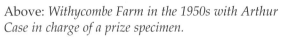
Above: Withycombe Farm in the 1950s with Arthur Case in charge of a prize specimen.

Right: Edgar Case entertaining the children around the time of the First World War.

as her housekeeper. The farm was being run by a bailiff, Henry John Thorne, and one of the two visitors there at the time was William Sleeman, a Bible Christian minister from Cornwall, so Sarah was keeping up her support for the chapel. She left the farm shortly after this; her body was brought back to Withycombe from Alcombe for burial in 1894. The man who took over from her was Robert Case who moved down from Sully's Farm nearby, effectively amalgamating the two properties into one.

Robert Case's father was John Case, blacksmith of Rodhuish, and it is thought that the James Case who built the new smithy in West Street around 1800 was Robert's uncle. However, the family's genealogy is relatively complex so this is not absolutely certain. Just about all of the men in that branch of the family – who were descended from John Case and Joan Oatway, married in Withycombe in 1751 – were originally blacksmiths, with several branching out as farmers in the nineteenth century. Of these Robert was by far the most successful, as his acquisition of Withycombe Farm shows.

He married the long-lived Lydia Ridler, daughter of the village miller, and the couple raised six boys and a girl on the farm. Robert was friendly with John Strong of Eastern Farm and Charles Withycombe of Townsend Farm, both in Carhampton, and several of his children married into those families. Son Herbert Ridler Case married Kate Strong before going on to farm at Higher Rodhuish, while son Edward Robert and daughter Laura Emma married Eliza Jane and John Watts respectively (thought to be stepchildren of Charles Withycombe). However, it was the youngest son, Edgar Frederick, who inherited Withycombe Farm after Robert's death in 1902.

Edgar, with his fashionable Edwardian moustache, is remembered by many of the older villagers, as he ran the farm and played a leading part in Withycombe life until his death towards the end of the Second World War. With his wife Florence Mary (née Babbage) he also raised seven children, of which one daughter still lives nearby. Their son Arthur Case took on the farm in 1945. Since his death in 1982 his widow Nancy has continued to play a leading role in the organised life of the village (she is one of the churchwardens at the time of writing), while son Anthony takes care of the farm.

As with Court Place, Withycombe Farm was a major employer of labour in the village, especially before mechanisation became prevalent, and it too had its own set of workers. We can probably detect the influence of Robert Case's farming beginnings at Sully's Farm in West Street in the fact that many of Edgar's workers lived in that area. 'Noble' Davey of Scout Cottage was one such, as were the Chapmans who followed after him. It is worth noting that it was not just the men but the women too: when hands were called for to gather in vegetables from the fields – such as the annual crop of 'cattle cabbages' – it was

the ladies living in the cottages around the old Sully property who regularly did the job. William 'Bowler' Nicholas, who made his home on the Causey after moving to the village from Bilbrook, was another Withycombe Farm regular, working there for 55 years. He successfully made the transition into the industrial age, mastering the art of operating the steam-powered traction engine.

Edgar Case embraced this relatively new technology and purchased the necessary machinery, not just for use on his own farm but also for contract work in the surrounding area. Many photographs of traction engines and threshing machines taken in the West Somerset area in the early decades of the twentieth century show Withycombe Farm machinery in action, usually with Bowler Nicholas at the engine's controls.

At least two of Bowler's boys followed in their father's footsteps. Harry and Fred Nicholas started working at Withycombe Farm from their thirteenth birthdays for 6s.0d. per week and they too worked there all their lives. Both drove the traction engines like their father, with Fred (the elder of the two) taking the threshing tackle out to Porlock to do contract work, while Harry worked closer to home. Later Harry drove one of the steamrollers, which had been contracted out to local councils for road surfacing work, rolling the first hard-surfaced roads in the area. The farm had seven of these machines, providing employment for other workers, such as Jack Cridland.

Only one more property is to be found on the west side of Lower Street, tucked between Withycombe Farm and the churchyard. An old house used to stand here, on or close to the site of the present one, but little is known about it before the nineteenth century, when it was Joanna Webber's Cottage. Judging by its location alone it must have belonged to the manor of Withycombe Wyke but it cannot be positively identified among the 1709 sale items.

The property is first identifiable in 1795, when it was almost certainly a house owned and occupied by John 'Hobs'. As we have seen, the brothers Samuel and John Hobbs had arrived in the parish a few years earlier and purchased or leased several properties, most of which were grouped together in Lower Street close to Withycombe Farm. This was another of these. The 1840 Tithe Map confirms the owner of the property, a house and garden (No.120), as John Hobbs, with the occupier named as widow Jane Hobbs. Jane was the widow of butcher William Hobbs, who was John's brother.

However, in the following year's census it was John Hobbs' widow Sarah who was living in the house. Sarah was described as a shopkeeper, but whether the shop was on the premises or nearby is not known. Several of John and Sarah's sons, including shoemaker Frederick and masons Richard and Ephraim, were living with their mother.

This photograph, taken in the early years of the twentieth century (Halswell, which replaced The King's Arms after it burned down in 1901, is just visible), shows the Pearses' cottage with the end of Myrtle Cottage to its right. Note the cart-sized entrance which is no longer there. Joanna Webber's cottage is visible on the right of the picture in front of the church, although it was not to survive much beyond this time.

Left: *The centre of the village during the 1930s, showing the house originally called 'Blalowen' and Withycombe Farmhouse. The church looks in need of limewashing – a regular chore throughout the centuries.*

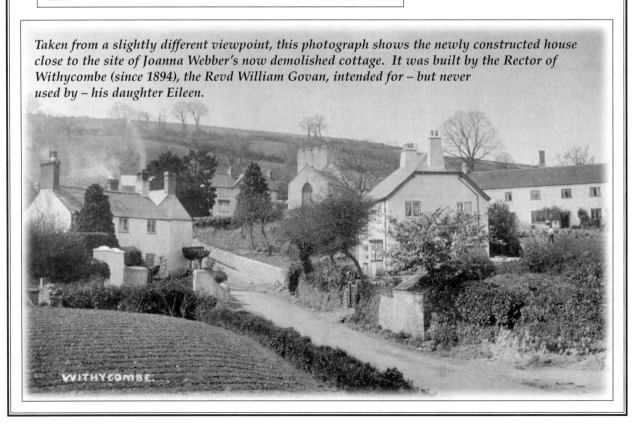

Taken from a slightly different viewpoint, this photograph shows the newly constructed house close to the site of Joanna Webber's now demolished cottage. It was built by the Rector of Withycombe (since 1894), the Revd William Govan, intended for – but never used by – his daughter Eileen.

Withycombe Farm's threshing team, including members of the Nicholas family, doing contract work on the Brendon Hills.

Below: *Joanna Webber, seen here by the entrance to The King's Arms or its replacement, Halswell.*

Left: *Admiral and Mrs Hope-Robertson, who lived in the house built by Rector William Govan and originally named 'Blalowen', pictured in the 1920s.*

Shopkeeper Sarah was still there in 1851 with son Robert (another mason) and her sister Ann Blake, who was described as a lodger. Both Sarah and Ann were daughters of Thomas and Joan Sully; and it appears to have been the friendship and familial ties between the Sully and Hobbs families that brought the latter to Withycombe in the first place. Sarah died in 1855 and the house passed to son Richard, who by then was married with a family of his own. They soon moved to West Street though, to run their own little shop there. Perhaps Richard was drawing on the experience gained while helping his mother in her shop when he decided to start such a venture himself.

By 1871 the house was in the hands of William and Joanna Webber, recently arrived from Old Cleeve. That parish had been William's home. Joanna was the daughter of Withycombe's William and Joanna Birth, christened in 1823. A widow by 1891, Joanna lived to a considerable age in the house, which was in a poor state of repair, so that eventually the old lady was forced to use a ladder in order to go upstairs to bed. Her son James lived with her but it was another son (probably Joseph, who in 1881 was a soldier in the 32nd Regiment of Light Infantry stationed at Aldershot) who used to be remembered by some Withycombe residents. He is said to have served in one of the Highland Regiments and caused some consternation among the village children when he appeared in the village wearing his kilt. They could not decide if he was a man or a woman!

Joanna was a source of interest to many of the village children at the turn of the century, in large part because her garden overlooked the school. George Maidment recalled that they directed some doggerel verse at her that went something like:

O' Slippy Joanna is picking her geese,
Selling the feathers a penny a piece.

Another boy, Tom Burnett, watched the old lady one day as she was digging a hole at the foot of an apple tree. He convinced himself that she was burying some treasure, and many years later, when he had occasion to be digging in the garden, he would watch every spadeful of earth for any sign of it. The rumours of Joanna's secret wealth were not confined to the children alone; she was rarely seen to spend money and so (it was reasoned) she must have had a big pile of it hidden away.

Joanna was probably fond of the children and glad of the attention they paid to her, if the tales of Withycombe's tradition of Begging Day are anything to go by. On 21 December the children would make a tour of the village, asking for Christmas presents. The better-off farmers, such as Robert Case and John Oatway, would give the children a basket of apples; but many would chase them off with a broom. However, Joanna would give them a basin of cold potatoes, which they consumed on the spot.

Both Joanna and son died in the early years of the twentieth century, with James being buried at Withycombe while his mother was presumably put to rest with her husband at Old Cleeve. When William had made that final journey himself some years earlier Henry Pearse had driven widow and son to the funeral. They reached the churchyard just as the bearers were preparing to unload the coffin. 'Quick boy,' she said to James. 'Jump down and give 'em a hand with Father!'

As with another of Withycombe's fine old ladies, near neighbour Betsy Dent, the passing of Joanna

Webber coincided with the end of her old cottage. It was demolished by two local workmen, who afterwards promptly set themselves up as farmers, one at Rodhuish, the other at Washford. The story quickly went around that the pair had found Joanna's secret hoard! A replacement for the house was built on the site by the rector, the Revd Govan, as a future home for his daughter Eileen. It was named Blalowen, clearly a name of some significance to the Govans as they also gave it to their house in Carhampton.

Eileen Dawson, as she became, never lived at the new house. Its first resident may have been one John Adair, who was listed at that address in 1914; then two Greek ladies named Perdikedes replaced him, being there in the early 1920s, followed in 1923 by a naval man, Lt-Commander Frank Crowther. By 1927 retired Admiral Charles Hope-Robertson and his wife had taken up residence and it is thought that they continued there until Bill Stevens brought his family across the road from the little house familiarly known as 'The Teapot' some time in the 1930s. It remained in the Stevens family for many decades, with son David taking over in the 1960s. Bill Stevens kept a little shop on the property, close to the Withycombe Farm entrance, which had previously been the village 'gas house'; while beside the road close to the church path a shelter was erected for a pair of petrol pumps.

On the road opposite Withycombe Farm is an area containing several structures: the building consisting of two dwellings, now called 'Squirrels'; the garage/workshop that was Albert (Jack) Chilcott's coachworks and which became Stevens' garage; and another dwelling that was built by Jack's son Charles Chilcott in the twentieth century. Most of this area used to be part of another of Withycombe's small farms, long known as Hoare's Tenement.

This was the third in a row of Withycombe Hadley's more substantial small farms, all of which paid goose money at the highest rate of 8d. However, Hoare's Tenement was not as valuable a property as the other two, only paying a manor rent of 11s.4d., possibly indicating that it did not include any meadowland. It has not been positively identified before the period 1604–17, at which time it was in the hands of Alexander Withey (alias Wheddon). His widow is known to have occupied the premises after him.

We know that by 1639 the Hoare family had moved in because the Glebe Terrier of that year describes its field called Oakey as adjoining a close 'called Rackclose being pte of the tenement of Elizabeth Hoore'. Rack Close is a large field running from the rear of the buildings mentioned above all the way up the hill to Great Wood Close, and it is known to have belonged to Hoare's Tenement.

Elizabeth's son John had taken over by 1655 and he continued until 1688, when he died and was buried in Withycombe. His widow Mary was presented to the Manor Court as the new tenant in the following year. A lease of 1715 transferred the

property to Mary's son John Hoare, yeoman, although mention of undertenants might indicate that others were actually working the farm. This lease strangely refers to Hoare's Tenement as being in Withycombe Wyke, which it certainly was not; and this error was then repeated in many later documents. This may have come about because the occupants of Hoare's Tenement had acquired the Withycombe Wyke cottage on the other side of the road, and may have chosen to live in it, causing the confusion.

When John Hoare died in 1754 the farm passed from the family into the hands of Withycombe blacksmith John Price, via a lease on his own life and that of wife Jane and son Robert. Being no farmer himself, he immediately sublet it to undertenant Robert Grabham, yeoman. Price remained the official tenant, however, paying such dues as the Church Rate (8d.) for what was now referred to as Price's Farm.

Grabham died in 1765 but the Prices remained in nominal charge at least until 1785, the year of John's death. This was the point at which the Hobbs family, in the persons of John and Samuel, arrived in the parish and took over Hoare's as their main base. At that time it was said to comprise nearly 24 acres of land, which must have included Rack Close and Home Orchard close by. However, other fields linked with it cannot be identified with complete certainty because those originally associated with Milton's Tenement were amalgamated with them under the Hobbs' stewardship.

At this point we will shift attention slightly from the farm to the semi-detached pair of houses that still stand on the site, which were definitely the homes and farmhouses of John and Samuel Hobbs and so can be regarded as belonging to Hoare's Tenement thereafter. However, it must be said that there is no absolute proof that this was the case in earlier times. The structure of this pair of dwellings is so unusual – the two parts joined at right-angles – and yet so appropriate for the Hobbs brothers that one suspects that the building may have been erected for them. Some dating evidence would be useful in order to determine the facts here.

In 1830 Hobbs' Farm, as it was now being called, was valued at £22.0s.8d. The occupants were again John and Samuel Hobbs, sons and heirs of the earlier two of the same names. The two were named again on the Tithe Award of 1840 for No.85, a house and garden, and No.86, a house, barton and garden. The former appears to have been the house facing on to Lower Street, together with the garden to the north of it; while the latter included the adjoining house as well as farm buildings in the area of the present garage/workshop. The following year's census lists the two men, both described as farmers, and their families living in what must be these two adjoining properties.

Farmer Samuel continued to live in his house until his death as an old man of 81 in 1868, with his widow Ann surviving for a further three years, but, following the death of John and his wife Mary in the 1840s, it looks like the family of Samuel's nephew John, a mason, moved into the other. He may have been joined there in 1861 by Samuel's son Robert, a butcher. There were certainly three families living in the two houses by 1871, when those of mason John and butcher Robert were joined by that of one Daniel Hurford.

Conditions were less cramped after John's death in 1876, so only Daniel Hurford and Robert Hobbs were to be found in residence in 1881, although lodging with Robert were two school teachers: Elizabeth Mathews, a 17-year-old pupil-teacher, and Margaret Tomlinson, 22, a schoolmistress from Yorkshire.

It is likely that Dan Hurford and Robert Hobbs (who had become Parish Clerk) were still there in 1891, although Robert was to die later in that year. Alfred Stevens from Morebath in Devon, who had arrived in the parish a few years earlier, may have moved in soon after Robert's death; certaiknly the house closest to Lower Street became his family home around this time. He was listed there in 1901 with wife Mary Ann and children Albert, Frank, Alice, Arthur and Alfred. The house behind was unoccupied, Daniel Hurford having passed on in February of that year.

The year 1901 also saw the destruction of The King's Arms, an event which made Jack Chilcott homeless and indirectly led to him coming to live in Hurford's house and setting up his wheelwrighting business and coachworks nearby. His family was there in 1920, while in the other house were Lydia Stevens and her children. She had been married to Frank Stevens before his early death two years previously. Among their children was Bill Stevens, mentioned above in connection with the nearby house known as Blalowen.

For much of the time that the Stevens family lived in the house (when it was called first Vine Cottage and later Ivy Cottage because of the creepers which covered its walls) it included a shop. Alfred's wife Mary Ann was listed as a shopkeeper in trade directories between 1897 and 1910, the year of her death; and after Frank's widow Lydia married Charles Gould those two carried on a similar business, later running it in association with Bill Stevens' own shop just across the road. Then after Charles and Lydia many will remember Bill's son Derek and his wife Maureen keeping the shop for many years.

Both this and the adjoining house were in the ownership of the Luttrell estate by 1951, when they featured in the grand sale. At that time Charles Gould was named as tenant of 'The Village Shop', which was described as 'an attractive old Cottage built of stone and cob', while Frank Burt had the other (having replaced Charles Chilcott after the latter had built his new house nearby). Both had a pigsty although neither had running hot water – the usual state of affairs in old cottages around this time. Some years later, when Frank Burt's daughter Joan lived in the back house, the author can recall her filling a tin bath in front of the kitchen range for her protesting son, who would much rather have been going out to play! Frank's widow, by that time a very old lady, was also still around and being cared for by Joan, who, between the young and the old, certainly had her hands full.

The extended Pearse family outside their Lower Street cottage in the late 1920s. Phyl and Ralph are on the left, Dick is on the right. Also there are mother Maud and Aunt Lizzie, as well as Kit and several young Moules.

Beyond Hoare's Tenement and its associated buildings, we pass from Withycombe Hadley territory to glebe land, and the first property we come to is Alderman's Cottage, later known as Rose Cottage (from the yellow *Rosa banksiae* that still grows in its front garden) and now as Christopher's Cottage. It is unusual and possibly unique in Withycombe in that no manor is ever mentioned in leases that contain references to it; and it appears to have been exempt from many taxes (such as Church Rates) until the nineteenth century.

All leases refer to the cottage as 'heretofore in the possession of [blank] Alderman', which is likely to have been Amos Alderman, who arrived in the parish and married Margery Knowles (alias Moore) in 1699. This date is consistent with the apparent age of the building and, because we know that the bride's family was responsible for much property development in the village at this time, we can speculate that it was they who brought Alderman to the cottage. The Aldermans raised a family there in the ensuing decade and then Margery must have died, because Amos married Mary Elliott in Carhampton in 1716. Amos was buried in Withycombe in 1735, his widow some years later.

George Davey was the next tenant, although his identity is something of a mystery. It is quite likely that he did not live there himself, perhaps taking the tenancy after the death of Amos and allowing Mary to continue as his undertenant throughout her widowhood. This seems probable because Mary's death in 1753 meshes with the marriage two years later of the next tenant, William Burge, to Joan Davey. The Burges settled down to raise their own family in the cottage and may have lived there until their deaths at the turn of the century.

Left: *Albert Chilcott's coachworks in Lower Street, near the 'new' entrance to the Rectory. The inexorable rise of the motor car saw the eventual replacement of this business by Stevens' garage/workshop.*

Below: *Frank Stevens (carter for Henry Pearse) with the horse and cart that took second prize at Minehead Horse Parade in May 1908.*

Below: *Ivy Cottage in Lower Street, photographed on 24 May 1931.*

Left: *Charlie Gould in gypsy costume, complete with barrel organ. This was Charlie's party piece.*

Below left: *Now called 'Squirrels', this was once Ivy Cottage and before that Vine Cottage, named from the foliage that covered its walls. The two cottages here were home to Samuel and John Hobbs after they came to Withycombe to farm in the late-eighteenth century.*

Below: *Lydia Gould outside her house in Lower Street, with Barbara Sully, who assisted in the shop.*

Right: *This is Charlie Gould's barrel organ, but the event and the people involved remain as yet unidentified.*

Below: *Some members of the Chilcott family at Cissie Chilcott's wedding. Dick Chilcott is third from the left, with Jack and his wife at the far right.*

Below: *This was the scene at Ivy Cottage four days after the photograph on the oposite page (far left, centre) was taken and following a severe storm.*

Left: *Here we are well and truly into the era of the motor car, with the petrol pumps at the foot of the church path in use.*

A very early example of the photographic portrait, this shows John Pearse proudly displaying his carpenter's square, the symbol of his trade.

Above: *These are Henry Pearse's daughters from his first marriage, photographed c.1910. Their names were Ada, Stella, Elsie, Hilda, Kit and Bessie.*

Below: *Maud, the widow of Henry Pearse, in the garden of what was then called Rose Cottage, the family home since 1851.*

By the river wall in the early 1930s are (left to right): *Joyce Griffiths, Tony Young, Bob Gould, Reg (?) Young and Thelma Young, with Donald Young in front.*

Left: *An early photograph of John Pearse's wife Jane (Staddon), who lived in the Lower Street cottage from the time of its purchase in 1851 until her death 40 years later.*

Right:
Henry Pearse as a young man.

Meanwhile, the ownership of the property had lain in the hands of Joseph Taylor, gentleman, and then his widow Elizabeth and son, also Joseph, a cabinet-maker, all of Bristol. A letter survives among the Luttrell documents which was sent by Joseph Taylor of Bristol to the Luttrells in 1777, in which (obviously in response to a complaint from the latter) he asserts that his house in Withycombe was not as badly dilapidated as had been suggested. We cannot say for certain that this was the cottage being discussed but it seems probable that it was.

In 1790 the Taylors sold the cottage to Thomas Milton the younger of Withycombe, yeoman, for the sum of £9. Thomas was the man who married Sarah Weetch in 1786 and who died in 1812. His death saw the property pass to widow Sarah and their son, another Thomas (born 1793), by occupation a carrier. Three years later the Miltons sold the cottage to Robert Cording, a labourer of Rodhuish, for £23; Hugh Escott of Sandhill advanced the cash.

Robert Cording was born to James and Grace Cording of Withycombe in 1779, but lived himself at Rodhuish, being described as of that settlement at the time of his Carhampton burial in 1825. A few years later the cottage first appeared on the new Church Rate list, as a house and garden valued at 18s.0d., in the occupation of Robert Cording, who was also listed as owner and occupier of No.80, a cottage and garden, on the 1840 Tithe Map. However, the following year's census shows John and Mary Cording in residence. Interestingly George Burge, a razor grinder, was also there: he was a grandson of earlier residents William and Joan Burge.

The entries after 1825 probably still referred to the original Robert Cording; they had simply not been updated. After that date the property was actually inherited by James Cording and John Lockyer Haddon (who had taken on the debt owed to Hugh

Escott), both of Old Cleeve. In 1851 James sold his interest to John Lockyer Haddon, who promptly sold the whole thing to John Pearse, carpenter of Bilbrook, for the sum of £49.15s.0d.

It was a rare thing in Withycombe for a property transfer to take place without there being some family connection between the two parties, and this was no exception. John Pearse's mother was Betty Cording, believed to be a cousin of Robert. In addition, John had been married to Sarah Yeandle, whose own family was closely linked to the Cordings, another Sarah Yeandle having been Robert's wife. The younger woman (John's wife) had worked at the Rectory for the Revd Verelst before her marriage and upon leaving was presented with a Bible, which remains in the Pearse family. She died in 1848 and John was re-married, this time to Jane Staddon of Wootton Courtenay.

John was the son of James Pearse of Bowden. He had trained as a carpenter at a Bristol coachworks before returning to practise his trade in the local area. However, Withycombe had its fair share of woodworkers and so he gradually began to branch out into other areas: first as a road contractor and then as a farmer. As mentioned above, the Hobbs' premises at Christopher's Farm were used as a base for these new ventures.

John and Jane had three daughters and two sons. Two of the daughters went into service in London where one of them, Fanny, while working as a nanny to a wealthy Hampstead family, saved the children from a fire, suffering burns herself in the process. The grateful parents awarded her a pension for life and she returned to live at Carhampton. The other, Martha, also returned and married steamroller driver Harry Luck, while the third, Lizzie, eventually became housekeeper to her father and later lived at Myrtle Cottage next door. Eldest son George emigrated to Ontario, Canada, in the 1860s, and many of his descendants live today in America. Henry, the youngest, stayed at home and inherited both the cottage and the family business after John's death in 1893.

Henry Pearse lived in the cottage all his life and raised many children through his two marriages. The first, to Emily Jane Andrews of Milverton, produced six girls, several of whom married into the Sully family of Carhampton and emigrated to Canada. The second, to Maud Evelyn Moule when Henry was almost 52 years old, produced a further six boys and two girls! When Maud's brother Jack married Bessie Pearse, one of Henry's daughters from his first marriage, this led to some complex family relationships, with Bessie's stepmother also becoming her sister-in-law!

Several changes were made to the property in John and Henry Pearse's time, not so much to the house as to its surrounds. Most spectacular would have been the changes made as a result of the building of the school next to it. The earliest maps seem to

Above: *The scholars of c.1887. The only child identified is Elizabeth Edbrooke, wearing a white bow and standing next to the teacher on the right. She was the future 'Teacher Lizzie' who taught at the school during the early part of her career before taking on the children at Carhampton.*

Above: *Withycombe School's Class II in 1902.* Left to right, back row: *Walter (?) Griffiths, Ned Davey, Fred Gratton, George Maidment, Tom Wyburn, Tom Baker, Bill Gould, Tom Williams, Sidney Hancock, George Griffiths;* fourth row: *Elsie Dyer, Hilda Case, Percy Gould, ?, Ronald Tyler, Ernest Gould, ? Baker, Annie Willis, Mabel Wyburn, Joe Williams;* third row: *Irene Maidment, Annie Dyer, Bessie Williams, Clara Gould, ?, ?;* second row, seated on bench: *Hilda Gould (standing), Annie Eliza Williams, Jane (?) Davey, Mildred Wyburn, May Griffiths, Mabel Keeble (teacher), Gerald Gould, Alice Gould, Leonard Gould, Wilfred Gould;* on ground: *Jack Gould, Edward (?) Griffiths, George (?) Webber, Stanley Hancock (?), Charles Dyer, Charlie (?) Gould.*

Above: The church played a major role in the setting up and running of the village school. It was built on land belonging to the glebe and there was a gate leading directly from it into the Rectory grounds. Here the Revd Govan himself makes an appearance in a class photograph taken around 1904. Mrs F. Smith is the teacher. Many of the children can be recognised from the picture opposite.

Above: Now in the church porch, this is the school bell and the plaque commemorating the foundation of that institution in 1866.

show that the village brook used to flow above ground, at the side of the road, from the Causey cottages to the point where it now emerges from a culvert below the Pearses' cottage. It must have been fordable here as it crossed the cart entrance to Hoare's Tenement and also that to the cottage, for in the nineteenth century it too had a wide entrance, on the north side of the current front garden. A little bridge (indicated on an 1820 estate map) was probably for pedestrian access to the front door of the cottage only. This had to change when the school was built. The waterway was channelled underground in an operation that must have caused considerable upheaval to the garden of the cottage, beneath which it now runs.

The twentieth century saw other changes, among them the removal of the cart entrance and the building of a little dairy. This still stands and was used as such well into the author's own lifetime. Before the Milk Marketing Board stepped in and centralised daily milk deliveries the author can recall the various processes of production going on there, from the washing and sterilisation of bottles and equipment to the capping of the filled bottles. This was done by hand, using a metal instrument with a rubber insert, into which the foil top was placed before pressing it onto the bottle. Cream was collected and butter made with butter-pats for the use of the household, but this was a laborious task that gradually died out as the convenience of buying it from the village shop became a time- and labour-saving option.

Henry Pearse died in 1936, leaving the cottage in Maud's hands. When Henry was on his deathbed, straw was spread on the road outside to deaden the sound of passing traffic – one of the last occasions when this village tradition was followed, as it could have had little effect on the motor traffic that was rapidly supplanting the horse and cart; and after he

139

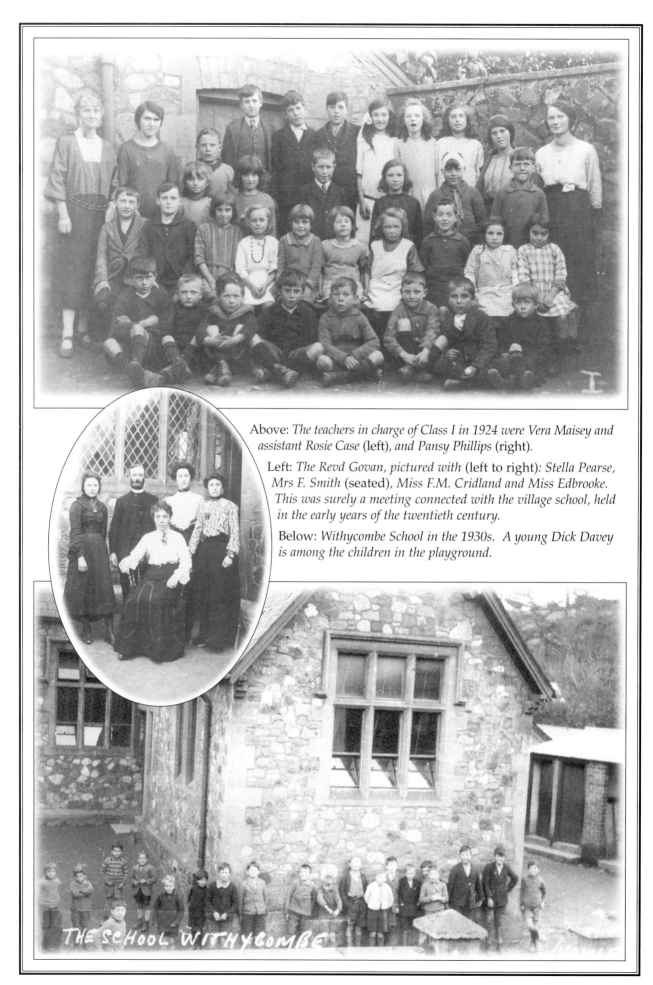

Above: *The teachers in charge of Class I in 1924 were Vera Maisey and assistant Rosie Case* (left), *and Pansy Phillips* (right).

Left: *The Revd Govan, pictured with* (left to right)*: Stella Pearse, Mrs F. Smith* (seated)*, Miss F.M. Cridland and Miss Edbrooke. This was surely a meeting connected with the village school, held in the early years of the twentieth century.*

Below: *Withycombe School in the 1930s. A young Dick Davey is among the children in the playground.*

Above: *Class II in the schoolyard, 1924. Left to right, back row: Pansy Phillips, Reg Pearse, Winnie Burge, ?, Ivy Cridland, Lilian Davey, Florrie Cridland, ?, Rosie Case, Vera Maisey; middle: Colin Pearse, ? Jackson (?), Ken Pearse, Ron (?) Burge, Willie Alderman, ?, Edna James, Kath Sully (?), ?, Arthur Case; front: Ralph Pearse, Billy Burge, Tom (?) Burge, Les Pearse, Violet (?) Davey, Kitty Cridland, ?, Herbert Case, Ronnie James.*

Above: *Among the children enjoying fancy-dress fun at the school in the late 1940s are thought to be Frances Davey, Josie Pateman, Johnny Davey and Duncan Stevens.*

Right: *'The Teapot' as the Post Office. Myrtle Cottage is on the other side of the school entrance.*

had died the church bells sounded a knell, tolling for every year of his life – another tradition that has since largely died out. Most of Henry and Maud's children married and moved away in the years that followed, so that eventually only Dick, the youngest son, remained. Since 1967, when Maud died after a fall in the little cottage, he has continued there alone, unusually having lived in the same house that his father was born in 145 years earlier.

When in the 1880s it became apparent that son Henry was intending to marry, John Pearse decided to build him a home of his own, which he erected close to the roadside on a part of his back garden next to the school. This became known as Myrtle Cottage. Henry and Emily Jane did live there for several years, but after John's death in 1893 they moved to his cottage. Myrtle is too small for all but the smallest of families and over the years it has tended to be home to elderly ladies.

In 1901 widow Elizabeth Parsons seems to have been living there and probably remained until her death in 1910, at which time Henry Pearse's sister Lizzie replaced her. Myrtle Cottage was Lizzie's home for the next quarter of a century. Bill Stevens and wife Beattie lived there briefly before moving to their house just across the road but then Les and Florrie Martin moved in (they were there by 1938) and it was their home for many years.

The village school, next along the road and opposite the path that climbs up to the churchyard, was opened in 1866 to remedy the serious lack of educational facilities that had existed up until that time. Only Hannah Gay's dame-school in West Street was operating prior to this, which could not have coped with the average of 60 children that Withycombe was home to at any one time. As mentioned previously, the Church played a huge part in the school's creation, not least in providing the land – originally part of the Rectory gardens – upon which the building was built.

Initially there were two classes divided according to age, invariably under the control of a pair of female teachers, assisted by a pupil-teacher. Pupil-teachers were invariably drawn from the brightest senior girls, who would frequently go on to become qualified teachers themselves. The two best-known examples of this were probably Lizzie Edbrooke and Rosie Case (later Hardin). Keeping discipline among the children who sometimes numbered as many as 80 was not easy, especially when the teachers themselves were young and inexperienced. George Maidment, a pupil there at the beginning of the twentieth century, fondly recalled some of his experiences, including the older boys being 'out of hand' and being locked in the infants' classroom, only to escape through a small window into the playground; and the relentless teasing of someone referred to as 'Pork Butcher Court', who lived next to the school in the house known as 'The Teapot', until the fellow's

temper got the better of him and he would storm into the playground with his carriage whip! The Revd Govan was quickly summoned, via the door to his garden, to restore order.

Fortunately there was usually one senior schoolmistress who was sufficiently daunting to keep things in order. In George's time this was Mrs Frances Smith, assisted by Harriet Stamford, both of whom were experienced teachers. Later generations of Withycombe children will remember Pansy Phillips and Vera Maisey, and then Rosie Hardin. While most of Withycombe's teachers came from far afield, Rosie (christened Rosetta Mary) was local, the daughter of Jim Case of Rodhuish. In the early years, when children as young as three were accepted, it is not surprising that most of the teachers were female. Nevertheless, there was the occasional schoolmaster, possibly the best remembered of whom was Archibald Foote, who taught at Withycombe in the years following the First World War. Regrettably the school was closed shortly after it celebrated its centenary in 1966, as a result of dwindling numbers. The school bell hangs now in the church porch, while the building remains, converted to a dwelling.

George Maidment's recollection of 'Pork Butcher Court' is the earliest reference to the little house jocularly known as The Teapot Inn, or simply 'The Teapot'. It is believed to have been built by the Case family of Withycombe Farm after the building of the school, on a small plot of land below the Causey cottages (which they owned), to fit into a small space at the side of the school gates – much like Myrtle Cottage on the other side. The 1887 map includes it, whereas the Tithe Map of 1840 does not.

Little is known regarding its early occupants, although the 1901 census suggests that George and Lavinia Gould might have stayed there briefly. We do know, however, that the building was used as the village Post Office before the First World War, prior to the opening of Beadon Case's West Street cottage in that capacity. Responsible for this was surely the whip-wielding Mr Court. William Court was a butcher who, with wife Emma, had previously lived in Alcombe before moving to Withycombe soon after 1901. It is quite likely that he initially started the shop as a butcher's premises (hence George Maidment's nickname for him) and that after his death in 1907 his widow continued to run it, but as the more familiar Post Office. She may have had some experience in this area because their Alcombe butcher's shop had been next to the Post Office there. Emma Court died in 1919, which ties in with the fact that Beadon's replacement was operating in the same year. Strangely though, the Courts were never named as sub-postmasters for the village; before Beadon Case took over, Mary Ann Stevens fulfilled the role. Did she run the shop at The Teapot?

Subsequently the cottage came to be used in similar fashion – and for similar reasons – to Myrtle

Cottage, being home to single ladies or families with few children. Sidney and Ada Irish are thought to have lived there between the wars, with Ada continuing after her husband's relatively early death in 1930.

Above The Teapot, as the road rises steeply towards the Top Cross junction, we come to Withycombe's most picturesque feature, the ancient Causey, with its line of old cottages perched on top. The lower section – as far as the sturdy buttress which supports the front wall about half way along – is the oldest and was originally Withycombe's Poor House. Before the 1834 Poor Law established the Union Workhouse system, villages were obliged to care for their own sick and infirm and this they did by providing a building for the purpose – the Poor House. Practically nothing is known about the operation of Withycombe's Poor House. Early photographs (albeit taken 70 years after it ceased to function in this capacity) show it divided into no less than four cottages, with as many front doors. This suggests that it may have been divided into several dwellings, in the fashion of almshouses.

The building and its adjoining garden were sold on 12 March 1839 at The King's Arms nearby. The buyer was miller John Ridler. He would have let the property, but it is difficult to say to whom, or even to assess the number of dwellings it was divided into. That there were four front doors is certain but that does not necessarily mean that there were still four dwellings: the census returns tend to suggest that it was let as two or three at the most.

Early tenants look likely to have included labourer William Scott and shoemaker Thomas Poole, and members of the Cording family, displaced from their previous home down the road since John Pearse's arrival there. Towards the end of the nineteenth century Henry Griffiths lived there for many years before moving to Rodhuish, where he worked at Lower Rodhuish Farm. His brother Uriah may have lived there briefly before him, although he soon moved on to his more familiar home at Oak.

While Henry lived on the Causey – across from the churchyard – he was handily placed to perform his job as sexton, which was his responsibility in the 1890s. He gave up the post after moving to Rodhuish, when it was taken on by first John and then George Gould, with Albert Sully taking over in the 1930s.

Coming into the twentieth century we find another of Withycombe's characters, Tommy Gould, living in the smallest house at the bottom end of the row. He is remembered as a tailor who used to walk to Bristol every year to buy material, although George Maidment remembered him as one of the village's stone-crackers – which may be how he ended up in his old age. George and the other boys occasionally played cards with him of an evening, trying their hands at such games as 2½d. Loo and All Fours, while others recall him sitting on his doorstep of a

Below: Village character Jack Kent, seated in the yard outside Anvil Cottage (?). Jack would drink cider from two flagons simultaneously and upon occasion would sleep outside his house, in a bush. Possibly these two facts were not unconnected!

Above: *Ann Kent (née Willis), Jack's mother, dressed for the weather (!) on a day out at what looks like Weston-super-mare.*

Below: *Gordon Fry with the splendidly bedecked 'Short'.*

summer evening, playing the flute. By 1920 Ann Willis and her son John (Jack) were living on the Causey: they also used the surname 'Kent' as Ann had been briefly married to someone with that name before she had been left a widow. Around this time the Maidments, working for Edgar Case, re-roofed the row of cottages, removing the thatch from all of them. It seems likely that Edgar acquired the buildings through his mother Lydia, John Ridler's daughter.

Others who lived there around the time of the Second World War included Bill Gould and Les Headford, while Gordon Gould and Gordon Fry were both residents during the postwar period.

The Causey cottages extend beyond the buttress in the form of two dwellings that look slightly newer than the Poor House section, although they are obviously still quite ancient. A little picket fence has spanned the frontage of both since the earliest photographs were taken. Nothing is known about them until 1840, when the Tithe Map reveals them to be 'John Smith's Houses'. John Smith owned them both, occupying one himself while William Pearse the

A group photograph taken at the school centenary celebrations. Left to right, standing: Miss James, Stephen Crossman, Rosie Hardin, Patricia Fox, Pat Parsons, Gladys Porter; on chairs: Ann Fielding, Norma Stevens, Gertrude Sully, Mrs Cridge, Lily Woodcock, Miss Edbrooke, Mabel Fry, Audrey Case, Ann Palfrey, Mrs Slater; kneeling: ?, Stewart Sully, Graham Burdon, Janice Badcock, Wendy Case, Jane Ralph, Camille Lewis, Jackie Potter, Carol Lewis, Julie Palfrey, Dennis Parsons, Rodney Porter, Philip Shopland; seated on ground: ?, Myra Bragg, Rosemary Bragg, Nigel Coleman, Julian Britten, Angela Fox, Mandy Parsons.

Inside one of the classrooms at the school centenary celebrations.

Above: *Miss Edbrooke is presented with a bouquet by young Stephen Crossman at the school centenary celebrations, with the Revd Watson on hand.*

Left: *Another picture of the school centenary celebrations. Left to right, back row: Audrey Case, Joan Davey, Rosie Hardin (?); middle: Lily Woodcock, Gertrude Sully, ? Cridge, Mabel Fry; front: Ann Fielding, Ann Palfrey.*

Below: *Villagers in the playground celebrate the centenary of the village school in 1966. Left to right, standing: Audrey Case, Jean Sully, Norma Stevens, Ann Fielding and Lily Woodcock; seated: Rene Lewis, Ginny Palfrey, Mary Jones, Mrs Badcock, ? Cridge, Gertrude Sully.*

A superb picture of the Causey, taken some years before the thatch was removed from the cottage roofs (c.1920). Harold Bryant is said to be the baker coming up the road with his horse and cart. Joanna Webber's cottage, with its tall chimneys, still stands near the foot of the church path, where one of the taps which supplied drinking water to this part of the village can also be seen.

Left: *The old cottages on the Causey, early 1960s.*

Below: *The man on the Causey in this picture may be Tommy Gould, who lived in the last little cottage in the row in the early years of the twentieth century.*

tailor had the other. It is not clear what was going on in the latter case, as William definitely also had Anvil Cottage next door. Perhaps by this time he lived in this one while running his business at the other.

John Smith was a millwright who lived only briefly in Withycombe during the 1840s, but it is thought that he had a workshop to the rear of the property and was responsible for the mill machinery that was discovered thereabouts some years ago, which gave rise to the theory that the village mill used to be sited here – which was certainly not the case.

Bearing in mind that the topmost house seems to have been used in some form by William Pearse throughout the latter half of the nineteenth century, this leaves the lower one free for occupation after Smith's departure. However, we cannot identify the occupants until Bowler Nicholas moved in. He was there by 1901. He had married Diana Willis in 1887, the daughter of Frederick Willis, who had been living somewhere close by a few years previously, so it is possible that it had been their home.

Bowler, the traction-engine driver whom we have met before, was a man of strong constitution. At election time, candidates would travel the villages looking to drum up support and on one occasion Bowler was selected from the small crowd that had gathered, being considered a key man to get on side.

'Would you take a drink with me sir?' asked the candidate, offering a nearly full bottle of whisky to the sturdy labourer. Taking advantage of the gentleman's unlikely-to-be-repeated-outside-of-election-time offer, Bowler lifted the bottle and drank... and drank... and continued until the bottle was empty. It is said that he swayed slightly before turning and walking away, leaving the candidate – for once – lost for words. Bowler died in 1940, his widow six years later, and the house was left in the hands of son Fred.

The final house in the row, which had been ostensibly in the hands of William Pearse, had become known as 'The Cottage' by 1894, when it was briefly occupied by Thomas Leversha, who was followed three years later by a Miss Coombes. It still bears that name-plate today. In 1901 it was briefly home to a late captain of militia, James Lesley, then by 1914 to a Mrs Lysons. It is best remembered though as the home of retired policeman George Hall and his wife Elizabeth, who resided there through the 1930s, George dying in 1943.

This brings us back to Top Cross for the final time and concludes the tour of the old parish of Withycombe. However, it is not quite the end of the story because, since 1884, Withycombe has also included the hamlet of Rodhuish, formerly in Carhampton, which we will consider in the next chapter.

Schoolchildren posing in the road (traffic was obviously not a problem) at the top of the Causey in 1920. Left to right, standing at back: *Florrie Cridland, Ivy Webber, ?, Ted Gould, Dick Chilcott, Herbert Davey, Ivy Dyer, Alfie Gratton;* standing middle: *Emily Cridge, Eva Ellis, 'Gribble' Davey, Billy Stevens, Rupert Chilcott, Florrie Burge, Reg Pearse, Alan 'Shiner' Burnell, Ivy Cridland, Winnie (?) Burge, Dorothy Gould, F. Davey, Florrie Nicholas, Phyllis Pearse, Violet Davey;* seated middle: *Ralph Pearse, ?, Florrie Davey, Kitty Cridland, ?, Herbert Case, Ronnie James, Winnie (?) Davey, Edna James, ?, Faith Gould;* seated, front: *Leslie Pearse, ?, Arthur Case, Walter Case, ?, Claude Case, Muriel Case, Harry Cridge, ?, ?.*

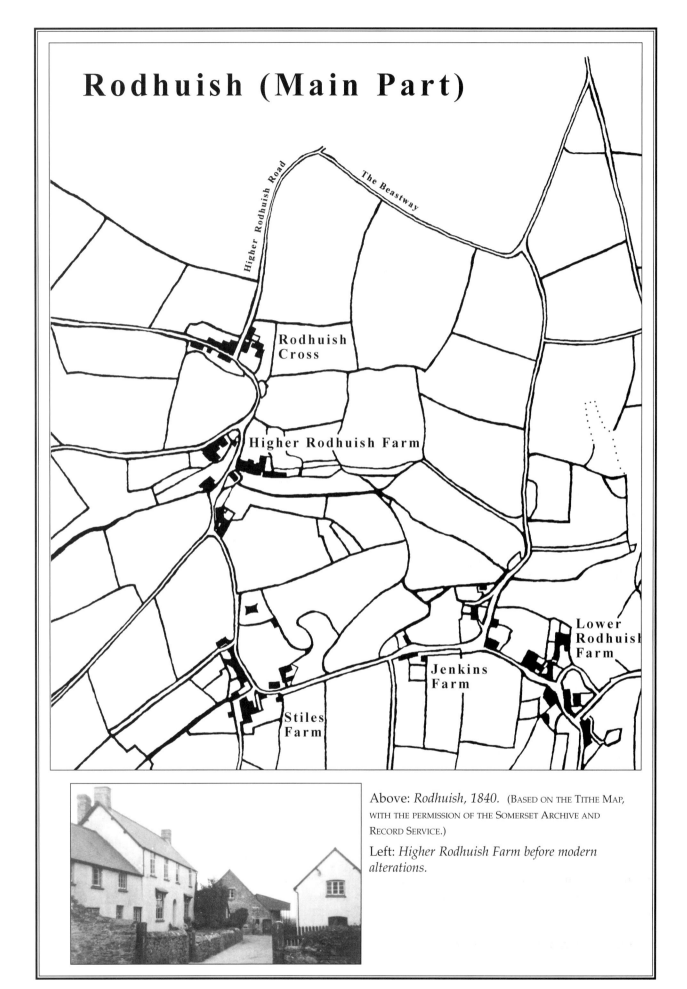

Rodhuish (Main Part)

Rodhuish
Cross

Higher Rodhuish Farm

Stiles
Farm

Jenkins
Farm

Lower
Rodhuish
Farm

Above: *Rodhuish, 1840.* (BASED ON THE TITHE MAP, WITH THE PERMISSION OF THE SOMERSET ARCHIVE AND RECORD SERVICE.)

Left: *Higher Rodhuish Farm before modern alterations.*

Eleven

Rodhuish

Lying on the edge of the Brendon Hills to the south of Withycombe is the hamlet of Rodhuish. Its ancient history belongs to the parish of Carhampton, of which it used to form a detached portion, so we will concentrate here on its story from 1884, when it became part of Withycombe.

At Rodhuish we see a typical hill-country pattern, with clusters of cottages arising close to farms, built as homes for the agricultural labour force. Although its Parish Church was at Carhampton, it is served by the Chapel of St Bartholomew, a very attractive ancient building constructed to save local inhabitants from having to make the long journey every Sunday; and it has also had more than one Nonconformist chapelry, including the Bible Christian 'Tin Tabernacle', a corrugated-iron building erected in 1899 not far from Lower Rodhuish Farm. Built at a cost of just £51

The Chapel of St Bartholomew at Rodhuish, from a postcard sent in 1907 to Blanche Vickery (possibly from her friend Annie Hagley of Combe Farm).

and timber-lined to provide some relief from extremes of temperature outside, it still stands. Tom Lewis, one of the last of the itinerant Methodist preachers, was a member there.

Approaching Rodhuish from Withycombe village, at the end of a long drag up the Higher Rodhuish Road we arrive at Rodhuish Cross, where a handful of old cottages can be found. In 1891 there were three dwellings, occupied by the families of farm labourers Richard Vickery, Dan Gould and George Willis. The former, who had lived previously at Lower Hill, was the son of Carhampton shoemaker William Vickery. He was in his seventies, as was George Willis, who had daughter Ann Kent and her children Jack and Maria living with him. Dan Gould had been born at Longcombe and seems to have been a grandson of James and Honor Gould: that lady, a widow of 88, was lodging with him at the time.

By the beginning of the new century only Eliza Willis, the widow of George, remained, together with Ann and Jack Kent. Dan Gould had moved to Oak (see below). Both families would eventually make the move down to Withycombe village. New arrivals were Charles and Elizabeth Williams, who had chosen to live close to Elizabeth's family, that of Joseph Hurford, who resided in one of the houses near Higher Rodhuish Farm. The little Williams children, like many raised in Rodhuish, made the daily journey down to Withycombe School. The third house was unoccupied in 1901.

There would surely once have been a small farm at Rodhuish Cross and in the 1920s there was one again, when Herbert Couzens farmed there. Fred Eames was one of the cottage tenants at that time.

Before continuing down the road to Higher Rodhuish Farm, a brief detour is necessary along Oak Lane, which breaks westward from Rodhuish Cross to link it to Bowden and Withycombe Common, and of course the house at Oak. The lane marks the boundary between Withycombe and Rodhuish, with Oak lying across from the fields known as the Gilcotts, with which it was once associated. When it became part of Withycombe it was in the hands of Richard Gould, a shepherd born at Aller, Carhampton, and his family. However, after his wife Maria lost her life in the Queen's jubilee celebration on Withycombe Hill in 1887, part of the house was let to a second family, that of Uriah Griffiths. Uriah was Richard Gould's son in law, having married his daughter Mary Jane.

Richard was gone by 1901, replaced by Dan Gould from Rodhuish Cross. The latter was still living at Oak in 1920, but Uriah surpassed him by a distance, still at home there in 1938, at which time he was 85 years old.

Right: *One of Higher Rodhuish Farm's workers, Geoff Dyer. The youngster perching on the shafts of the hay cart is Alan Thomas, the farm owner at the time of writing.*

Lots 124 and 125 comprise two Cottages in the Hamlet of Rodhuish, which lies about one mile South of Withycombe.

LOT 124

(Coloured Pink on Plan No. 4)

Area 2 roods   16 perches

A WELL BUILT COTTAGE

Situate near Higher Rodhuish Farm, this Cottage is semi-detached. Built of stone and cob with a slated roof it contains :

GROUND FLOOR: HALL, PANTRY, SITTING ROOM, KITCHEN, with single oven range. Estate Water stand pipe by door.

FIRST FLOOR: LANDING, THREE BEDROOMS, two communicating.

OUTSIDE: Old Cider House, Coal House, good Garden, Orchard with Pig Sty.

Let on a weekly tenancy to Mr. J. W. Case at a rent of £13 1s. 10d. per annum. Landlord pays rates—£3 8s 6d. last year.

Tithe Redemption Annuity 3s. 4d.

LOT 125

(Coloured Pink on Plan No. 4)

Area 32 perches

A Semi-Detached Cottage

known as

No. 1, PINS COTTAGES

Built of stone and cob with a thatched and tiled roof.

GROUND FLOOR: LIVING ROOM with single oven range, WASH HOUSE with copper, SMALL PANTRY with sink (cold water).

FIRST FLOOR: THREE BEDROOMS, two communicating.

OUTSIDE: Closet, Coal House, Garden. Estate Water. Let on a weekly tenancy to Mr. C. T. Meddick at a rent of £7 5s. od. per annum. Landlord pays rates—£2 1s. 2d. last year.

Left and below: *The two Rodhuish items included in the 1951 sale of former Luttrell properties.*

Above: *Joseph Mark Hurford, standing behind his wife Eliza (Scott). Beside him is daughter Elizabeth, who is behind another daughter, Bessy. A 'cabinet portrait' by H.H. Hole.*

Above: *Cuthbert Thomas in the saddle outside his Higher Rodhuish Farmhouse.*

Right: *Two lads driving a horse and cart out of Higher Rodhuish Farm.*

Left: *A good flock of sheep and a neatly thatched hayrick; farmer Cuthbert Thomas of Higher Rodhuish had every reason to record this moment with a photograph.*

Below left: *Rene Lewis (née Needs) in the bus shelter beside the Tin Tabernacle at Rodhuish.*

Below: *The old farm buildings (now demolished) at Higher Rodhuish Farm.*

Below: *Modern times at Higher Rodhuish Farm. Where horses and carts used to trundle, tractors and huge lorries now provide carriage.*

Higher Rodhuish Farm before alterations. Part of it was once a cider house used by drovers and other travellers passing through the hamlet on their way to the market towns to the south of Exmoor.

Returning to Rodhuish Cross, a little further on we come to Higher Rodhuish Farm and its surrounding cottages. The farm itself, which is said to have once had its own water-mill and an adjoining cider house which served passing drovers amongst others, was in the hands of Herbert Ridler Case, the son of Robert and Lydia of Withycombe Farm, when the area became part of the parish. Initially it may also have been occupied in part by Thomas Leversha, who farmed at Higher Rodhuish into the early 1890s before returning to Withycombe village.

Herbert Case was only a young man when he started at Higher Rodhuish but by 1901, recently married to Kate Strong, he was in sole control. Children Nora, Austin and Robert were born there in the early years of the century. William Surridge had replaced Herbert by 1906, then in 1916 Fred Thomas

took over. Since then it has remained in the Thomas family, farmed by Fred, son Cuthbert and then grandson Alan.

Close to the farm lived Joseph Mark Hurford and his family. As a young man he had lived in West Street, Withycombe, lodging with Thomas Court (both men were originally from Wootton Courtenay); but soon after his marriage to Eliza Scott he moved to Higher Rodhuish, where he acquired the contract to maintain the roads. By the 1880s Joseph and Eliza were also running a shop there. Most of the others who lived nearby were farm workers, such as Thomas Chapman and Thomas Willis in 1891, and John Gould and George Davey ten years later. The last three certainly lived in Pinns Cottages (now just one dwelling), situated opposite the bottom of Stout's Way Lane.

Several families of Cridlands, including blind James Cridland and his wife Annie, also lived in the area, but perhaps closer to Styles Farm, which had its own farm cottages. John Chubb definitely lived in one of the latter, later lodging with William Welsher; and one was home to Bill Wakely in more recent times.

Styles Farm was worked by a Devon man named William Brook in the 1880s, but John Watts took over

Left: *Lester Watts of Styles Farm, flanked by brothers Cuthbert and Cyril Thomas at a gathering of the hunt.*

Below: *These very old cottages above Styles Farm in Rodhuish were probably built for the farm workers and their families. The furthest was used briefly as a chapel.*

in the next decade, following his marriage to Laura Case who, like Herbert just up the road, was a child of Robert of Withycombe Farm. Their son Lester had succeeded them by 1927. He retired to Blue Anchor in the 1950s and the farm passed to Tom Baker of Briddicott, who had married Lester's daughter Audrey. Nowadays the farm is famous for its ice-cream, unusually made from sheep's milk, and it remains in the Baker family.

Next we come to Jenkins Farm. Before the 1880s it was home to John Case, who was one of the sons of James Case, the man who built Withycombe's West Street smithy. After John's death in 1873 his son Caleb took over from him, continuing until his own death in 1919. Caleb's son was Jim Case, whose daughter Rosetta was the Rosie Case (later Hardin) who taught at Withycombe School. Edwin Pope replaced Caleb at Jenkins Farm in the 1920s, then John Norman took over, moving the short distance from Lower Rodhuish Farm. Later Bill Case farmed there, and then Cyril Burge. During the Second World War Claude Case and Cyril Burge were two who searched for the crew of a German bomber that had crashed nearby, parts of it landing in a field belonging to Styles Farm: they discovered one of their parachutes but the crew were apprehended near Luxborough after giving themselves up. Their efforts to surrender earlier were apparently thwarted when a Rodhuish farm-hand, hurrying to milk the cows, refused to have anything to do with them, being already late for work!

We have dropped down now to Lower Rodhuish, where Sandrocks Lane can lead the traveller back to Withycombe, the thoroughfare terminating at the top of Rattle Row, near its junction with Sandhill Lane. As the names suggest, the hill that the lane traverses was once a valuable source of sandstone and it is peppered with old quarries. Most of the farm cottages at Lower Rodhuish stand or stood alongside the southern end of this lane, in an area known as Park Steep.

We have encountered many members of the Case family in Withycombe and Rodhuish and it is thought that one of their earliest homes was in this part of the hamlet. Here blacksmith John Case and wife Joan came and set up their smithy towards the end of the eighteenth century. It is believed to have been the dilapidated building at the end of Sandrocks Lane, close to the Tin Tabernacle. Son James would later move to Withycombe village to set up the West Street smithy, while son John continued the family business at Rodhuish. He married Ann Poole and they raised a family here, which included Robert, who went into farming and eventually took on Withycombe Farm. Another son, Thomas, continued the blacksmith's business before eventually also branching out into farming. He never married and died in 1903. As we have seen, descendants of both James and John returned to live and farm not far from the family home.

One of a pair of cottages, now demolished but associated with Lower Rodhuish Farm, was William Gratton's from around 1890. His son Jack later came to live at Anvil Cottage in Withycombe's Mill Street, daughter Ada married Charlie Needs and daughter Bessie married yet another Case – William Henry, a descendant of West Street blacksmith James. Charlie Needs lived there later. The other one of the pair may initially have been occupied by John Farmer, whose daughter Lavinia was later to marry George Gould and become a well-known figure in Withycombe. By the early 1900s though it had become home to Harry Griffiths when he moved in the opposite direction, coming up from his house on the Causey to work at Lower Rodhuish Farm.

Where one finds a blacksmith, a carpenter or wheelwright is likely to be close by. Carpenter James Greed was the man at Lower Rodhuish for many years, replaced by 1901 by Thomas Willis, a carpenter and wheelwright. Tom had trained under the Greeds many years earlier but then worked as a farm labourer, living at one of Pinns Cottages, before returning to take over their workshop on Park Steep. He made coffins, among other things, and brewed his own cider, so that his workshop was often jokingly referred to as 'The Carpenter's Arms'! His wife Ann was the local midwife.

One more old cottage can be found in the vicinity, this one beyond the farm, where the road starts to

Two unidentified ladies outside Waterwheel Cottage at Lower Rodhuish, possibly pictured around the time of the Second World War.

Outside the now demolished cottages near Lower Rodhuish Farm is a gathering of the Gratton clan, c.1930. Left to right, standing: Alfie Gratton (son of Jack), Nellie Gratton, Fred Gratton, Ada and Charlie Needs; seated: Bessie Case, Muriel Case with dog Bonzo, William Gratton, Mary Gratton, Catherine Case and Jack Gratton. Bessie and Ada were daughters of William and Mary Gratton, while Muriel and Catherine were daughters of Bessie and William Henry Case. Jack Gratton lived down at Anvil Cottage in Withycombe village for many years.

This picture shows the now demolished Lower Rodhuish Farm cottages. Charlie Needs lived in the one on the right, Harry Griffiths next door.

Mortimer Thomas making the presentation to Gertrude Sully on her retirement from the post of clerk to the Parish Council.

climb up Rodhuish Hill. This is Waterwheel Cottage, which may have been shepherd Bill Cridland's home at the turn of the century.

Most of these dwellings had been built to house the workers at Lower Rodhuish Farm nearby, which worked a substantial 350 acres of land at the time it became part of Withycombe. It was then in the hands of William Tyler, a young man who had been born in Jamaica, and he ran it for many years. He died after being crushed against a bank by a bull that he was leading.

John Norman farmed there for a while from around 1914 before moving to Jenkins Farm; then Mortimer Thomas, whose wife was Effie King of Sandhill, took over. Dick Pearse remembers pulling mangels for him, along with Tom Lewis and Charlie Needs, around 1930.

With the exception of Oak, all of the Rodhuish properties mentioned so far have been close enough to each other to make up something of a coherent community: but now we venture out into some of the more isolated areas. Included here, perhaps surprisingly, is Escott Farm at the western end of the hamlet, said to have been the original site of the manor-house of Rodhuish. Indeed, the demesne fields surrounding it may well be the reason why it is somewhat isolated. William Lutley, from Wiveliscombe, was the farmer there from the 1850s to beyond the turn of the century. He and his wife Elizabeth (Withycombe) raised a large family there, employing a private tutor to educate the children in the 1870s and '80s. The farm then consisted of some 230 acres, making it considerably smaller than the other major Rodhuish farms.

By 1914 Thomas Vearncombe was the farmer at Escott's but after the war he was named as bailiff

there. By 1927 Sidney Takle was doing the same job. Later it was owned and farmed by the Babbage family. Nowadays Escott's is just a house, the land having been taken on by its nearest neighbour, Lower Rodhuish Farm.

To the south of the main inhabited part of the hamlet the land climbs steeply to a ridge, reached by several narrow ways, such as Stout's Way, Stringland and Felon's Oak Lanes. At the top of the last of these is said to be the site of a place of summary execution, although older sources frequently refer to the site as Fellow's or Felloes Oak. Here there used to be a cottage on the Rodhuish side of the parish boundary, which was home to the Edwards family, but it seems to have fallen out of use in the 1880s. Beyond the ridge the land falls away towards Luxborough and Treborough, and it is on the way down to the Washford River in the valley bottom that we encounter several of Rodhuish's isolated properties.

Three hill farms used to be found on the southern slopes, almost certainly built on the spring line. From west to east, they are Eyreland, Culverwell and Fowlwell.

Eyreland, probably named after the Eyre family, although sometimes called Higher Land, was reaching the end of its useful life by the time it became part of Withycombe parish. Richard Vickery had been living there in 1881 and he may have been the last to do so: as we have seen, by 1891 he had moved to Rodhuish Cross, leaving Eyreland vacant. Even then it had ceased to be a farm for some time and was just a dilapidated cottage.

Culverwell fared a little better, with two cottages surviving into the 1880s. John Farmer (with daughter Lavinia, mentioned above) lived in one, while

James Sutton and wife Mary (Gould) had the other. However, one of these soon fell out of use, so that by 1891 only one was occupied, by William Sully of Watchet. Thomas Cridland and wife Ruth had replaced him by 1901. Cyril Burge lived there before his move to Jenkins Farm, when a family of Jehovah's Witnesses named Radford took over. Nowadays only some sheds mark the site.

The third, Fowlwell, entered its Withycombe era as the home of John and Anne Gould. An elderly couple even then, both born in the 1820s, they lived on at the isolated cottage into the early years of the twentieth century. John had lived there all his life, as it had previously been home to his parents Thomas and Jane Gould. The Robert Gould who married Elizabeth Vinnicombe and lived in Withycombe village around the turn of the century was a son of John and Anne.

By 1927 Harry Griffiths had moved up to live at Fowlwell; and it was Tom Lewis' home in the mid-twentieth century. Little remains there now.

Another cottage that seems to have stood somewhere on the south side of Rodhuish Hill was High Park, also occasionally referred to as Hyde Park. It was most associated with John 'Noble' Davey and his wife Elizabeth, who moved there from their home in West Street in the early years of the twentieth century, reputedly because they found life in the village a bit too hectic! John was the son of villagers George and Harriet Davey, and he was frequently referred to as John Davey senr to distinguish him from his son of the same name, who remained in West Street. It is believed that John senr continued to live at High Park until his death in 1926. Later a family named Taylor lived there, as briefly did Bill and Bessie Case.

Fowlwell was reached via a lane that branches off Greenland Lane, which runs south from Felon's Oak. This road leads to a group of dwellings called Greenland. In 1881 there were three homes, two of which were inhabited by young men of the Warren family, who worked as labourers at Treborough slate quarry nearby. Greenland had probably been the Warren family home since they moved into the area in the early 1800s. By 1891 though, two of the cottages were unoccupied, and only William Warren and his family remained. William changed his job to carpenter and continued at Greenland for most of his life, still being there in 1927. A couple of houses remain at Greenland today.

At the bottom of Rodhuish Hill we come to the Washford River, close to which can be found three more very old properties, all of which have survived in one form or another. Although technically the parish of Withycombe extends even beyond the river, taking in Langridge Wood to the south, we are now very much in the territory of Roadwater.

The cottage at Pitswell or Peterswell Lake was the home of Treborough gamekeeper Robert Parsons and his wife Hannah. Their son Archie was also a gamekeeper who lived there at the turn of the century.

More important though was Langridge Mill, once a corn-mill powered by the Washford River. John Greed, carpenter and miller, had operated the mill until his death in the 1850s but by the 1880s his son George was calling himself a farmer, with 81 acres to his name. However, trade directories continued to refer to him as the miller there for some time after this. From 1914 Herbert George Case was named as a farmer, living at Langridge Mill. His identity is not known with certainty but he may possibly have been the 'George Herbert' Case who was a son of Joshua Case, who in turn was the older brother of Caleb of Jenkins Farm. In the middle years of the twentieth century we know that a Sid Case farmed at Langridge Mills; and that George Herbert not only had a son of that name but also another – named George – who was living at Roadwater when he died in the 1980s.

Farming at Langridge was a tricky business, as virtually all of its fields were very steep. Consequently sledges were used rather than carts to carry hay, etc. to and fro. This was an old hill-farming method, employed on Exmoor and elsewhere since the earliest of times.

It was also quite an isolated farm and this particular Case family was regarded as somewhat 'hillbilly' in nature. Nevertheless, when the Crown Estates invited a selection of their tenants to a royal garden party in London in the 1950s, Sid Case was one of those chosen. Upon being presented to the Queen Mother, he was asked how farming was progressing down in the West Country. 'Very good, ma'am,' he replied. 'The early teddies be all round-hoed up!'

There is one final property to consider, and that is Druid's Combe, in past times invariably contracted to Drucombe. This is now a farmhouse that stands close to the river, in the south-western corner of the parish. It was home to the Nethercott family probably since Daniel and Grace arrived in Carhampton in the 1780s: another Daniel – possibly their son – was killed in 1825 when he fell into the mill-wheel at Langridge, just a little way downstream. When it became part of Withycombe it was home to William Nethercott and his wife Matilda. William, who had been born at Drucombe, was initially described as a gamekeeper but soon moved into farming. He was named as a farmer at Drucombe as late as 1910, but by 1927 it was home to Herbert J. Webber.

Incidentally, it is not thought that this property is the same as that which belonged to the manor of Withycombe Hadley and was also referred to as Drucombe: that was the grander property at nearby Slowley.

This concludes our brief look at Rodhuish, and completes our historical tour of the parish of Withycombe.

Subscribers

Chris and Teresa Adams, Withycombe

Stephanie Aitchison, granddaughter of Violet Webber of Withycombe (1901–66

William E. Allen, Lyndhurst, Ohio, USA

Mrs Judy Back, Saskatoon, Canada

Suzanne Badcock, Challacombe, North Devon

Gerald and Marion Badcock, The Ford, Withycombe, Somerset

Mrs I. Baikie (née Davey), Bridgwater, Somerset

Clive and Audrey Bateman, Withycombe, Somerset

Mrs Carolyn Bates, Burnham

Mr Loxley Iszekel Bernard-Humber

F. James Binding

Margaret and Edward Blewitt

Richard and Caragh Blewitt

Mr and Mrs John R. Bonser, Blue Anchor, Somerset

Derrick Bott, Minehead

Gerald and Kathleen Bull, Bishops Lydeard

Dorothy Bulpin, South Australia

Richard Alan Burge, Bournemouth

Michael and Myra Burnett, Withycombe

Mrs E.M. Burns (née Griffiths), Withycombe, Somerset

H. John Butterworth and P. Jean Gilbert, Withycombe, Somerset

J. Owen Case, Basingstoke, Hants.

Nicholas Case

Francis Norman Case, Alcombe, Somerset

Anthony C. Case, Withycombe Farm

Mrs Anita J. Chadwick

Pete and Pat Chinnock, Rodhuish, Somerset

The Chinnock Family, Rodhuish, Somerset

Danae H. Clark, Rodhuish, Somerset

Simone Cook, formerly of Withycombe, Somerset

Violet M. Cridland, Carhampton, Somerset

J.I. Crossman, Withycombe

Mr John N. Davey, Stogursey, Somerset

Florence Mary Davey, Withycombe, Somerset

Thelma Davey, Carhampton, Somerset

Mrs Margaret A. Davies, Huntley, Gloucestershire

Verna Dawson, daughter of Violet Webber of Withycombe (1901–66)

Mrs J. Derrick (née Griffiths), Taunton, Somerset

Peter and Wendy Dickinson and William George Lewis Gould, Withycombe

Stan and Michele Dische

Moira Dlugosz, Aylesbury, Buckinghamshire

Peggy Pearse Donovan, Chula Vista, California, USA

C.M. Dyer, Carhampton, Somerset

Gerald Dyer, born Hill Cottage, Withycombe, 1943/Los Lobos, Spain

Rosemary Edwards, Ebbw Vale, Gwent

Stephen E. and Audrey J. Eley, Withycombe

Irene H. Fennell, Minehead, Somerset

May and Michael Ferris, Great Easton, Essex

Barbara and Bob Ferris, son of Kathleen Jane and Lewis Cedric Ferris,

Ruth P. Fox, Rodhuish, Somerset

Stanley R. Fry, Watchet, Somerset

Judith Garrard, Rodhuish, great-grandaughter of Anne Willis

Leslie J. and Aileen M. Gill, Withycombe, Somerset

Godfrey and Joan Godsell, Dunster, Somerset

Steve and Mandy Godsell

M.L. Gooders, Kent and Somerset

Michael William and Vanessa Gould, Withycombe

Graham C. Gower, Clapham Park, London

Mark J. Gratton, Wells, Somerset

Lynn Gratton, Naseby, Northants

Maurice J. Gratton, Dunster. Son of Jack Gratton

John Gratton, Timberscombe, Somerset

Mrs Cherry Green, Ipswich

Jonathan Greenhow

Mr Geoffery Griffiths

Gordon I. Griffiths, Dunster, Somerset

L.A. and D.R. Griffiths, Dunster, Somerset
Ms Beverley Griffiths
Derek I. Griffiths, Dunster, Somerset
Mr Edward Griffiths, formerly Withycombe
Eric Hagley, Verwood, Dorset
Richard and Geraldine Hagley, Basingstoke,
    Hampshire
Roger Harrison, Old Cleeve, Somerset
Lilian Hayhoe (née Cridge), Watchet, Somerset
Brian Hicks, Cookham, Berkshire
Mavis I. Hill, granddaughter of Mrs Amelia
    Maidment
Mr Michael Hodge, Bristol
Mark S. Hostetler, St Louis, Missouri, USA
Carolyn W. Hostetler, Wooster, Ohio, USA
Peter and Jean Humber, Withycombe
The Hutchings Family, West Street,
    Withycombe, Somerset
Annie James, Withycombe
Tim James, Withycombe
Mrs V. Jones, Minehead, Somerset
Mike and Christine Jones
Liz Jones, Southsea, Hampshire
Brian Jones, Dallas, North Carolina, USA
Pamela Kelly, Surbiton, Surrey
Jean Knight, Withycombe, Somerset
Simon Lee and Fiona Freshney, Finlay Freshney-
    Lee, Withycombe
Diane J. Lewis, Minehead, Somerset
Mrs Marjorie Lockyer, Leatherhead, Surrey
Donald and Beryl Mash, Withycombe,
    Somerset
The McKee Family, Rodhuish, Somerset
Michael A. Miles, Withycombe, Somerset
Steve Milton, Salisbury, Wiltshire
David J. Milton, Auckland, New Zealand
John L. Nicholas
Violet E.M. Nicholas, Withycombe, Somerset
Andrew Nicholas, Williton
Wilfred J. Nicholas, Swansea
Betty O'Neill, formerly of Withycombe,
    Somerset
E. Palfrey, Moorcroft, Withycombe
Mrs Marjory Parker
Donald F. Parsons, Withycombe, Somerset
Mr and Mrs A. Parsons, Withycombe
Richard W. Pearse, Chicago, Illinois, USA
Richard Pearse, Withycombe, Somerset
K. Pearse, Wincanton, Somerset
Belinda Pearse, Sydney, Australia
Keith N. Pearse, Sydney, Australia
Robert E. Pierce, Rockville, MD
Nigel and Sue Pike, Bilbrook, Somerset
Rachel and Phil Pope, Carhampton, Somerset

Victor C. Poppy, Carhampton, Somerset
The Prentice Family, formerly of Witheridge,
    Devon
Mr and Mrs C. Price, Williton, Somerset
Martha and Alan Proctor, formerly of Merton
    House, West Street, Withycombe
G.H. Pugsley, born at Withycombe
Mary F. Ross (née Case), Withycombe
Alan Sanderson, Crediton, Devon
Roger J. Scudamore, Bournemouth (formerly of
    Withycombe)
Ainsley Scudamore now of Bristol, and Joan
    Scudamore of Withycombe
C.P. Sharp OBE, Maulden, Bedfordshire
Richard Sherrin, Carhampton, Somerset
Janet Shortland (Gooders)
Mrs Joan T.M. Silverthorne, Withycombe
B. and J. Skudder, Doniford
Wendy Slaymaker, Oxford
Dave Smith, Chingford, London
David Stevens, Withycombe, Somerset
Duncan Stevens, Minehead
Geoffrey J. Stevens, Carhampton
Derek J. Stevens
Mandy J. Stevens (née Parsons), Carhampton
Mrs Jennifer Stuart-Steel, London
Mrs Glynn Sully, Saskatoon, Canada
Mrs J.M. Sully Morgan, Raglan, Monmouthshire
Ruth Sully-Lawless, Withycombe, Somerset
Carolynne A. Sully-Lawless, Withycombe,
    Somerset
Sarah Sully-Lawless, Withycombe, Somerset
Mr A. Swift, Exeter, Devon
Mrs J.M. Swift (née Griffiths), Withycombe,
    Somerset
Mr and Mrs F. Tarr
David Lyddon Thomas, Bristol
Mrs Jacky Thomas, Watchet
Mike Tidball, St Albans, Herts
Sandra V. Upham (née Martin), Bristol
Gordon Edward Uppington, Harpenden
Terry Vaughan, Watchet, Somerset
John F.W. Walling, Newton Abbot, Devon
J. Waterfall, Stamford, Lincolnshire
Stephen J. Webber, Carhampton, Somerset
John and Betty Wellstead, Withycombe,
    Somerset
Raymond J. White and John Clamp, Rodhuish,
    Somerset
Liz and John Williams, late of Squirrels
Jillian Young, Walton-on-the-Naze, Essex
Donald R. Young, Frinton-on-Sea, Essex
Nigel J. Young, Wimbledon, SW19
Raymond T.H. Young MBE

Community Histories

The Book of Addiscombe • Canning & Clyde Road Residents Association & Friends
The Book of Addiscombe, Vol. II • Canning & Clyde Road Residents Association & Friends
The Book of Axminster with Kilmington • Les Berry
and Gerald Gosling
The Book of Bampton • Caroline Seward
The Book of Barnstaple • Avril Stone
The Book of Barnstaple, Vol. II • Avril Stone
The Book of The Bedwyns • The Bedwyn History Society
The Book of Bickington • Stuart Hands
Blandford Forum: A Millennium Portrait • Blandford Town Council
The Book of Bramford • Bramford Local History Group
The Book of Breage & Germoe • Stephen Polglase
The Book of Bridestowe • R. Cann
The Book of Bridport • Rodney Legg
The Book of Brixham • Frank Pearce
The Book of Buckfastleigh • Sandra Coleman
The Book of Buckland Monachorum & Yelverton • Hemery
The Book of Carharrack • Carharrack Old Cornwall Society
The Book of Carshalton • Stella Wilks and Gordon Rookledge
The Parish Book of Cerne Abbas • Vale and Vale
The Book of Chagford • Ian Rice
The Book of Chapel-en-le-Frith • Mike Smith
The Book of Chittlehamholt with
Warkleigh & Satterleigh • Richard Lethbridge
The Book of Chittlehampton • Various
The Book of Colney Heath • Bryan Lilley
The Book of Constantine • Moore and Trethowan
The Book of Cornwood & Lutton • Compiled by the People of the Parish
The Book of Creech St Michael • June Small
The Book of Cullompton • Compiled by the People of the Parish
The Book of Dawlish • Frank Pearce
The Book of Dulverton, Brushford,
Bury & Exebridge • Dulverton & District Civic Society
The Book of Dunster • Hilary Binding
The Book of Edale • Gordon Miller
The Ellacombe Book • Sydney R. Langmead
The Book of Exmouth • W.H. Pascoe
The Book of Grampound with Creed • Bane and Oliver
The Book of Hayling Island & Langstone • Rogers
The Book of Helston • Jenkin with Carter
The Book of Hemyock • Clist and Dracott
The Book of Herne Hill • Patricia Jenkyns
The Book of Hethersett • Hethersett Society Research Group
The Book of High Bickington • Avril Stone
The Book of Ilsington • Dick Wills
The Book of Kingskerswell • Carsewella Local History Group
The Book of Lamerton • Ann Cole & Friends
Lanner, A Cornish Mining Parish • Sharron
Schwartz and Roger Parker
The Book of Leigh & Bransford • Malcolm Scott
The Book of Litcham with Lexham & Mileham • Litcham Historical & Amenity Society
The Book of Loddiswell • Reg and Betty Sampson
The New Book of Lostwithiel • Barbara Fraser
The Book of Lulworth • Rodney Legg
The Book of Lustleigh • Joe Crowdy
The Book of Lyme Regis • Rodney Legg
The Book of Manaton • Compiled by the People of the Parish
The Book of Markyate • Markyate Local History Society
The Book of Mawnan • Mawnan Local History Group
The Book of Meavy • Pauline Hemery
The Book of Minehead with Alcombe • Binding and Stevens

For details of any of the above titles or if you are
interested in writing your own history, please contact: Commissioning Editor Community Histories, Halsgrove House,
Lower Moor Way, Tiverton Business Park, Tiverton, Devon EX16 6SS, England; tel: 01884 259636;
email: katyc@halsgrove.com